ARE YOU THERE, CROCODILE?

Michael Pennington

ARE YOU THERE, CROCODILE?

INVENTING ANTON CHEKHOV

OBERON BOOKS
LONDON

First published in 2003 by Oberon Books Ltd.
(incorporating Absolute Classics)
521 Caledonian Road, London N7 9RH
Tel: 020 7607 3637 / Fax: 020 7607 3629
e-mail: oberon.books@btinternet.com
www.oberonbooks.com

A catalogue record for this book is available
from the British Library.

ISBN: 1 84002 192 6

Cover Illustration: Andrzej Klimowski

Author Photograph: Mark Pennington

Proofread by Prufrock – www.prufrock.co.uk

Printed in Great Britain by Antony Rowe Ltd, Chippenham.

FOR LOUIS AND EVE

CONTENTS

ACKNOWLEDGEMENTS

Shaw, George Bernard, *About His Mother*. Reprinted with the permission of The Society of Authors, on behalf of the George Bernard Shaw Estate.

Strider – The Story of a Horse by Mark Rozovsky from a story by Tolstoy, in a version by Peter Tegel, unpublished script from the National Theatre, London production in 1984. Extracts from this version reproduced here with kind permission.

Stryk, Lucien, 'Chekhov in Nice' from *And Still Birds Sing: New and Collected Poems* by Lucien Stryk (1998). Reprinted with the permission of Swallow Press / Ohio University Press, Athens, Ohio.

AUTHOR'S NOTE

When I first played my one-man show, *Anton Chekhov*, at the National Theatre in 1984, there was some surmise about the fact that I had completely ignored the plays that most people remember when they think about Chekhov. I had my reasons, chiefly Chekhov's own defensive tendencies: his unease in the role of great playwright is interesting in itself, and I was mimicking his grudging attitude towards them. However, as the show has developed over the years, the plays have begun to creep in, in what I hope is a humorously parenthetical way.

Now they are in this book, as a sort of harmonic. This is not the place to look for a critique of these great pieces: in twenty-five years of working out what Chekhov might have been like, they have been, I should say, no more nor less important to me than they were to him.

In common with most of the English-speaking world, I first encountered Chekhov and his contemporaries in a language he had so little interest in that he resisted all offers of translation. By now however, there is such a dynasty of versions of the plays, from Constance Garnett to Peter Gill, that they seem to have an independent English life; there are countless translations of the stories, among which I happen to favour Ronald Hingley's and Harvey Pitcher's; and as for a rarity such as *The Island of Sakhalin*, I have been particularly grateful to the work of Luba and Michael Terpak. I also know Gorky through Moura Budberg, Tolstoy through Rosemary Edmonds and so on. It is no reflection on the work of any of them that I have used them as pointers back to the originals, which have then been retranslated for my purposes from their source. My Russian being what it is, I have depended here on generous help – especially from Frank Williams of the BBC Russian Service, and from Irina Brown and Teresa Cherfas, who have also acted many times as my Russian conscience and authenticators.

As will become apparent, if it was not for Lucien Stryk, none of this, almost certainly, would have happened.

I have formal debts for many matters of reference. I have always had Ernest J Simmons' biography of Chekhov near at hand, and Simon Karmolinsky's selection of his letters; not long ago Donald Rayfield's brilliant biography arrived and refreshed me no end. I have also read David Magarshack's authoritative work on Stanislavsky and Michael Frayn's commentaries on the plays, as well as his translations. Dr John Coope's *Doctor Chekhov* is a most interesting source for medical matters. Laurence Senelick's *The Chekhov Theatre* and David Allen's *Performing Chekhov* are indispensable performance histories, and I am specially grateful to Senelick for alerting me to Doctor Kurkov's reactions to the original *Uncle Vanya*. Likewise, Harvey Pitcher's *Lily* is the only source I know for the activities of Lily Glassby in inspiring the character of Charlotta in *The Cherry Orchard*.

The Russian (Julian) Calendar, which is used throughout, was twelve days behind that of Western Europe until 12 March 1900. Thereafter it was thirteen days behind: and one delightful if slightly fortuitous result of this is that on our Twelfth Night you can celebrate Russian Christmas Eve in London, perhaps at the Orthodox Church off Brompton Road, peering through a mantle of narcotic incense to see the city's Russians moving with incantatory slowness – babushkas from Dostoyevsky, venture capitalists of the new dispensation, winkle-pickered shysters in sideburns and shades, and righter-than-right English gentlemen who happen to have White Russian blood somewhere in their veins.

Meanwhile, if you want to know the state of the world's news on the day *The Seagull* opened, or, like me, what your grandfather was doing when Chekhov died, it is necessary to remember that 1900 turning-point.

MP
London
December 2002

INTRODUCTION: MELIKHOVO

March 1897

I passionately love anything called an estate in Russia. The word still hasn't lost its poetic sound to me.

                                    – Anton Chekhov

On 22 March 1897, Anton Chekhov sat down to dinner with his publisher Alexei Suvorin at the Hermitage Restaurant on Petrovsky Boulevard in Moscow. As they began to eat, Chekhov went to say something, but suddenly covered his mouth with his napkin while blood poured through it. Suvorin rushed him to his own suite at the Slavyansky Bazaar Hotel, but it was obvious he should be in hospital. At first Chekhov, a doctor himself and a singularly bad patient, refused to go, but three days later he was to be found in a clinic on the other side of the city, ominously close to the Novodevichy Cemetery, under observation at last for the tuberculosis he surely knew he had.

At the time, diagnosis of this disease was rough and ready – although X-rays had been discovered, they were only used for detecting fractures – and so the sufferer might be able to deceive himself for quite some time. Chekhov was not an easy man to mislead, but he may have been used to living on a narrow ledge between fear and dismal certainty. Treatment was also vague – the patient was stuck with ice packs, with eating high-fat meals up to six times a day to counteract weight loss, with instructions to avoid sunlight but to find a dry climate if possible, and sometimes with the revolting *koumiss*, a concoction derived from mare's milk. In the clinic, despite orders from his medical colleagues, Chekhov ordered caviar and scent from his visitors, chose new lenses for his pince-nez, and continued to spit blood. His sister Masha laboured through the snow to see him, and was shocked to find, among the get-well gifts, a doctor's sketch of a pair of blue lungs almost completely overtaken by the red of disease. As Chekhov lay in bed, there were some signs of spring: on one visit, Suvorin reported conversationally that the ice was breaking on the Moscow River. This was, perhaps, a mistake, and Chekhov's face darkened at last: his brother Nikolai had entered the last stages of consumption eight years before at just this time of year. Chekhov reminded Suvorin that when his own peasant patients died of the disease, they always said the same thing: 'There's nothing to be done; I'll go in the spring, with the melting of the snows.'

Chekhov's secret, diligently kept since he first discovered blood in his sputum thirteen years before, was well and truly out – he must have been furious. The literary world grew anxious: Tolstoy visited Chekhov in hospital and wore him out talking about immortality. Many others arrived, insisting that the patient didn't speak and then plying him with questions. A fortnight later, on Good Friday, Chekhov, now very weak, returned to his estate at Melikhovo, fifty miles south of Moscow. For some time he fished and idled and injected himself with arsenic, which was much trusted for pain relief. The painter Josef Braz arrived and appropriated Masha's bedroom to work on a portrait of the writer that nobody would ever like, least of all its subject. Such a thing must have seemed more like a memorial than a celebration:

> I sat for three weeks, eating cherries twenty at a time (which is the best way to eat cherries, by the way), and still it makes me look as if I were eating grated horseradish...

Perhaps it is in a break from one of these despondent sittings that Chekhov is famously photographed sitting on his verandah steps, stroking the ears of his dachshund bitch, Quinine. He wears a long double-breasted coat and a cap even though it is May, but he looks healthy enough: his face is open and friendly and far more relaxed than it would have been for Braz. Whoever took the picture was trusted, or perhaps a lover of dogs: it is hard to imagine a great writer looking more easy and natural.

Quinine was an odd name for a dog, like calling a cat Morphine: quinine was recommended for advanced tuberculosis, and the sight of it in bottles, together with the smell of lysol, must have pervaded the room when Nikolai met his wretched end. Chekhov had kept a three-month vigil in Moscow, patiently doctoring him, before suddenly giving up and going to the country, leaving his eldest brother Alexander in charge with inadequate medicines. Depending on which authority you read, he was either taking a well-deserved break from the sickroom or inexplicably deserting. Either way, Nikolai died in Alexander's arms a few days later: according to Alexander, only Anton's eyes were dry when the family gathered for the burial. Chekhov spoke little of the tragedy later, though it may have been one reason for his self-punishing trip across Siberia to Sakhalin Island the following spring: with the man, as with his characters, oblique action often spoke louder than words.

Quinine had a brother called Bromide. It happens that a grandson of his, named for some reason Box II, became the pet of another Russian writer, Vladimir Nabokov, and ended his days in Prague with Nabokov's widowed mother, waddling furiously along in a wire muzzle, 'an emigré dog in a patched and ill-fitting coat'.[1] In a way the two writers represent extremes in Russian sensibility – Nabokov, the privileged intellectual from western-looking Petersburg (he never once visited Moscow) and Chekhov, who rather disliked Petersburg, from the peasant stock to which intellectuals owed an obligation. Nabokov shares with Chekhov a fanatical eye for detail and a gift for letting it bloom on the page, but he is a far more self-conscious, more Proustian writer, working in complex English, while Chekhov perfects native understatement. My guess is that Chekhov would have appreciated Nabokov's ability to find comedy in the cruellest situation (*Lolita*), but would not have approved of his capture and impalement of butterflies on a board as a hobby (*Speak, Memory*). Most connections between the two great stylists are as quaintly circumstantial as the matter of the dog: as a boy of five Nabokov was on holiday with his parents in Wiesbaden while further up the Rhine Chekhov was dying at Badenweiler. More to the point, Nabokov records a meeting between his great-aunt Praskovia, one of the earliest women doctors in Russia, and Chekhov, at which the latter was surprisingly uncouth: Praskovia, a pioneer of psychiatry and women's education, was later dismissed by him as not only 'a non-doctor' but 'a lump of meat – if you stripped her and painted her green she'd look like a frog'. However, this was in a letter to his sister, to whom Chekhov said a number of things he might have preferred to keep off the record.

Chekhov told his wife once that he would rather live with a crocodile than with a cat (his respiration was not good, after all), but he loved his dogs and was exceptionally fond of Quinine – he didn't care quite so much for Bromide, who had a tendency to vomit. According to his brother Misha, the writer would set the table on a roar for half an hour at a time talking to Quinine, assuming for her the pitiful voice of an old man. Pet-lovers do this, but Chekhov's version would have been de luxe, as if his visitors were listening to a new short story: The Doctor and the Little Dog. After a hard country life, away from the camera and often mauled by the farm dogs, Bromide was put down, foaming at the mouth, when Chekhov finally left Melikhovo in 1898. But Quinine, immortalised by his favouritism, continues to sleep in the crook of his left arm: a hundred and one years later, I am looking at the verandah steps, hardly able to believe that the two of them have gone.

February 1998

The custodians of Russian heritage sites are something of a breed apart. They are, typically, charming and eloquent middle-aged women with an encyclopaedic knowledge of their subject, and they often give the impression that they are survivors of the celebrated family in whose house you are standing.

1. Vladimir Nabokov, *Speak, Memory*, Weidenfeld & Nicolson 1967, Penguin Books 1969.

Since Chekhov's sister and wife both outlived him by fifty years, this is a pleasant fantasy. One of the guardians of Konstantin Stanislavsky's house in Moscow, showing a more than academic affection for her subject, burst out with joy yesterday when I said that the big stove in the corner of the room reminded me of the emblematic family stove on which everybody scratches daily messages in Mikhail Bulgakov's novel *Days of the Turbins* – which Stanislavsky adapted for the Moscow Art Theatre as *The White Guard*. When I arrived at Melikhovo today, word soon got out that I was an actor from England: immediately a group of German visitors was hurried through their no doubt expensive tour and the equally large party of waiting Americans was held at the door, so that I could be left in Chekhov's house for a precious half-hour completely alone. All the slings and arrows of English theatre life are deflected by such moments: in Russia we are taken almost too seriously. For a time, I moved among the immediacies of Chekhov's life that I knew as well as the photograph with Quinine – the sofa in his green wallpapered study, Isaak Levitan's painting of Lake Udomlya on the wall. I could see the handwriting on his letters and hold the pince-nez he bought just before the disastrous Petersburg premiere of *The Seagull*, his hypodermic and the battered satchel in which he carried the district census he was working on when he had his attack at dinner. It was like being left alone with William Blake's etching plates or Mozart's piano.

As Chekhov testifies, his L-shaped house offers an arc of beautiful views. At once I grasped his delight at being able to fish in a pond while sitting at his bedroom window, and imagined him bustling down the path to the little summerhouse where he wrote *The Seagull*, running up a flag to show he wasn't to be disturbed. Back in his study, I remembered a photograph I had seen of a gathering here in the spring of 1892. Chekhov loved photography, set at its junction between science and art: Russia had recently seen its first major exhibition and cheaper equipment was becoming accessible to the amateur. Putting it to a rather more generous use than Tolstoy, whose interest was in self-portraits, Chekhov assembled a huge personal archive, and this particular shot resounds with enjoyment. He is sitting with two of his brothers and his sister and assorted admirers. His hands almost completely cover his face as if he were giggling: though he is the house's new owner, it looks like a student party or a squat. The wave of chatter drops as the camera lens opens (not for long, judging by the spontaneity of the picture, which is remarkable for that time in limited indoor light), then rises again before fading into the distance as I move into the dining room. Here Chekhov always sat at the end of the table by the connecting door, so that he could slip away without fuss: many times, with a new idea forming in his head, he would complain of feeling 'like a crayfish in a net with crayfish'. These two were the big rooms, the heart of the house. They get smaller as you move through the sleeping quarters: Masha's pink-walled room, with a portrait of Anton (as if she didn't see enough of him already) on the wall; the constricted premises where their father struggled to keep alive a constricted faith, with a violin on the wall and a disproportionately large icon. This was a man so frantically religious that he celebrated Passover as well as Easter, when he would walk the Melikhovo corridors swinging a censer. I pass Anton's and his mother's bedrooms: the hallway is lit by bright diamond-shaped stained glass windows in the Russian *Modern* style (the equivalent of our Art Nouveau), which animate the rather heavy furnishings. In such rich light, it is easier to visualise people here with their tramping feet, their careless breathing, their raised voices and small exclamations. Today's American visitors have become restive: as they are let in, feeling something of Chekhov's urgency I move on into the garden, where there is a foot of snow. And these steps are where he sat all right, with Quinine one summer morning, glad to escape the intruders.

This is my first visit to Russia since the collapse of the Soviet Union, though I was here twice before. I'm not just sightseeing, but doing a job. I've been commissioned by the *Independent* newspaper in London to write a piece about Russian theatre in its new circumstances: particularly I'm to report on Yuri Lyubimov, director of the subversive Taganka Theatre, who has now had to define a new role for his company. He has just turned eighty, and has been a personal friend since I played Raskolnikov and aided him somewhat in bringing his celebrated version of *Crime and Punishment* to London in 1983. At this moment, all the dizzying images of the new Russia are evident. The Iversky Gates into the Kremlin, taken down not so long ago so that tanks could pass through, have been restored and replaced. Beyond them, what used to be Gorky Street, a dour avenue of low voltage street lamps, little traffic and unadorned buildings, is now (as Tverskaya) like Madison Avenue in the rush hour – Tiffany's, Christian Lecroix, Yves Rocher, a Pizza Hut, you name it, all blazing with confident neon. If the heart lifts, it is only to drop again as you realise that only a small middle class able to swim with the tide of corruption and graft can afford the merest of this merchandise; and that beneath the Mary Quant tulip cuts and black lipstick the sales girls are the same angry, humiliated citizens as before. The Soviet Scowl, perfected when a friendly word to a Westerner could be seen as sleeping with the enemy, is also alive and well on the faces of bank tellers and petty officials. The cashier on the metro demands that you unfold your money bills before submitting them. The gentlemen's lavatory attendants (female) sternly charge three roubles a visit. Loudspeakers in the streets may no longer exhort pedestrians to eat bread or remember to breathe, but the same hectoring timbre can be heard as theatre commissionaires boss you into your seat. In the old days, you might succeed in making a formal complaint because your antagonist was afraid of their superior; now you encounter a kind of impudent anarchy. Muscovites in a body (one to one is quite another matter) have always achieved definitive standards of boorish discourtesy to the outsider: but perhaps discourtesy is the wrong word, since it implies the existence of its opposite, and there is no sign of that. As, after a week, you shove in the metro with the best, you might reflect that the brutality of the nineteenth century has bled into the humiliations of the twentieth to produce a truly barbaric brew beneath Marlborough Country billboards.

The *Independent* will love me.

Mayor Luzhkov has declared war on the icicles that hang from the house-eaves and occasionally drop on passers-by. More seriously, he has changed the city's skyline by building a new Church of Christ the Saviour with traditional onion dome and cross, as if to say that now the Soviets have gone, Russia is reconnecting with its religious past. Like hell it is – you can smell the Mafia everywhere: the manager of the Rossya Hotel has just been murdered, that of the Radisson a year ago, and I heard of the owner of quite a small bar who pays over a thousand dollars a day protection. Contract killings (a tremendous growth industry as a means of settling business disputes) are cheap – especially by the time the request has filtered through the syndicate to the man who pulls the trigger, who might get a couple of hundred dollars. Multi-millionaires under thirty risk their lives daily, and the annual murder figure for Moscow is 30,000 and rising. Facing this lethal delirium, the militia can barely operate without the full-time support of SOBA, a self-regulating fast response SAS-style team manned by Soviet diehards. At this moment Boris Yeltsin has failed in Chechnya once and will shortly fail again, and a great financial crash lies a few months ahead. A Russian friend sums it up – for a moment after perestroika there was freedom and money; now there is only freedom.

At Melikhovo you plunge into smaller but still eloquent paradoxes. In Soviet times it was virtually impossible to come here alone. A foreigner's visa only allowed for travel within thirty-five kilometres of the centre of Moscow: so Melikhovo was out of bounds without many official clearances and accreditations, or the probability of being tailed – not, I suppose, because of the effect of the place itself, but of the unimpressive things you would see on the way. Today I've had plenty of leisure to study these dispiriting suburbs while my car broke down not once but three times. The relief of seeing a sign on the Kharkov motorway, 'Chekhov 500 metres', was great and surreal, as if the M1 out of London suddenly diverted you to 'Dickens'. This renaming of the town Chekhov knew as Lopasnya would have depressed him, turned him in on himself, made him cock his head perhaps, in that appraising way of his.

He was always scathing about what we would call the cult of celebrity, having himself perfected a blend of faux-naiveté, genuine modesty and prickly pride. He knew what he was worth all right, but canonisation, even on a map, would not have sat well.

Chekhov has survived two revolutions as a hero, though the Soviets had to bowdlerise him to keep him in the club. This is not only due to literary merit, but to a civic seriousness as great as that of the messianic Tolstoy, though far more squeamishly acknowledged. While Tolstoy might thunder from on high about the need for civilised man to put his feet squarely into the shoes of the poor, Chekhov can be imagined struggling through the night like Astrov to doctor yet another family of sick peasants, the scientist in him reproving the writer:

> I lack a political, religious, philosophical view of the world – in fact
> I change it every month. So I must confine myself to describing how
> my people love, marry, give birth, die – and how they speak.

You can hear both sincerity and subterfuge in this. He would easily have grasped the role of the artist of conscience in the Soviet era, forever resisting and implying – endorsing Solzhenitsyn's assertion that writers were Russia's second government while flinching from such self-importance. Perhaps he would have been more dismayed by the new Russia, where literature and the theatre, like many arts, are seen as they are in the West – nice but strictly unnecessary. The Soviet Union, like all regimes that deny free speech, held such things in wary regard, and the homes of the approved were scrupulously maintained. In these liberated days the public funds to sustain them are dwindling, and they are indefatigably held together by private individuals, a few of whom I am about to meet.

One way and another, however, when Chekhov moved to Melikhovo in 1892 a writer was as important a thing as anyone could be. He was joining a charmed circle of literary men expected to address the painful destiny of Russia as best they could; and though he'd not paid for his pre-eminence by exile like Pushkin, or by the masquerade of a firing squad like Dostoyevsky, he could point for credibility to his investigation of Russia's notorious penal colony on Sakhalin two years previously. He was also making some money at last. His long story 'The Duel' had recently been published in full in *New Times* to the exclusion of all other contributions, and he was being taken seriously after nine years on Grub Street in which he'd turned his hand to any kind of humorous journalism to keep his family going. An irony he must have appreciated was that while his efforts at serious drama – *Ivanov* and *The Wood Demon* – had been spurned, his theatre luck currently lay in vaudevilles and one-act farces, the dramatic equivalent of his abandoned fiction style.

Chekhov sometimes described his first Moscow house on Sadovaya Kudrinskaya (on the Garden Ring) as 'a chest of drawers' – and at other times, because of its pink hue, as a bastion of liberal politics, but that was a joke. Melikhovo was both a practical upgrade and a modest assumption of status. Still, as he prepared to confront his 'six hundred acres of pasture, birch forest and nasty little river', his suitcases full of agricultural manuals, he was leaving a city he had come to love. He stalled his uneasiness by comparing himself to the Roman Emperor Cincinnatus, who gave up the public life he was born to and became a farmer.

February 1892 – October 1896

Chekhov, his father and mother, the family cook Maryushka and his sister Masha ('without whom the porridge would not boil') arrived at this time of year, which then as now saw the place covered in snow. Cincinnatus was two and a half hours by train from Moscow, nearly six miles from the railway station and twenty from a post office. The outhouses were dilapidated, the main building crawling with bugs, and the surrounding land neglected. In fact, as with many of his formal transactions, impulse had led to a bad deal. The price was high, at 13,000 roubles (£1,600 then, and close to what my grandfather would soon be paying, in the last days of the Welsh coal boom, for a very much grander house). Improving fortunes or not, Chekhov was much indebted to the soberest of his brothers, Misha, for negotiating a reduced mortgage, and to *New Times* for an advance to start the payments. There was no bathroom, the horses were starving, and the pond really a cesspit, but never mind: at the age of thirty-two, Chekhov was one of Russia's literary landowners, just like Turgenev and Tolstoy.

The peasants around his new home were a threatening presence. One of the first incidents was 'the miracle of the horse', when a mare that had been left out at night was quietly switched by them for a broken-down gelding. Chekhov must have felt most odd, being, unlike his genteel contemporaries, a distant cousin of the thieves – he was a serf's grandson, born in the year before Alexander II's 1861 Act of Emancipation. However, twenty years before that, his paternal grandfather Yegor Chekh had managed an astonishing feat. Gathering together his savings from a lifetime of parsimonious work, he had bought his and his children's freedom from the service of a Count Chertkov – grandfather of Tolstoy's most fervent disciple, as it happens. As well as enterprise, vision, an unusual quality of literacy and exceptional eccentricity of dress, Yegor seems to have had a harshness of character, making him known far and wide as the Viper – it was a quality which his son Pavel, Chekhov's father, inherited more readily than his progressiveness. Pavel, bad tradesman and religious bigot, was so obsessed with choir-singing that his sons' childhood memories were dominated by paternal thrashings and by being dragged out of bed on winter mornings and over cold flagstones for the first of the day's several church services. It was, in fact, 'no childhood at all'; and when Chekhov was sixteen, Pavel's bankruptcy broke up his family. However, by apprenticing his children Yegor had propelled them all from the peasant to the merchant class, and Pavel had been able in turn to provide an education for his, even if the younger ones depended rather on the generosity of relatives.

As well as Yegor's gift, Chekhov was the beneficiary of a wider instinct for progress. Apart from the Emancipation, Alexander had brought in a startling range of reforms; among them trial by jury, and a new remit for local councils (*zemstvos*) to provide medical services and free education. Chekhov would spend much of his life sustaining that progressive impulse as darkness began to close in again – first with the accession of the reactionary Alexander III to compromise the reforms, and then with that of Nicholas II, whose idea of progress was to throw medieval court balls, dress his ministers in kaftans and reintroduce the ancient Slavonic language. Politically wary but genetically engaged, something about Chekhov is wryly symbolised by the fact that he lived his forty-four years from 1860 to 1904. Shift a year forward from each date and there are the Emancipation and the first Revolution to bracket perhaps the most crucial forty-four years of Russian history before 1917. It is as if he were acknowledging but demurring from the highly-charged dates.

Chekhov didn't care much for the peasants, but affection didn't come into it. He had a keen sense of their lives:

> terrible labour that makes the body ache all night, cruel winters, crop failure, overcrowding, no help or anywhere to look for help…

Digging himself into Melikhovo, he let them cut hay on his land and he set up a free clinic in a nearby village, where he soon found himself treating five hundred cholera victims in a month:

> They bow respectfully to me, as Germans do to their pastor, and the old women cross themselves when they see me coming, as if I were a saintly half-wit…

As time went on, he would ease the peasants through a winter of famine in the complete absence of Government help; organise their participation in the national census (in which Tsar Nicholas truthfully signed himself 'Landowner'), and build three schools, a library and a fire station. He sponsored a post office in the next village, keeping it going almost single-handed with his copious correspondence; and he dreamed of (but didn't realise) a 'People's Palace' comprising a theatre, library and museum. He even imported a priest so that the old wooden church on the edge of his land could be reopened and where, despite all the bitter memories, Pavel could have the satisfaction of leading the choir.

Chekhov's friends, in guarded approval, soon began to people Melikhovo – and indeed his imagination. One of his first visitors, in April, was Levitan – as great a landscape artist perhaps as Monet, but to this day relatively unknown in the West, and Chekhov's fast friend. Levitan was to the countryside what Chekhov was to the language, a passionate witness who never painted a human face. In Melikhovo, he would come looking for Chekhov, knocking at his window with their regular call – 'Are you there, crocodile?' – and Chekhov would break off to walk with him or even do a little shooting. One day the artist half-killed a woodcock. An absurd scene developed, in which Levitan, 'twitching and shaking his head', asked his friend to finish off the grounded bird. But he couldn't bring himself to do it, and as they bickered, the woodcock looked up at them 'in wonder'. Eventually Chekhov did the deed, and recorded:

> And so two idiots went home and sat down to dinner, and there was one beautiful enamoured creature less in the world.

At the time Levitan was busily courting Chekhov's friend Lika Mizinova, and Chekhov, with the artist's criminality, parodied their relations in 'The Grasshopper' – nailing both the moody painter ('How can I get on with my sunny landscape when the sun won't shine?') and his admirer ('Her greatest talent was for making friends with celebrities'). When Levitan read the story, he didn't speak to Chekhov for three years. Then, without fuss or explanation, they were reconciled, in 1895; whereupon Chekhov, as if afraid that his original point had been missed, did it all over again. In *The Seagull*, as well as parodying once more the blind glorification of talent in Nina's attitude to Arkadina and Trigorin, he allows his explosive friend to leave a mark on the character of Konstantin. It is likely that Levitan once shot a bird and laid it at Masha Chekhova's feet, in the manner of Konstantin with Nina. At another time he turned his gun on himself; and with an affection perhaps not innocent of the instinct for research, Chekhov left his work and travelled three hundred-odd miles to Novgorod province, near the Gulf of Finland – an area in which seagulls wheeled and squalled continuously – to look after him. As for Lika, despite her dealings with Levitan, she had always been deeply in love with Chekhov; but he always ducked away from her, giving himself such merry titles as The King of the Medes. In truth, he was exercising a Platonic *droit de seigneur*. After Levitan, he introduced her to the musician and playwright

Ignati Potapenko and watched his seduction and impregnation of her – suggestively presenting the couple with one of Quinine's first puppies, Catarrh (the medical refrain continues). Potapenko, who was married, took Lika to Paris and abandoned her, echoing Nina's fate at the hands of Trigorin. Lika wrote to Chekhov that 'not a trace of the old Lika is left': in 1896 her baby died, like Nina's. However Chekhov didn't steal that event – the play had been written by then.

In other ways too, Chekhov had stayed close to home with *The Seagull*. Alexei Suvorin's son Vladimir had killed himself in 1887 largely because his father never read a play he'd written – just as Arkadina, at the end of *The Seagull*, shockingly admits that she has never had time to read a word written by her doomed son. A woman called Lydia Avilova, who for years made a great to-do about what she took to be Chekhov's secret love for her, had recently sent him a medallion inscribed with a line from his story 'Neighbours' – 'If you ever need my life, come and take it' – Nina's exact message to Trigorin. The author's signature is sometimes so broadly written that it seems like a private joke. On Dorn, for instance, one of Chekhov's sequence of doctors who, like him, are attractive to women and good at the job: the contradictory fact that Dorn can be cavalier with his patients – 'Oh, take some Valerian drops' – would only remind Chekhov's friends of his own professionalism.

To put all this private matter into *The Seagull* was sailing close to the wind, but there's no sign that Potapenko minded his immortality as Trigorin, or that Chekhov much objected to his behaviour, despite a few token pieties. In fact they were soon to be found travelling down the Volga together. Potapenko was punished only by being made to supervise the typing-up of *The Seagull* and being charged with getting the play accepted, as it had to be, by the Imperial Theatres Committee. The Committee sniffed for a bit, thinking the work inconsequential – they found its 'Ibsenism' unpleasant, declared the seagull superfluous to the play, and said the idea of a woman taking snuff and drinking vodka was 'unnecessary'. They didn't mind *per se* that the heroine was living openly with a man, but they couldn't accept that her family didn't seem to object. The silly remark is revealing – the Committee and the public, at home with stereotypes, rarely encountered work in which the author suspended moral judgment as spectacularly as Chekhov. It must have seemed scandalous that the trespassing Trigorin is accepted and even liked by Masha and the rest of the family, just as Chekhov had forgiven Potapenko. Chekhov made the required changes (reversing them when the play was published), and the Committee authorised the Alexandrinsky Theatre in Petersburg to proceed with a production.

It flopped, spectacularly, near enough hissed off the stage. It was as if the theatre was full of wasps and bumble-bees, said a critic, and his fraternity described the piece as 'pointless', 'not a play at all', with 'a plot borrowed from a lunatic asylum'. The horrible adventure provoked in Chekhov both anger and self-loathing, as bad reviews do. Although he dismissed critics as horse-flies – harmless enough but a distraction from the horse's work – it was another thing to be attacked by a swarm of them. He swore off repeating the humiliation, convinced to some extent that he was no playwright. So – no *Three Sisters*, no *Cherry Orchard*; where does that leave us?

May 1898

Eighteen months later, Chekhov is sitting in the study I have just left. Since *The Seagull* fiasco, the haemorrhage at dinner and his photograph with Quinine, he has wintered in the south of France, where the indefatigable Braz has tracked him down for more sittings. Returning to Melikhovo, he has found everything in chaos. Bromide, apparently infuriated by the presence of two new puppies, has bitten Pavel Chekhov, and all the doctors in the district have been called. Meanwhile a letter is waiting, on this very desk, from Vladimir Nemirovich-Danchenko, playwright, novelist and drama teacher, whom Chekhov knows a little through Nemirovich's brother, a gambling acquaintance. Nemirovich is writing to him wanting to revive *The Seagull*.

What Chekhov doesn't know is that the previous June he has written another unsolicited note, to Konstantin Alexeyev (stage name Stanislavsky), a talented amateur actor of private means, inviting him to lunch at the restaurant of the Slavyansky Bazaar in Moscow where Suvorin had recently nursed Chekhov. Stanislavsky had been much stimulated by the 1890 visit of the company of the Duke of Saxe Meiningen, whose work combined historical verisimilitude with a range of visual effects new to Russian audiences – not to mention the role of director as autocrat. Under the Bazaar's great vaulted ceiling, in its Easter-egg decor, the lunch went on for eighteen hours (the restaurant was open all day and night) while the two men discussed the founding of a new People's Theatre, based on admirable ideas both great and small, all of them completely unknown in Russia at the time – adequate rehearsal periods, punctuality of performance, accessible prices for the poor, comfortable individual dressing rooms, chessboards in the Green Room, acceptance among the carefully-chosen actors of 'ensemble' casting (Hamlet one day, a messenger the next) – all evidence of a seriousness of intent as much ethical as aesthetic. Stanislavsky declared later that not even the Versailles Peace Conference had discussed world matters as intently as he and Nemirovich their grand project. Nemirovich was to be what we might call the producer-administrator, responsible for choice of repertoire with literary veto; Stanislavsky the director of productions, with 'artistic control'. Their recruits would be drawn from Nemirovich's students at his Moscow Philharmonic School (including Olga Knipper, who would one day marry Chekhov), and from Stanislavsky's colleagues at his Society of Art and Literature (among them his own wife Maria Lilina).

Up until 1882, all Russian theatre companies had been licensed by the state, but with the surrender of this restriction private groups had begun to mushroom – one of them was being run by Fyodor Korsh, an astute Moscow impresario who put on Ibsen and Tolstoy for young people's matinees and had premiered Chekhov's *Ivanov*. If you consider that the powers of the Imperial Theatres Committee included not only script veto but casting approval (rather like the television networks now), and the calling up of props, costumes and decor to its own official taste, the whiff of freedom was bracing. The company born at the Slavyansky Bazaar would be the latest independent, destined of course to become the most significant. Nemirovich, a wily and magisterial figure, does not mention in his letter to Chekhov that Stanislavsky is as yet no enthusiast for *The Seagull* or indeed for the author, whom he rather dislikes. (For a great future teacher of acting, Stanislavsky could easily be deceived by the outward manner, failing to recognise Chekhov's habit of looking above his head as shyness.) Nemirovich, on his behalf, promises Chekhov an 'artistic triumph…in a most careful production, declaring war on the establishment' and as much money as he can afford.

The weather in Melikhovo is warm. It has taken six summers to renovate the house. A cherry orchard has been planted, freshwater fish bought, there are plans to keep bees and chickens: Chekhov is in the sort of natural rapture that often seems his only hold on a precarious life. The company of actors can be delightful and theatre politics entertaining; but they can also be turgid and repetitive, and no match for the countryside at this time of year. He certainly doesn't need reminding about the failure of *The Seagull*, even though subsequent performances have been far more successful. He sends a message through his sister to Nemirovich so non-committal that it amounts to a refusal. Within a week Nemirovich is back to him, almost suicidal – this is the only play he wants to do, the only author he wants to work with. He will come to Melikhovo and show Chekhov his plans for the production. Chekhov refuses again. Nemirovich writes a third time, pointing out that *The Seagull* can in fact be done anywhere – and has, like Chekhov's new *Uncle Vanya*, been performed rather successfully in the regions. Why should Moscow be denied a first-class version? Chekhov now replies that if Nemirovich must come to Melikhovo, he'll have to hire his own horses at the station.

In the end, of course, Chekhov parts with the play in a burst of enthusiasm, and certain things follow. At the end of the first performance at the new Moscow Art Theatre in 1898, there is a deafening silence, to the horror of the actors. But it is the moment's pause for recovery before theatre history is made – as, for instance, it will be fifty years later at the final curtain of Arthur Miller's *Death of a Salesman* in New York. Then the house erupts, and *The Seagull* soars into our lives for good. The author embarks on a new existence, and Melikhovo, neglected, begins to fall apart, as if its heart has stopped beating: shortly before the play's opening Pavel Chekhov has died and Anton's own health is pointing him towards the warmer South. Having hastened to buy the estate, he sells it badly, purchasing a property in the Crimea. He returns briefly the following summer to show Olga Knipper where he wrote the play that brought them together, and in its very last days he digs up any transplantable shrubs and strips the house down to the wicker chairs. An escaped convict roams the grounds. Quinine dies as painfully as Bromide. The buyer defaults on the hurried instalment deal Chekhov has arranged – and in fact he will never get paid, though Masha will ultimately secure something when she repossesses the house and begins to sell it on to an admirer in the last months of Anton's life. Meanwhile, the news that the defaulter has cut down the Melikhovo cherry orchard will reach Chekhov in Yalta as he contemplates his last play.

So the consequences of Nemirovich's wooing and Chekhov's frail decisions here extend well beyond his short life. Apart from introducing him to Knipper, *The Seagull*'s revival saved the new company, which after a bright start had seen a series of alarmingly rapid flops. (As with the English Stage Company in London in the 1950s, the big hit associated with the theatre was the third or fourth show, not the first.) The Moscow Art Theatre would never have been formed except as a protest against the theatre practices that destroyed the earlier premiere and nearly finished Chekhov's playwriting life just as it began, and it is forever connected with him, a seagull still on its curtain even now that the company is sponsored by Philip Morris. We know Chekhov's dramatic masterpieces only because of these precarious facts, and I and countless others have lived certain kinds of lives because of them. For that reason I am standing here shivering in the snow, trying to get all the dates straight in my head, almost hallucinating by force of will.

It is nearly forty years ago that I fell for my first Chekhov play, and about thirty since it occurred to me that he might matter to me as much as Shakespeare. About fifteen years ago I briefly became known as London's 'Russian actor' – even though my appearances in Chekhov had been limited at that time to a condensed radio version of *The Seagull* and a touring revival of *Three Sisters*. So I have loved this writer all my grown life – well, hasn't everyone? My fervour for the great plays is an orthodoxy, but there's always been something else, born of fidgety nosiness or a desire for authentication. Twenty years ago I attempted a real identification with Chekhov and only last year relinquished it, thinking the obsession done. During that time, like a wordfinder programme, I could almost tell you how many times in his life he had referred to cherries, say, or crocodiles. To my surprise, after all those years of tracing his outline, second-guessing him, begging his pardon, sometimes seeing a twinkle in his eye and finally letting him go, I now find myself in his garden, trying once more to push myself into the life not just of a great writer but, among those I could never meet, of perhaps my favourite man.

PART ONE

SEVERAL HUNDREDWEIGHT OF LOVE

> There was a sense of shame in the theatre. People turned their backs, and somebody cried out: 'Why is that young man carrying a dead duck around?' The company didn't know their lines, they weren't interested, so why should the public be? Oh, if only they wouldn't all *act* so much.
>
> – Anton Chekhov, on the Petersburg premiere of *The Seagull*

That's it, blame the actors.

What did he expect? I trudge through the frosty streets behind the stricken playwright – out of the theatre onto Alexandrinsky Square, along the Nevsky Prospect to the Griboyedov Canal and into Romanov's Restaurant, remonstrating, able to do what neither Potapenko nor Suvorin was in a position to in 1896 – apply a long hindsight.

Propelled from the auditorium after the first Act 'by the first law of physics', Chekhov has taken refuge in a dressing-room belonging to Elizaveta Levkeyeva for the rest of the show – rather inconveniently, I should have thought, but perhaps actors were more easy-going in those days. Overwhelmed, he has then snubbed the official reception and started this solitary walk. I park myself next to him in Romanov's. It's not quite what I expected in here. Despite its grand name this is no more than a grocer's run by a man called Romanov – and the first name, unfortunate on this occasion, of Konstantin – who has acquired an innkeeper's concession. I do my best. The Alexandrinsky may have been a bad choice for *The Seagull*. Petersburg audiences had more appetite for French farce than for such a stubbornly Russian play, and it might have been as well to recall the almost identical fate of Gogol's *The Government Inspector* at this theatre in 1836. But, Chekhov retorts, the company gave him 'a phenomenal success' seven years ago with *Ivanov* when Moscow had been hard on it; so they had a good pedigree, and Levkeyeva had once been an *ingénue* in Ostrovsky, even if she was now better known for broad comedy dowagers. *The Seagull* had been part of a double bill (imagine it) and the whole event her benefit performance: but she herself was never going to be in the Chekhov, only the second show. Her fans, who had paid high prices to see her, didn't know that or hadn't taken it in, so they can't have been pleased. Nor was it the Alexandrinsky's fault that the Imperial Theatres Committee had ordered no new scenery for the occasion, leaving them with used box sets and old forest flats. Those were the rules, as hard to grasp now as if the Arts Council were to design productions at the Royal National Theatre out of their own used stock.

The litany of disaster is about to become history, and of course history hasn't finished with this play. The production was inadequately planned, and the actors what we would call unprofessional, crude and lazy – but that's how things were then, there. Chekhov must have known something of what to expect. As a young man he had been a diligent theatre critic and he knew the game. In fact he must have propped up the bar here in Romanov's in those days too, honing his invective, as he is now sitting grumpily, refusing to listen to my reasoning. A further part of which is that two of tonight's performances – Vera Komisarzhevskaya's ravishing Nina and Modest Pisarev as Dorn – will in the event be accepted as better than those of Roksanova and Vishnevsky with the Moscow Art Theatre two years later, when the play will – yes it will – be redeemed. And tonight's Sorin, Vladimir Davydov, is the known strong actor who played Ivanov: too bad that in the last Act his wheelchair gently slid down the raked stage, to the delight of all. The same thing has happened to me with a hospital trolley. Not to mention chairs on castors. And armoured tanks. Chekhov turns back to his supper.

Of course he could have withdrawn the play. He hadn't really been attentive to rehearsals. There were (only) eight in the nine days before the premiere, but he didn't come to the first three even though he was in town – preferring to concentrate on keeping Lika Mizinova and Potapenko apart in the first night seating arrangements, organising the publication of *Uncle Vanya*, and going to see other shows. During his absence, the production lost its Nina. Forty-two and a star, Maria Savina baled out because she judged that the character would have to be a blonde and she, Savina, didn't care to wear wigs. I wonder if she didn't fancy the older part of Arkadina, the benefit of playing which, as Olga Knipper was to find in Moscow, was that you might end up marrying the author and having roles such as the Masha of *Three Sisters* and Ranyevskaya written for you. But I'm getting ahead of myself, not to mention Anton Pavlovich. Savina's defection turned out to be a stroke of luck: Komisarzhevskaya, ten years younger, with her pale face, mournful eyes and exceptionally musical voice, almost saved the day and made her own name. Savina meanwhile had toyed with the idea of playing Masha instead, a part which Levkeyeva also belatedly thought of claiming. Savina sounds like a colleague to avoid: eight years later, she was asked to play Arkadina in a revival at the Alexandrinsky and refused because she felt it was Nina's play and she did not wish to 'violate' herself.

Chekhov later became quite tough about re-casting after rehearsals had begun – to meet his own requirements, that is, not the actors' – but on this occasion the internal shenanigans seem to have passed him by. One way and another, the cast knew in their bones that they were in for a flop, which is no fun. When Chekhov finally came to rehearsals he was unenthusiastic: think of that face in the stalls, looking like the Braz portrait. You'd be discouraged.

By the second performance, with Chekhov gone, the Petersburg intelligentsia started to fill the house. Komisarzhevskaya wired to report a huge and continuing success. The fact that the play was taken off almost immediately (some say after five performances, some eight) may reflect more on the management's nervousness than on its real legs; and it was revived in Kharkov, Kiev, Taganrog, Astrakhan and even Prague within the next year. Just as the Alexandrinsky is condemned in hindsight, so the Moscow Art Theatre is hailed for finally saving the play. There is also a view that the extent of the Petersburg catastrophe has been talked up by the Moscow Art Theatre's founders to make themselves look better. They hardly needed to gild their lily: that second premiere in 1898 was some night, up to the communal intake of breath in the auditorium at the end, like the pause between the landing of a blow and the body's reaction. No wonder Prince Alexander Urusov rejoiced that 'life itself spoke from the stage'; no wonder Maxim Gorky, quite in love with Chekhov, wrote to him that he felt 'terribly fine and merry'. Apart from anything else, a Russian audience had smelled real cigar smoke for the first time – it had always been mimed before – and in the interval complete strangers felt able to approach and ask each other what they thought of the play. A little boy even asked his mother if they could go for a walk in the wood he saw on the stage. A community was being formed, a constituency for a theatre of real life, getting at least a glimpse of Chekhov's vision thanks to communal application and entrepreneurial daring.

Not that Chekhov would call it real life: the triumph also initiates a life-long dispute with Stanislavsky about the nature of truth in the theatre, which I'm not sure Chekhov always comes out of well. It is certainly a pity that a great playwright was reaching a point of refinement at the moment that an innovating director was still feeling his way. Confronted by Stanislavsky's insistence on verisimilitude, Chekhov had snorted:

> Imagine a painting of a face by Kramskoi [a particularly realistic artist].
> Suppose you cut out the nose and put a real one in its place. You'd
> have a realistic nose and a ruined picture

– and later, asked whether he'd liked the lake the designer had created for the play, he said, 'Oh well, it's wet.' It's easy to warm to the writer's charm and wit in such asides, but there are moments when Chekhov rather exceeds his brief, especially on the subject of Stanislavsky's acting. Apart from directing the play, the unfortunate man had been persuaded – by the author – to take over Trigorin and abandon the easier role of Dr Dorn. But Chekhov held very particular views about Trigorin, not so much about his behaviour but how he should dress: here Stanislavsky seems to have transgressed by wearing too elegant a pair of trousers. At any rate he got small thanks for all his efforts: Chekhov's final judgment was that he had acted like an epileptic and would have benefited if the rest of company had given him a sperm injection.

What standards do we apply here? Stanislavsky is thought by many to have been a fine actor, though, throughout his life, he also demonstrated an endearing clownishness. Anecdotes have crowded as close around him as around John Gielgud. For one of his parts he simply could not be persuaded to shave off his life-long moustache, and for a while had it waxed down and pasted with make-up (what can it have looked like?). He was finally persuaded into the right course by the gift of a false one that he could wear in the street. Chekhov no doubt was irritated by him, but there is something that goes beyond the artistic here, and I wonder if he didn't resent his unearned wealth – Stanislavsky was descended from serfs as he was, but his father's family, most unlike Chekhov's, had amassed a fortune in the manufacture of silver thread. For his part, Stanislavsky still wasn't that keen on Chekhov, thinking him proud, haughty, and not entirely without guile. As a director, meanwhile, his rehearsal methods at this stage were decidedly odd, since for most of the time he seems to have stayed on his estate, sending in plans for each Act which Nemirovich had to implement with the cast. But the fact is that for every over-zealous lighting effect and self-conscious sound cue, for every instruction for a pause of twelve seconds precisely, as if the play were a particularly rigid musical score, a marker was put down for matters we now take for granted – ensemble playing, the inner life of the characters, precision of thought and feeling, an essential seriousness. We probably wouldn't be doing these plays if it weren't for the idealism and stubbornness of this remarkable man.

The Seagull is really about all this, of course. Expectations of the theatre and Chekhov's literary preoccupations riddle its central relationships. The achievement is great because self-referenced plays of this sort form a not very compulsive genre. Chekhov had warned in advance that as well as 'several hundredweight of love' there would be much talk of literature in the play; but it is more than talk, and more than the fact that *The Seagull* is heavy with quotations from Shakespeare and Maupassant – apart from the obvious *Hamlet*, its famous opening lines come from *Bel-Ami*, and the book that causes an argument between Arkadina and Dorn in Act Two is the same author's 'Sur l'Eau'. At a deeper level, Konstantin's struggle with his mother, both Oedipal and professional, Konstantin's and Trigorin's battle for Nina and Nina's ambitions are all articulated within the question of how best to write, how to act, what can be hoped for from the forms.

The play's two authors, in a manner both evident and evasive, write in Chekhov's own hand. Trigorin is a literary star but by his own account a second-rate writer, whom Chekhov dares us to identify with himself. His counterpoint, Konstantin, starts the play by saying Trigorin is not as good as Zola or Tolstoy, and then Trigorin says it himself, one enchanted afternoon by the lake with the admiring Nina:

> I'm clever and charming, but nothing like Tolstoy…on my grave it'll
> say: here lies Trigorin, a good writer, but not as good as Turgenev…

Chekhov puts into this man's mouth, without mercy or special pleading either, his own self-deprecation, his enthusiasm for fishing, and even one of his fine natural descriptions. When in Act Four Konstantin resentfully admires Trigorin's account of a moonlit night, some at least of the audience would have recognised the quote from Chekhov's 1886 story 'The Wolf':

> The neck of a broken bottle by a weir is glittering next to the dark
> shadow of a mill-wheel.

Above all, and redemptively (for he would be the villain of the piece if Chekhov were to deal in such things), Trigorin shares with his author an almost sacred love of the Russian world around him:

> I love this lake, the trees, the sky, I feel for nature…but then I'm not
> just a landscape painter, I'm a citizen; I also love the Russian people,
> and I must deal with their sufferings, their future, science, the rights
> of man.

The very rhythm of his lines sometimes finds an echo in Chekhov's private conversation. The author once wrote to Lika Mizinova:

> I am never free of this idea: I have to write. It's an obligation. I have to
> write and write

– and Trigorin opens up to Nina, with the same disastrous effect on her heart:

> I'm haunted by it. It's an obsession: I must write, I must write.

Konstantin meanwhile has some of the same resonances. As his mother dresses the wound he has inflicted on himself, he confides:

> Just lately, these last few days, I've loved you as tenderly as when I was
> a little boy

– rather as, when Chekhov had ministered to Levitan by the Gulf of Finland, the debilitated artist wrote to him in the same cadence:

> I don't know why, but the few days you spent here were the most
> peaceful I've had all summer.

As for professional practice, we might wish, as with Chekhov in his early days, that Konstantin would find the courage to publish without a pseudonym. Perhaps it is inverted vanity: Trigorin's two-edged compliment that his identity is being discussed in Petersburg as excitedly as if he were the Man in the Iron Mask is similar to the rebuke delivered by the literary doyen Dmitri Grigorovich when Chekhov persisted in hiding behind the signature Antosha Chekhonte. And like Chekhov, we surely approve Konstantin's reforming ideas for the theatre but are uncertain about his ability to deliver. On the one hand his exemplary play is eccentric – apparently less than half an hour long were it played through (that's all the time Nina has to give it, at any rate), an abstract meditation with olfactory and visual effects, sulphur and the devil's red eyes. On the other, Chekhov's own assault on theatrical vulgarity, the innovations of *The Seagull* in fact, imply some sympathy: in its sincere, uncertain way, Konstantin's work prefigures a future of profuse Stanislavskian atmospherics and Symbolist gestures.

> You know what? The theatre ought to be got out of the hands of the grocers.

Chekhov's contemporaries, wrongfooted at every turn, seem to have bristled at *The Seagull* with the same bafflement that later audiences felt at the arrival of Samuel Beckett and Harold Pinter. Apart from the biliousness of the critics, Tolstoy, who never condemned one writer when he could condemn two in the same breath, dismissed the play as utterly worthless ('like Ibsen') and Nemirovich's gambling brother took the view that it contained 'nothing theatrical… Chekhov is no playwright.' The fact that *The Seagull* contained some traditional appeasements – the final revolver shot, and one soliloquy to the audience per Act – failed to disguise a deep disruptiveness, and its natural enemies smelt the fact. The sheer measure of offence must have had something to do with its combination of unfolding literary credo and mischievous unpredictability.

In the first of many surprises, Medvedenko, a man so mundane that he normally thinks about nothing but his low teaching salary, finds himself discussing the union of souls through artistic endeavour. This is because of his love of Masha, who replies, 'There'll be a storm tonight' – but instead of the terrible portent it might be in Ibsen, this is, as in life, simply an evasive observation about the weather. When Konstantin arrives to put on his play, he points out that his uncle Sorin's beard needs a trim, to which Sorin says, 'It's the tragedy of my existence' – high dramatic language again, but used for a joke. When Sorin says sincerely how he too would have liked to be a writer, the dedicated young playwright ignores him because he can hear his beloved Nina coming. Meanwhile a character of exceptional contradictoriness has been announced, whom you can never quite align either with the devil or the angels – Konstantin's mother Arkadina, an egotistical actress who weeps over poetry, is tight-fisted, has a religious belief in the theatre but is jealous of other actresses, and who 'ministers to the sick like an angel'. When she arrives, this star is guilty straight away of hideous bad manners: at the very moment her son's play begins, she says, quite unnecessarily, 'We're fast asleep.'

Having himself tampered with the vocabulary a little, Chekhov now sets a radical dramatist to work. Konstantin has arranged on the stage not only his play but a traditionally-minded audience, of whom two are theatre professionals. We, the ultimate spectators, peer past them at a set with no backdrop, just a view of the lake, at a performance to be cued only by the moon going up. Almost inevitably, important characters are coming on and straight away turning their backs on us, which even nowadays is quite startling: it must have been remarkable when Stanislavsky did it and the Moscow Art Theatre's crude footlights illuminated the backs of threadbare jackets and cheap dresses. In this unfamiliar arrangement, we begin to form an oblique relationship with the 'real' characters by comparing their theatrical taste with our own.

Konstantin's leading lady Nina – his play's only actor, it seems – is also his sweetheart, a stranger from the other side of the lake (her family name, Zaryechnaya, means 'beyond the river'). When she arrives, she is excited about a number of things, all at the same time. To her father and stepmother, who have forbidden her coming, these summerfolk are 'bohemians', so the first exhilaration is at running away to join a more exciting set – especially as she is minded to go on the stage herself, like Konstantin's mother, whom her parents presumably view as the worst of the bunch. At the same time her heart is full of Konstantin, though she tends not to concentrate when she is with him, noticing the shape of an ominous dark tree over his shoulder when he tries to kiss her and asking him for its name. It is difficult to gauge either her love or her rebelliousness, since neither might beat so strongly were it not for the adrenalin of putting on the play. Schoolchildren and amateurs get worked up like this, a taste of independence and romantic yearning heightening everything. Life seems so pallid afterwards: going back to a desk on the Monday morning, to learn or to earn, is very hard. Actually, professionals know it too: the same exhilaration leads to inadvisable love affairs and friendships apparently formed for life which buckle on the last night. It is all part of the theatre's eroticism, and you get used to it, sort of. As for Nina, it's her undoing.

Hers is not the only split attention. Konstantin's play is to take place in Arkadina's garden where, from time to time, she and her guests can hear music, causing her to reminisce, somewhat through tinted glasses. Ten or fifteen years ago there were six estates around the water, and always 'laughter, shooting, fun and love affairs', in most of which the worldly Dr Dorn seems to have starred. These memories interest her, an actress, far more than the play she is to see. Among its other unruly spectators are further contradictory types: an estate manager with artistic pretensions, Shamrayev, who imitates opera singers and keeps talking about actors Arkadina probably wouldn't acknowledge in the street while being over-familiar with the ones she would: to call Pavel Chadin by his diminutive name Pashka is like an English fan talking about 'Pauly Scofield'. Shamrayev will spend the play grovelling to Arkadina in this way but truculently refusing everything he's asked to do in the way of his job – to release the dog, to provide horses. He is married to Polina, but even before he is seen she has been begging Dr Dorn for love and fussing at him in a wifely way for not wearing his galoshes. Dorn meanwhile hums little tunes to himself and denies an interest in the girl who is to appear on the stage by declaring, unrevealingly, that he is 'fifty-five years old'. Polina's and Shamrayev's daughter Masha is in love with Konstantin, having declared from the start that she is 'in mourning for her life'. Dorn's attitude to her is interestingly paternal: and in fact, Chekhov implied in an early draft of the play that Masha was Dorn's and Polina's daughter. Nemirovich-Danchenko, exercising his veto, advised him either to explore the idea further or to drop it, and he let it go, leaving behind a trace in the vehemence with which Dorn reproves Masha for taking snuff, calling her 'my dear child'.

Dorn will find Konstantin's play genuinely original, but the others, when pressed to the point (or, in Arkadina's case, unpressed), will surely think it wildly pretentious. Medvedenko certainly believes it would be better if Konstantin wrote a play about schoolteachers. The fact that it is as great a catastrophe as the first *Seagull* is largely the work of the author's mother, whose destructive mockery utterly humiliates him. He will now need all the help he can get; but when Dorn alone takes the trouble to offer him friendship, Konstantin, as inattentive as with his uncle earlier, breaks off to ask where Nina has gone and rushes after her. Moving into the second Act with these ungovernable people, we might hope for some orientation, but no: right away Masha eloquently accounts for her wasted life –

> I was born a long time ago, I drag my life behind me like a dress with an endless train

– and a few moments later is complaining that her leg has gone to sleep. The entire proceeding, wayward and askew, could leave you fretful even if you weren't a fan of Levkeyeva. It is no reflection on the plays of Ostrovsky or Tolstoy or Gogol to say that Chekhov's audience is being drawn into a new kind of bargain.

Chekhov is also bringing from his journalism a sharp eye for the obsessive, for the ludicrous ease with which we ignore other people's needs. This is a farce technique, but now used for something a farceur hardly aspires to: a hymn to our doomed, resentful interdependence. It is as if he had suddenly seen how communities are formed in spite of themselves, in the length and breadth of Russia. All his plays from now on involve a local group dealing with visitors from somewhere else who then go away, leaving Vanya and Sonya, the three sisters and old Firs struggling. In *The Seagull* the departure comes an Act early and is followed by a calamitous return, but the idea is the same: the local rootstock has been part enriched, part damaged by its seasonal dressing. When the community breaks up and everyone shrinks back into their ordinary lives, think what the winter must be like here. The town is left with the schoolteacher, his unhappy wife and unfortunate child; with the staff of the now quiet house gossiping occasionally about Arkadina's meanness in having left one rouble to be divided between the three of them; with Sorin working out his last years in a rotten job nearby, glad of a civil servant's small bribes; with Konstantin (had he lived) mailing his anonymous stories to Moscow; and with the triangle of the dangerous bachelor Dorn, Polina, ashamed of her husband, and Shamrayev, keeping up appearances.

Chekhov himself was forever unsure whether he belonged with life's travellers or its residents; and though he might not like his theme of communality and dispersal attributed to his new life in Melikhovo, he might not be able to gainsay it either. To achieve *The Seagull*, he had to escape an unmanageable flux of visitors, patients and rubberneckers in the gardens and rooms of his new house. Later, the Soviet Union was to exploit a profound need for connection: in this enormous country, the impulse is always to seek company, any company, and the idea of living alone is still, in the twenty-first century, bewildering. So, in *The Seagull*, as sometimes in Chekhov's house, disconnected people criss-cross, bear down, ignore, collide, their emotions contained in tiny spaces, and sometimes congestion produces the opposite of intimacy. Improbable encounters are sustained by a rough courtesy. In Act Two, in the garden, Polina for a second time begs Dorn to return her love, apologising for her husband while Dorn, refusing to change his life, meaninglessly repeats his age. By chance Nina enters with some flowers and offers them to Dorn, simply because he is there. This so enrages Polina that she grabs the flowers and tears them into pieces. The effect on Nina must be like watching some inexplicable tragedy at a bus stop. At the beginning of the next Act, Trigorin is having lunch on his own before leaving for Moscow when he is discovered by Masha, who is now drinking as well as taking her snuff. He joins her for some vodka while she tells him of her despair of securing Konstantin's love and her plans to marry Medvedenko instead. These two have no general dealings to speak of: like a stranger on a train, Trigorin expresses polite concern at her plan – 'Isn't that going rather far?' – and confides in return that Konstantin has challenged him to a duel. Before leaving, Masha tells him to send her one of his books and to add a personal inscription, which she dictates with unexpected sweetness:

> Don't sign it just 'Good wishes', but 'To Masha – who knows where she's from, who knows why she's here.'

Trigorin is left with his notebook and the memory of a small friendship typical enough in the life of a reasonably alert writer. That's all there is to it; when the two of them briefly meet again in the last Act, Trigorin will ask Masha if she is happy but won't wait for an answer, and we will feel something of her disappointment. In this world, men and women can be simultaneously kind and oblivious; as they part, they often declare to each other that they'll probably never see each other again rather than hopefully insisting that they will; and if they ever do, they have forgotten a great deal. Nothing settles. Most things disappoint.

> I've offended the conventions terribly. A view of a lake, not much action, and after starting forte the play ends pianissimo.

By the beginning of Act Four, Masha and Medvedenko are calamitously married. The drawing-room in Sorin's house has been adapted into a study for Konstantin. At the end of his life Sorin feels he must be in the same room as his beloved nephew, so a bed (or a wheelchair) is being prepared for him here. The change in the domestic layout has made things too cramped for the various needs of the people: and it hints at a larger topsy-turvydom, as if other rooms in the house and heart had been closed up, the outside world's right to them much reduced. Though Konstantin is relatively successful now, in another way his wings are as broken as those of the seagull he shot in Act Two, since he has lost Nina, the woman to whom he reproachfully offered the dead bird – and, worse, to the dubious Trigorin, who is his mother's lover as well as his literary bogeyman. But the family's desire to gather round Konstantin, to protect and respect him, won't preclude their welcoming Trigorin a few minutes later, and even celebrating his ironic victory at Lotto.

Sorin is seriously ill, however. A fourth-grade civil servant (there were only five ranks, but at least he had to be called Your Highness), he describes himself in the past tense as 'L'Homme qui a Voulu', beautifully explaining his disappointments in a style that anticipates Olga's in *Three Sisters*. He had always wanted to be a literary man but had not succeeded. He had wanted to be a good speaker but was hopeless at it. He had failed to get married, and, preferring to live in the town, is dying in the country. He has spent his life as a master in thrall to a servant, as can happen. Shamrayev has had him in a vice-like grip, and all the projects Sorin entrusted to him were fated:

> The bees drop dead, the cows die, they won't give me any horses…

Sorin managed his small rebellions, but his standard response to humiliation or impasse was to whistle a tune to himself, like the Masha of *Three Sisters*: if he had played billiards, he might have ended up muttering like Gaev in *The Cherry Orchard*. Now he is reaping the rewards of a deferential life.

As for Medvedenko, I have a feeling Chekhov very much liked this man, whom he based on a Melikhovo neighbour called Mikhailov, who had gone grey at thirty with the effort of supporting four children on a teacher's salary of less than £3 a month. Now the character's marital misjudgments spill into the confined space. He tries to persuade his wife to come home, where their child is being cared for by a nanny: to add to his difficulties, it is a stormy night, and he feels he won't be able to secure any horses for the journey from his disobliging father-in-law – though he hasn't yet dared to ask him. However Masha wants to stay near Konstantin, even though her baby will be without her for the third night running. When her husband makes this point, she tells him he's a bore and that she wishes she'd never met him. Indeed there is something about the decent and worthy schoolteacher that, with the injustice of life, irritates everybody. When he predictably fails to raise a horse and decides to walk the four miles, he tries to say goodnight to the company but nobody pays him any attention, least of all his mother-in-law Polina, who is eager that he should be cuckolded by Konstantin. Shamrayev, the husband she has herself betrayed, has no compunction about not helping him with his transport: 'Look, he's not a general.' However, Medvedenko is used to walking: at the end of the previous act, while everyone else prepared to drive to the station to see Arkadina off, he saved space in the carriage by going ahead on foot – 'It won't take long.'

Meanwhile, the wind blows. For everyone, it is better to be here than most other places: they chafe away, while outside, infinitely it seems, there is nothing but steppe. They are probably somewhere between two and three hundred miles south of Moscow, on the edge of the Ukraine. So this is not as bad as for the three sisters in Perm, but still so lonely that it is easy to believe a tall story I once heard, or read, that such a household kidnapped a passer-by – the first in a week – and brought him in for compulsory dinner, vodka and several days' conversation.

They all need a way out, want it but fear it, and are both disturbed and glad if somebody describes such a thing for them. Dorn is at hand, attending on Sorin, if that is not too strong a word for a doctor who tells his patient little more than that everything in nature has to die. Dorn, who loves to travel, has recently saved two thousand roubles (£250) from thirty years of medical practice and blown it all on a European tour. Medvedenko spots the chance of a word with him. After an edgy preamble – he takes the doctor to be undeservedly rich – he manages for once to ask a question that interests everyone:

> Doctor, which town did you like best on your travels?

The company gathers round, as intrigued as a group on the docks at Liverpool or Cape Town looking at the exotic destinations of the liners. The answer to Medvedenko's question is Genoa, which must sound like Shangri-La to ears bruised by this weather. The writer is specially curious:

> Konstantin: Why Genoa?
>
> Dorn: The life in the streets is so wonderful. You just go out in the
>   evening and drift with the crowd, anywhere. You share its life,
>   enter its spirit. You begin to think there could be such a thing as a
>   world soul, like the one Nina once acted in your play.

Everyone understands this: even the cynical Dorn is obsessed with community, alienation, corroboration. For a moment we can hear Chekhov's own voice, twenty years younger than his:

> ...It's so good to travel abroad, just to see how much kindness and
> civility one can meet...

Dorn would have had to apply for a passport, and his ability to secure one would be specially noted by Konstantin, whose father is described in his papers as 'an artisan from Kiev', so that Konstantin is not even free to travel to the capital, unlike his mother and Trigorin. Chekhov, low-born and now living outside Moscow like Konstantin, also had to struggle for the right to journey at will, even inside Russia. Two years before writing *The Seagull*, he had been obliged to obtain one passport to stay in Petersburg (by entering government service for the moment), and then a second for Moscow; another time he got as far as Odessa but was refused permission to board ship and go abroad, until by good fortune the Mayor got to hear of it and sent his men to break into the Passport Office.

Once there, Chekhov's views on Italy were more mixed than Dorn's. He thought the Venus de Medici would look hideous in modern clothes, that Rome was 'just like Kharkov' and that Naples was a 'filthy city'; he found Pompeii boring though he enjoyed riding a horse round Vesuvius. The balance was really swung, as for many visitors, by La Serenissima, though not for quite organic reasons:

> I remember Venice very well. A poor degraded Russian who listens to
> the organ in the cathedral immediately wants to become a Catholic.

There is a note of shame in him, of self-consciousness and exclusion, together with a refusal to be changed:

> what nostalgia we all feel for our homeland…when I'm abroad I
> think constantly of the southern steppe of my childhood. Levitan
> once went to Italy and as soon as he got off the boat he became so
> homesick he turned round and came back again.

For a Russian, the need for home and desire for flight are painfully entwined. Andrei Tarkovsky, near enough an exile himself, closes his 1983 film *Nostalgia* with an astonishing sequence that Chekhov, Levitan and Dorn would all have approved. The hero, a Russian writer isolated in Italy, sits in front of a poor dacha, perhaps where he was born. He can hear dripping water, and, as if part of a childhood memory, snatches of song and the barking of a dog. The sound of the water gives way to the sight of falling snow; the camera pulls back over two minutes to frame this Russian image within an overarching Italianate church. Tarkovsky called nostalgia not a sadness but an illness, the debilitating loss of part of oneself: you may always have to be somewhere other, but you carry Mother Russia in your heart like a lost relative. However, for six people and an invalid in the makeshift space of Act Four of *The Seagull*, a chance to experience the emotions of Levitan or Tarkovsky's writer-hero would be a fine thing.

Chekhov finally returns to his preoccupying theme – personal catastrophe defined by the theatre. Dorn asks Konstantin bluntly for news of Nina: her life has become the source of sly speculation. Konstantin hedges – it is a very painful subject for him. Dorn prompts him – he has heard she is leading 'an odd sort of life'. Konstantin dodges again ('it's a long story') but Dorn won't have it:

> Then make it short. (*Pause.*)

Dorn may give no more of a hoot for Konstantin than he does for anyone else: he simply wants to know the facts, whether the sensational gossip about Nina is true. While Konstantin speaks, everyone thinks about her: nobody has seen her for two years, though it seems far longer. In due course, she decided to turn professional – with the minimum of encouragement, but what there was came from a deadly source, not Trigorin but Arkadina. She destroyed Nina's performance and then did the worst kind of dressing-room routine, pretending that the girl would be welcome in her profession:

> You've quite a gift, do you hear? You should go on the stage.

With this insincere sentence she sealed Nina's fate as surely as Trigorin did by telling her his address in Moscow. Better perhaps to be blunt and cold-hearted like Dorn, hardened by the dreadful life of a Russian doctor and who knows what other disappointments, than such an agent of calamity.

In fact Arkadina saw a rival in Nina, and much of the play has hung on the implicit contrast between the two actresses, who at this moment are converging on this house where they met. It is hard to define their talents, though we continually consider them, thinking of one while we watch the other, sometimes seeing them through the prism of the man they have in common. Trigorin himself may have spotted the one quality in Nina's acting that he might question in his Arkadina:

You did it with so much sincerity.

As a jobbing theatre critic Chekhov used to lambast Arkadina's repertoire – plenty of Maupassant, and toffee-nosed melodramas like Markiewicz's *The Fumes of Life*, which he had dismissed as 'written with a lavatory brush'. At that time, he was given to denouncing actors as capricious fools and actresses as cows who think they're goddesses; he was extremely casual about Sarah Bernhardt ('just an acting lesson carefully learned by heart'), though wildly impressed by Eleanora Duse. Did he imagine Arkadina to be like one or the other or neither, or perhaps as one of the Petersburg divas who would give him so much trouble? She is certainly jealous of Duse, but is even that a presumption on her part? Arkadina may be a second-rater, or, more likely, good in a certain way, in a style that is still around. Nina, with her progressive associations, is another matter – or is perhaps there to show that better intentions can lead to the same mediocrity. Not all that much better, though. We may turn to her as the play's heroine, seeing Arkadina as vain and self-absorbed: but Nina has something of the wilful fanatic about her – old-fashioned in her sentimentalities about the actor's life and intolerant of those who do not understand the supremacy of the stage. Arkadina on the other hand is too experienced for sentiment or special pleading: she is just what many older performers have always been, egotistical and generous to the same degree. Many of her failings are harmless: and her famous meanness is contradicted by the generosity Konstantin remembers her showing in the old days to the children of their washerwoman neighbour. Even better, Arkadina herself has forgotten this kindness. This side of her inspires great love in her son, and we can feel some of its warmth.

Huddled together, the company listens to this writer-hero broken by two actresses, continuing to establish where Nina's controversial talent has led her. Trigorin has been as good as the word he gave her as a warning, his fishing-rod parked, the heat-haze shimmering:

A young girl has lived by a lake all her life. She loves the lake like a seagull, and like a seagull she is happy and free. But then a man comes along, and for lack of anything better to do, destroys her. Just like a seagull.

He recognised the deadly scenario better than she did: in due course he seduced her and abandoned her with their child, who then died. And he is expected here shortly, with Arkadina. Prurience mixes with the listeners' sympathy: but Dorn, typically, seems to care more about her acting career than her disastrous young life. Is she any good now she is a professional? Konstantin finds it hard to judge – it's all mixed up for him with his attempts to visit her, when the hotel manager wouldn't let him through. Distressed, he contradicts himself:

> She played the leads – but her acting was coarse, not competent – all shouting and overacting. She had good moments – a great scream, a good death scene. But they were just moments.
>
> Dorn: Well then, she must be some good.
>
> Konstantin: Hard to say. Yes, I suppose so.

Nina has never acted in Moscow, but by some extraordinary coincidence is here in the town, staying at an inn because her parents will have nothing to do with her since the scandal. In a horrible repetition, they have set guards around their house against her. She has an engagement for the winter in the one-horse town of Yelets – a place Chekhov described elsewhere as so dull that even the germs fall asleep – to which she has to travel third-class with the peasants, while, a hundred and fifty miles south, Arkadina has been playing in the Ukrainian capital, Kharkov – not one of Chekhov's favourites either but certainly better than Yelets, which was a famously bad theatrical venue. While Arkadina will claim to have had a fantastic reception – flowers, gifts of brooches – Nina will only say she has 'a rough life' on the road: after the show she is having to fight off the attentions of the local businessmen. In Konstantin's muddled assessment, we still don't know whether she – or Arkadina – deserves better.

The picture moves into close-up. Medvedenko has seen Nina in the fields – for once, he is the one with the news. Within minutes Nina is in the room, alone with Konstantin. She is here to attempt a reconciliation parodically anticipated by Arkadina's and Trigorin's shaming reunion in Act Three, after Trigorin begged for his freedom. Partly because of this, another pulse can be heard as she sits with Konstantin: the sound of generations athwart each other. The lovers' anguish is punctuated by exclamations from the middle-aged dinner next door: the company has negotiated Trigorin's arrival and even his astounding announcement that he wants to have another look at the spot where Konstantin and Nina once did their play, and they have all sat down together. These young lives have been blighted, somewhat like Romeo's and Juliet's, by their fumbling elders, with their self-aggrandisement, their emotional dishonesty, their temporising jollity.

Nina seems to have developed a kind of 'rep' veneer, a low-level professional savvy – but she often sounds genuinely wiser than Konstantin:

> Come on, let's sit down together and talk and talk, just as we used to.

She says she might be the seagull (or 'a' seagull – no definite article in Russian) – the creature Konstantin shot for her, that Trigorin warned her she was. The idea of this bird, used by both men in their pursuit of Nina, keeps puncturing her thoughts – sometimes she voices the obsession as an actressy catch-phrase, sometimes her sorrow is as raw as the seagull's cry. It is in any case a dubious symbol: as anyone who lives by the sea can testify, this is not a pretty bird but a raucous scavenger. To the debunking Chekhov it was an innocent fact of the wild countryside; Trigorin perhaps calls it a beautiful bird because of its trueness rather than its prettiness. Nina grew up entranced by the flight of seagulls across the lake, and she imagined herself one as she rushed from her parents' house to Konstantin; but when presented as a prey to her, it turned out to be a clumsy, dead and ugly thing, going flop at her feet. Now, as she tries to identify herself, she remembers both her dream and the ungainly reality:

> I'm the seagull. No, that's wrong. I'm an actress. Ah well...

In the end, she escapes into a wider loneliness, leaving both her predators behind. Her ability to take flight has helped her see something neither of them could:

> No matter whether we act or write, the great thing isn't glory or fame, not what I used to dream of, but simply stamina. You have to bear your cross and have faith. I have faith and things don't hurt me so much now.

A few moments later Shamrayev, with the utmost inappropriateness, offers to bring out the actual seagull, now stuffed, to show Trigorin. The unlovely thing looks all wrong in a sitting room. One would hope it is the last thing Trigorin wants to see – though he seems to be a man remarkably untroubled by tact. He is a little circumspect:

> Shamrayev: Konstantin shot a seagull that time and you asked me to have it stuffed.
>
> Trigorin: I don't remember. (*Thinks.*) I don't remember.

Unaware, Shamrayev returns crudely to the subject in the final moments of the play, to be answered in the same way:

> Shamrayev: Just as you ordered.
>
> Trigorin: I don't remember. (*After some thought.*) I don't remember.

On this cue, a gunshot cracks out – Konstantin, driven to despair, has killed himself in the next room. He is as lifeless as the stuffed thing we're looking at: the original has taken wing.

This gunshot is already halfway out of Chekhov's life. In the sprawling untitled play now known as *Platonov*, it had been used almost satirically – when Sonya shot Platonov in the chest he commented:

> Wait a moment, what's all this?

– then collapsed, only to rise momentarily when he realised a messenger needed paying:

> Give him three roubles.

In *Ivanov* it was more portentous, when the hero closed the play by running 'to one side' and shooting himself. Beyond *The Seagull*, the sound will recede like an echo: even here its real interest lies beyond, in how Konstantin's suicide is to be dealt with. In the play's marvellous coda, Dr Dorn, forced out of his general indifference at last, pretends a bottle of ether has exploded, and gives the word quietly to Trigorin, who is then (the great moral coward) left with the problem of breaking the news to Arkadina. The two compromised men could not have been better chosen for their burdens: a director is left to decide how much or little of their efforts is to be seen before the light fades.

A familiar face is beginning to form. One eye cast quizzically on our tendency not to listen, Chekhov has trained the other most seriously on how little we can manage alone. He has queried the power of his profession to give meaning to a chaotic life and, while at it, he has looked at the practical limits of the theatre, mocking its personalities. He has shown how a doctor can travel and yet learn little; and how those who suffer most may survive. His ambiguous seagull has discredited the symbolism that comes so easily to another kind of writer. And he has broadcast all this only by admitting that he supposes, after all, that a hero about to shoot himself normally expects to say a few words of farewell. But in Petersburg he obviously preferred not to witness the innovation whereby this is replaced by the long silence of Konstantin methodically tearing up all his work. He favoured his own company, and mine in my dreams. After Romanov's, rather than going to the Hotel Angleterre where Masha and Lika Mizinova had been waiting to have supper with him, he began to face the music by trudging home across the canal to the Suvorins, with whom he was staying. Their house, which resembled a medieval castle, or perhaps Citizen Kane's Xanadu, was on what is now Chekhov Street – an odd memorial for one of his more ignoble moments.

At one in the morning, the two patient women guessed what he'd done and went there. Chekhov wasn't yet back, but an hour later he slipped in and sloped off to bed, where he pulled a blanket over his head and refused to speak to anyone. In the end Suvorin managed to start a conversation through the blanket, though Chekhov wouldn't let him turn on the light. Suvorin's wife, Anna, reports that Chekhov swore that he was 'a very coarse word' if he'd write for the stage again in the next seven hundred years. Not for the last time, a future collapses for all of us.

In the morning, as if little had happened, Chekhov borrowed some books about peasant life from Suvorin's library and left before the house was awake, having first written notes to assure everyone he was in a perfect humour now, but ordering Suvorin to hold up the planned publication of his plays. His companion as far as Petersburg station was Potapenko, perhaps recommending himself at that mortifying moment because he had not himself been at the premiere (thus solving the problem of his wife encountering Lika). When a newsboy offered them a paper Chekhov, comically, told him he was not a reader, and turning to Potapenko commented: 'That boy has a kind face, hasn't he, but his hands are full of poison.' They parted. Chekhov took the slow service to Moscow (a day and a night, three hundred and fifty miles), changed trains and was home in Melikhovo by early the next day, betraying his distrait state by leaving his luggage on board. Later Suvorin accused him of cowardice over the whole affair, but Chekhov compared himself, unanswerably, to a man who has proposed marriage and been refused. However, after a cold bath and some castor oil he was ready to write another play, or better still a story – 'What bliss! No actors, producers, no audience.' It turned out to be a great work, 'Peasants' – no personal thefts this time, but a more savage view from the windows of his Melikhovo home at the landed gentry who destroy the lives of the poor around them.

A writer called Alexander Sumbatov-Yuzhin wrote to Chekhov after reading this story:

> I can feel what the weather was like on such-and-such a day, where
> the sun was, the way the ground slopes towards the river. I can see it:
> I don't need it to be described.

In truth, it's that gift of his that has allowed me to imagine myself tagging along on his Petersburg walk. There is something very intimate about Chekhov;

his response to disaster and his humour are so accessible that you want to talk back. To have been with Gogol after *The Government Inspector* flopped (much more highly-strung, he in fact ran away abroad) might have been quite wearing, and I doubt if I would have cared for Dostoyevsky's querulous mutterings about his enemies as he slunk through the Petersburg Haymarket. Even the astonishing end of Tolstoy in that station-master's cottage would be for me a second choice. But Chekhov is so familiar and true of eye that you see the streets and gardens, the hotel rooms and cherry orchards that he sees himself. I recognise his first-night sulk, and the hesitation over reading the reviews, of course; and it's easy to imagine the bad word he used. But I can also, almost, see Suvorin talking through the blanket and Lika's and Masha's faces as they sit in the Angleterre. And I can make a fair guess at what he ate at Romanov's and what coat he was wearing, how he addressed the owner, whether he then went on to another bar or a brothel. For once, genius seems the most natural company. The fact is simple and, in Russia, almost proverbial: Tolstoy and Dostoyevsky are giants, but Anton Pavlovich Chekhov is a friend.

SIBERIA

A writer is not a pastry-cook. When he takes the rope he mustn't say
he can't pull.

– Anton Chekhov

And of course a friend has rights. My notion of breaching the privacy of
this proud but reticent man, of presuming to do a stage show about his
life in fact, grew out of a conversation with an American poet and zennist in
1975 on the Trans-Siberian Express, which was certainly a good start. I was
dawdling home from a Royal Shakespeare Company tour of Japan, satisfying
a long curiosity about Russia that amounted to a mild, sweet obsession. In
fact it was over-ripening a little into sentiment, as if I believed that the very
fact of standing on Russian soil and smelling Russian wood-smoke would
itself prove something. But didn't Stravinsky say that the smell of Russian
earth was different, and that you could never forget it? I used to wonder
tremulously in Bayswater what it would be like to arrive at Omsk at two in
the morning in November: less whimsically, I was inquisitive to see what
Irkutsk, the Paris of Siberia, was like, and I wanted to get a respectable idea
of the vastness across which three sisters could dream of Moscow, Moscow.

The Trans-Siberian is not what people think it is, a tourist fantasy like the
Orient Express. For one thing, in 1975 the westward journey started not at
Vladivostok, as legend would have it, since the Soviets kept that city a military
secret, but at the unfamous port of Nakhodka, seventy-five miles up the track.
Here a foreigner would be soothed by one night of burnished brass, buttoned
red plush and lace curtains, before changing trains in the morning at the city
of Khabarovsk, to the north, onto the Trans-Siberian proper. This was and is
one of the world's busiest and least ceremonious transit routes, during which
many passengers wore pyjamas and both the food and the toilet facilities
slowed to a dribble within a couple of days. Times have moved on. Vladivostok
has reopened with a banal flourish: once home of a great fleet, it has been
impoverished by defence cuts, nuclear waste from its decommissioned
submarines is carelessly dumped in the sea and it is plagued by homelessness
and crime; but still there it is, free. The journey from Moscow now takes a
day less; a new line has opened, running from Irkutsk round the north of
Lake Baikal, and another mammoth has been dug out of the Siberian
permafrost. But then Russia too has emerged from its permafrost to find
itself, some would say, dying from exposure to the heat. The Trans-Siberian

is to be recommended only cautiously, but it can still be a real odyssey for the impressionable, and if you are as lucky as I was in my travelling companions, probably unforgettable.

I set out from Tokyo's port of Yokohama with three days and 950 miles at sea, moving northwards along the east coast of Japan, through the straits between Honshu and Hokkaido and westward to the Soviet Union. There were dolphins and a great deal of rain, and, for fantasists like me, one truly Russian presence on the boat, the Moiseyev dance troupe of Moscow returning from a tour: but they were firmly cordoned off, their romantic musk neutralised by Soviet orderliness. As we executed our left turn into the unsheltered ocean, *MS Baikal*, creaking furiously, heaved and fell through space as if flicked by a magisterial hand, and I reeled almost alone above decks while even the dancers took queasy refuge. Then, as the seas grew calmer, I fell under the intense scrutiny of a grizzled man in a grey duffel coat – invariably there, ten yards or so away, his gaze trained frankly on me whenever I sought to catch a Moiseyev eye. He looked as Burt Lancaster might, playing a secret agent in a John le Carré story. At these times I remembered that my mother had told me I was quite mad to take this journey, for those crazy Soviets would never let me through. Paranoia racing, I supposed Lancaster had a special cabin with a sea telephone from which to make his reports to the Lubyanka. I happened to be trapped in the sharp end of the boat when he finally approached me: I backed against the rails and thought urgently of home.

He was, in fact, Lucien Stryk from Illinois, the gentlest of men and a theatregoer. He announced that he had seen me on the stage in London and wanted to pay his compliments. I had the feeling, once the delight had worn off, that he might be overestimating me – what he had seen was not so remarkable a thing – and it took me some time to realise that I was dealing with a man of exceptional generosity and charm, and enormous talents of his own. A lifelong zen scholar in a field too glibly entered by many, his poetry (still too little known outside the US) is deeply influenced by masters old and new – Basho, Takahashi – but entirely personal. In 1975 he was returning from a spell in Japan on a Fulbright Research Fellowship, in his bag the manuscript for his new work, *The Penguin Book of Zen Poetry*, together with notes for another, *The Awakened Self.*

I have the Soviet authorities to thank for this great figure and for the friendship that has lasted ever since. Once on Russian rails at Nakhodka, we were billeted together all the way to Moscow in a two-berth compartment – the reasonable assumption being that the American writer and the English actor would talk the hind legs off each other, rather than wandering through the train embarrassing citizens with unanswerable questions. We were further insulated by having other foreigners to either side of us the length of the carriage, which thus took on an ominously detachable air: but that was the way things were ordered then, down to the tiny detail. In some ways we were relieved to conform. Beneath such adventures lies a great need for comfort, for the guilty pleasure of occasionally gossiping in your language.

I had taken with me, for the eight-day, hundred-stop journey, one large book, Ernest J Simmons' biography of Anton Chekhov – not foreseeing Lucien, I had imagined it would be the ideal companion. I am sure I already wanted to know more than anybody in the world about Chekhov: I know the reason, and it has to do with my student days. Undergraduate theatre (Cambridge 1961–4) was a perfect preparation for my profession, since the survivor was unlikely thereafter to come across anything like the same rivalry and malice or the same ideological factioning – the constituency being small and the testosterone, for it was mostly male in those days, very high. Needless to say, the more overweening the voice the greater the professional obscurity that generally awaited it; but it was tough at the time. Absurdly, one could sign up with the Ibsen camp or be a friend of Chekhov, wear a Meyerholdian or a Brechtian badge, and there were even small attempts to pit Arthur Miller and Eugene O'Neill against each other. As for Chekhov, the works of this most tolerant of men were cited for the most unyielding aesthetic postures, mostly based on a wild misreading of Stanislavsky. Although much of the talk was theoretical, conducted in the standard smoke-filled rooms and coffee-houses of the early sixties, it must be said that there was a good deal of practical activity too, the same dozen or so people forming the nucleus of half a dozen dramatic societies – a means of avoiding the university rule against any one society staging more than one show a term. By this manoeuvre, in a simulation of three-weekly rep, we could all keep on continuously with what we described, to the bafflement of our tutors and of visiting professionals, as our 'work'.

Though a Chekhovian myself on balance, I found to my disappointment that that didn't qualify me to act in the plays, the casting of which by some of my director peers was the subject of stern invigilation. I was thought to have not enough of the Asiatic gene for Soliony, to lack the introspection for Konstantin, to be too little aware of the Marxist future for Trofimov – in any case, having a West End actress for a girlfriend at the time, I was hopelessly compromised from an intellectual point of view. Striving to improve myself, I got into a terrible tangle about Stanislavsky's Magic If, and even investigated the movement theory – its bound and free flow and eight 'efforts' – of Rudolf Laban, but to no avail: better that Pennington be confined to Shakespeare and Shaw. With a certain worried nobility, I convinced myself that this was just, and watched undergraduate Chekhov productions in puzzled awe, sure that the largely inaudible *Ivanov* before me held the secret, if only I could strain my ears for the clues. There was one way out – all the debate was a good limbering for the English tripos, which I negotiated by writing about nothing much except the theatre; my speciality was to link Chekhov with Beckett and Pinter, and all of them with the Italian New Wave, and I finally published a much-vaunted article in *Granta*, 'Pennington on Pinter', which now nestles, to my embarrassment and his courteous glee, in the latter's archive. Actually it was pretty good: and I was formally rewarded with a 2:1 and the benefit of the considerable doubt, while some of my ideologue colleagues, I must say, did rather less well. But I still couldn't get a part in a Chekhov.

It all sounds very silly, I know, and so it was: but a memory of these dismal skirmishes was part of what I carried up the gangplank to Lucien eleven years later for our journey across Siberia. As we rolled along, he told me he had written a poem called 'Chekhov in Nice', not so much about the great writer as about the roamer and gambler; and one day, somewhere near Ulan Ude, he recited it to me in his grave, sympathetic tones:

> Were he less the son, he'd have come
> Here twenty years ago. Before those
> Germs, swarming, had carved
> A kingdom of his chest, before
> The flame had risen from his bowels
> To fan within his head. Were he less the son…

A little later, between Irkutsk and Cheremkhovo, as if he had been cunningly circling the subject, Lucien asked me if I realised that in 1890 Chekhov, already tubercular, had made the reverse trip to ours, in far worse circumstances of course, to do a survey of the penal colony on Sakhalin Island. Indeed, he had stopped at many of the same places as we had, before the railway of course. The journey flew in the face of health and personal safety, not to mention a burgeoning literary career: it took him three months to get there, Lucien told me, leaning back contentedly on his pillow. I hadn't reached that part in Simmons' biography, and I gaped at him. Chekhov's scandalised report on what he found on Sakhalin has now taken its place in the translated canon, but it was little-known in English in 1975; and although I was aware in a general way that Chekhov had a conscience, I had assumed that he exercised it from his armchair. At Novosibirsk, Lucien pressed the friendly advantage, declaring that having watched me carefully all these days, he believed that I should set about doing a one-man show on the writer. I scoffed, in a pro-y way. The subject was too difficult, the man too elusive; who needs one-man shows anyway? Poor helpful Lucien, I smiled, so unacquainted with the peculiarities of my industry: dear kindly Lucien, how could he understand? We parted in Moscow, he promising to nag me thoroughly, I still pitying him. He then called me once a year for nine years – more often, because we were fast friends now, but once a year strictly on this point. For eight years I continued to mock him – by the ninth, I'd done it.

I do have a slight aversion to solo shows – so easy to envisage and so difficult to pull off. So strategic, too – in an uncertain profession, anyone can do this kind of DIY, and, with a bit of graft, get it on somewhere. God knows why, really – it is a strain on the memory, and can be excruciatingly lonely, especially on tour. Why do without the exhilarating interaction of a company, instead summoning yourself alone to a rehearsal room and then waking on some distant shore in the arms of the British Council? While back at home your enterprise is not taken seriously at all: 'Are you working?' 'Yes, on my one-man show.' 'Ah. Well, let's hope something comes along soon.' It's not a proper job, just one in the bag.

More precisely: the choice of subject, the long research, your taste in theatre practice, uniquely sit up for the marksman – there is nobody to blame, though it can also be bracing to be so alone, a spider spinning out wild thread. Novels don't always adapt well to the stage, the reader's imagination being better, and in the same way the solo performer has to be doing something beyond the reach of the best-written biography. The real nub of it is animation – at any given point, why continue to speak at all? Because this is a monologue and there can only be one full-stop. The constant move forward will depend on cues inside the subject's personality, so it is not enough to find a favourite character, but rather one in some unresolved relationship with themselves or the outer world (the audience). Some characters are definitely best left in the wings. The most interesting account of the actor Edmund Kean I know is not one thespian's attempt to impersonate another, but the discreetly scandalised diary of his company manager, as strait-laced a character as such men tend to be, forever trying to keep the unruly genius to the mark; while Shakespeare hovers over Peter Whelan's play *The Herbal Bed* but, delightfully, is about to make his first appearance only as the play ends.

Chekhov was a secretive man in many ways; but, I began to reason, his wariness might have masked a reasonable self-regard. Once asked to account for himself, all he could manage was:

Among Russian writers I am number thirty-seven

– a characteristic joke which reminds us of what we know, that he stood a great deal higher than that. It is, after all, not conceit in itself that a man fears, but letting it show. Away from his desk Chekhov seems to me one of nature's reactors – even a little, as we might say, passive-aggressive: his correspondence is full of passionate opinion expressed on his own terms, but when pushed to a confession by someone else he is inclined to shift into satire. Alone on a stage, the feeling that something was expected of him could make him subversive or downright childish, as when once, approached by a eulogising official, he pointed out that the man's fly-buttons were open. In a show like this I should use his reluctant credos not for their felicity – making both him and me seem very self-satisfied – but as a measure of resistance. In this, I'd only be taking the same care of him as he took of his characters. In a bad production of *The Cherry Orchard*, Gaev willingly serenades his bookcase or talks about billiards because he's a funny old thing. In a good one you see that the pain of his nostalgia, and his discomfiture in his present company, is forcing him into foolishness.

It was tricky, but I began to see that it could be interesting. I got hold of a copy of *The Island of Sakhalin*, without telling Lucien.

A surprisingly young and robust face looks out from a photograph taken in 1890 on South Sakhalin Island. Chekhov is only thirty, true enough, but you don't expect to see such vigour, even sportiness, in him. Wearing a sort of student's cap, he seems to be sitting at the edge of a picnic in this unlikely setting – hamper, bottles and samovar – but the picture claims to show the formal presentation of some medal to the Japanese consul. Perhaps this is the most ceremonious it gets in this terrible place, though in fact the southern is the more temperate of the two islands – even mildly farmable, like the Falklands. The contentiousness of Sakhalin's history as a small political football between Japan and Russia is a surprise. No doubt what is not being discussed at this gathering is the fact that fifteen years earlier, Japan ceded it to the Russians (perhaps Japanese consuls were now appeased with many decorations). It would revert after the Russo-Japanese War of 1904–5 and remain Japanese until Russia got it back after the Second World War. In any case, the place seems to have little profit in it but the name, like the patch of Polish land Fortinbras is after in *Hamlet*, but from a Russian point of view, it chose itself for the type of convict colonisation programme the British had already undertaken in Australia.

As Lucien surmised, the work Chekhov did in the heart of Sakhalin's darkness – not to mention the preceding journey – is the Big Fact confounding what I thought I knew about the man. His 'Mania Sakhalinosa' baffled his contemporaries as well – especially the men of letters, who guessed that he was hurt by the failure of *The Wood Demon*, or was on the run from a love affair – and critics have taken up the speculation. According to taste, Chekhov made the journey in a spirit of enquiry, just wanting to have a look; or he felt needled by criticism that he had undertaken no missions to irritate the Government in the manner of Leo Tolstoy; or he was coming to savage terms with the death of Nikolai. Some say the experience permanently ruined his health and peace of mind, others that he was tougher than that. In fact there seems little reason to doubt what he said himself. First the veil of picturesque self-deprecation –

> When I thought about my work it was as if I were eating cabbage soup from which a cockroach had been taken – if you'll forgive the comparison…so I'm studying Sakhalin till it's coming out of my ears: the soil and the subsoil, the loamy sand and the sandy loam

– then the fact, angry and righteous:

> Exile. What a terrible thing for a Russian. We've let millions of people rot in prisons all across the continent, we've driven them through the Siberian cold for thousands of miles and infected them with syphilis and debauched them, and then blamed it all on the red-nosed prison warders. But it's not the red-nosed prison warders who are to blame. It's us. All of us.

There's an interesting feint here. A philosophical overview was certainly expected of the medical man. As a student Chekhov had planned a doctoral thesis in the Darwinian manner called *A History of Sexual Authority*, as well as a more orthodox history of Russian medicine (in the event he abandoned both). His interest in the conditions in which ten thousand souls survived or did not on Sakhalin was so evidently in line with this that he was able to secure some official support from the Russian Empire's Central Prison Administration in Petersburg. On the other hand, he was an artist, and a morally engaged Russian writer was ever a dangerous thing, a deep-seam miner alerting an unfree people. So it was that the Administration's promise to him of unlimited access to the prisoners was accompanied by a private instruction to the island's Governor to watch him closely. No doubt Chekhov was suspected of a little disingenuousness, as if the anger in his private correspondence could be smelt on his breath. Still, at least he wasn't Tolstoy.

He was in any case not allowed to contact the minority of political prisoners who lived on Sakhalin; but the criminal population in their five hard-labour settlements, the equal number of men with families who guarded them, and the few hundred Ainu and Gilyak aborigines were fair game. What Chekhov also found were former convicts (many of whose women had followed them into exile) making a hopeless effort at colonisation, on soil generally little better than bog-land, infested with mosquitoes, granted the briefest of growing seasons, in fog, rain and sub-zero cold. At first he felt as much at a loss, he said, as a crayfish stranded on the sand; but by the time he left, every stone in this God-forsaken place seemed to have been turned over by his stick, every feature of the soil noted, each settlement scrupulously analysed and tagged with a statistic. Completely alone for three months, he had compiled a census in which ten thousand convicts had their own detailed cards – with no short cuts, of course: his method was to visit every hut and look in the prisoner's eyes.

The astonishing *The Island of Sakhalin*, four years in the subsequent writing and his longest prose work by far, shows an applied scholarship as remarkable as its grave, mature style. A view persists (keeping the book off the bibliographies for a long time) that this is the scientific, not the literary Chekhov – as if there could be such a division; but its apparent unreadability from any other point of view than the factual is, paradoxically, the emotional making of it. It is a masterpiece precisely in the Chekhovian style. The more rigorously the author disguises himself the more you find yourself in the heart of the matter; and you get more of Chekhov himself than in any but his most intimate letters. Though not the first to draw attention to Sakhalin, his combination of science and eloquence made him the most influential witness yet, and his findings led to some cosmetic reforms – the chaining of convicts to wheelbarrows and the shaving of their heads were abolished. As a modest tribute, there is now a little one-storeyed wooden Chekhov Museum, and the main street in Alexandrovsk, where he landed, is named after him.

Bent over his pen, this unlikely witness keeps glancing up at you. Noting Sakhalin's average monthly temperatures, the dates when the ice might be expected to thaw and the density of the sea-fogs, he comments:

> Cold people become brutal, and the weak-spirited lose any hope of a good life if they never see the sun.

He spots the bleakness beneath the small celebrations:

> Evening – bright lights, the band plays, but there's no merriment, people walk like shadows, quiet as shadows. Music in the ears of a man without a home increases his misery. The reflections of the coloured lanterns in the dirty water of the river Duyka are beautiful and ludicrous, like a cook's daughter dressed up as a countess…

Observation turns to outrage, then dries into scientific ink. There are no books in the 'schools', and when Chekhov himself undertakes an operation to lance an abscess all the scalpels are blunt and there is no carbolic. How can this have come to pass? To the Ainu and Gilyaks a drinking bout has become more important than a marriage, and Chekhov sympathises. A tunnel is being built through some mountains, even though there are perfectly good high roads through the area and in any case no engineers – the result is a huge waste of convict labour, something crooked and filthy:

> A first class example of our Russian tendency to use all our resources
> on trifles, ignoring the necessities.

Note the deadly use of 'our Russian': the authorities were wise to watch him.
One day he rides through a forest and meets a group of prisoners. Knowing
that he at least is unlikely to shop them, they quietly complain about their
inedible bread. Looking into the matter, Chekhov finds that the daily ration
is three pounds of the wet, doughy stuff, undercooked with bad flour: and that
by some 'Russian' mystery its quantity tends to reduce between arriving at
the baker's and leaving, mixed up with clay. He sees blind children, and
convict women – and sometimes colonists' wives – being allocated to settlers
like domestic animals; girls working as prostitutes as if it was 'a municipal
enterprise' even before they have started menstruating, and becoming pregnant
as soon as they have.

Chekhov claims no superhuman stamina, though he often seems to have
it. Just once he pleads frailty, admitting that he was unable to cover one
settlement as thoroughly as he might because that week he was simply 'so
tired, so tired'. The weary man vigorously trudging in his heavy moist
overcoat, half-known to his hosts and a stranger to the settlers, has his own
battle to fight, daily, with the unexpected. On this sliver of land, he finds
himself surrounded by water in a way a Russian is unused to, and it laps into
his narrative as it rarely does into his fiction:

> This is the Pacific…far away over there, the coast of America. Not a
> living soul near you, not a bird, not a fly. You ask yourself who do
> these waves thunder for, who hears them at night-time… It is terrible,
> but at the same time I want to stand here forever and stare at these
> boring waves…

He also has secret anxieties – identifying at what age the convict population
generally succumbs to tuberculosis, he can hardly fail to observe that it is
precisely at his own time of life. He describes himself shivering like a boy
whose blanket has fallen off in his sleep: then he is severe, then crankily
addicted to small pleasures. Sometimes the lonely figure smokes in a corner
and allows himself to think of home:

> The northern scenery here is vivid and reminds you of Russia. Nature
> in Russia is mournful too, but mournful in a Russian way. Here it
> smiles and mourns at once, and creates a sadness hard to define.

Then he warms himself with a trade joke or two, noting that the Gilyaks are
such misogynists that the dramatist Strindberg would be given a warm welcome
by them. When he lodges with a prison doctor, he sees that his host looks like

Henrik Ibsen; eating soup, chicken and ice cream with this man, he hears with one ear the prisoners' clanking chains outside and with the other the cosy chirping of canaries in the room.

Chekhov has been recognised as an important writer for two years, and springing character from overlookable detail is a reflex. Now he stands in the rain in a burial ground. The newly-dug grave fills up with water, the coffin-bearers sweat in the wet and talk irritably about other things as they drop the coffin in and toss the sods of clay after it. One of the dead woman's children, Alyosha, is three or four, in blue patched trousers and a blouse much too big for him. He gazes into the grave. Chekhov, watching like Hamlet or Horatio, asks the boy where his mother is: Alyosha looks speculatively at the coffin, makes a gesture 'like a man cleaned out at cards', laughs and waves at it:

> Shovelled away!

Next the short story writer sees the important details of a typesetter's wedding: the indifferent choristers, the congregation looking impatiently over their shoulders for the bride to arrive, the best man in his white tie a typesetter too – all of them managing to forget that they are not at home but in a prison church thousands of miles away. When they leave there is nothing but the smell of burning candles inside and melancholy returning like a fog. Outside it is raining. And, in the last sentence, what of the officiating priest?

> Father Yegor settled into his carriage and was driven to the home of the bride and bridegroom.

It is like Chekhovian fiction, down to the flat, factual ending with its slight burden of omen or psychological weight.

His summary of all this is a simple, cleansing litany. It is self-evident that hunger, slavery and fear produce their own vices, and that exile is really capital punishment given another name. By the time a prisoner is released, the citizen in him is finished and he has lost the very instincts that might have helped him colonise – which proves, simply, that the sentences are too long. It is obvious that convicts will thieve like 'consummate artists', since exercising skill in making off with a live sheep or the Governor's compass is their last form of self-respect. Anticipating his Vershinins and Tusenbachs to come, Chekhov is sure that in fifty years these things will be viewed with horror, but at present the judges are not educated enough to be interested.

He leaves the prison island uncertain whether he has grown up or gone out of his mind. Before he went away Tolstoy's *Kreutzer Sonata* had been a great event, but now it seems ridiculous. Emphasising his limitations, he nevertheless has the air of someone standing up straight at last:

> I've worked for three months from five in the morning until late at night and I still feel like a man at a zoo who's seen the insects and missed the elephant... I have enough for four doctoral dissertations and a feeling in my innards as if I'd been eating rancid butter.

There is another photograph from Sakhalin, taken as Chekhov was embarking on the *Petersburg* steamship for Hong Kong and Europe. There are good times ahead as well as some *coups de bas*, such as the burial at sea that would inspire his first story for months, 'Gusev', about a tubercular soldier who dies on board ship and is then eaten by a shark. But Chekhov will be proud of not having been seasick in a great storm, and will enthuse naively about Hong Kong and Singapore, swimming in the Indian Ocean and gleefully boasting that he has

> ...had a black-eyed Hindu girl, and would you like to know where? In a coconut grove, on a moonlit night...

Hardly back in Russia, he will be off again to Vienna, Italy and France – again at rather touching pains to stress his Dorn-like worldliness:

> To take your own wife to Paris would be like taking your own samovar to Tula.

Standing on Sakhalin's dockside with all this to come, he looks as alert and vigorous as he did at the picnic. No doubt he will never forget the reproach in the face of one convict who, far from appreciating his coming, has accused him bitterly of leaving; but what more could he do than file the experience and move on?

> I'm glad this rough old convict's uniform is hanging in my literary wardrobe. Let it hang there!

However, the boyish figure, two thirds of the way through his own life, is hiding a new power inside him, the fuel for nearly fifteen years' work. How can you tell, from these awkwardly posed (and somewhat foreshortened) images, the weight of his new conviction? How, in any case, to tell the mind's construction from the face?

CATCHING HIS EYE

Do you think that looks like me? It's not me, it's some Frenchman.

— Anton Chekhov

Chekhov was never well captured in a painting, but he was often photographed: the pictures are mostly so well-known that there is a jolt of pleasure in the unexpected ones. Apart from the two on Sakhalin, I've now seen the medical student almost lost in a crowd in 1883 and the good doctor being pushed in a wheelbarrow in Melikhovo; I've caught a distant glimpse of him shielding his face from the sun as he talks to the builder of his Yalta house (complaining, perhaps – he described it as a sardine tin) and driving in a carriage up the path towards it, tiny and hunched in thick overcoat and hat. These pictures, failing to cut the biographical mustard, refreshingly place him in a world of which he is a small part, not the Great Object.

But mainly I depend on these quite frustrating close-up shots, with their fleeting impression of life: a veil of negative scratches and watery blurs intervenes between my eye and his, allowing him to edge into the background. You get little impression of his height of course, but the broad Slavic brow is striking, the eyes have a tendency to hood, and as time goes on you can get a fair idea of his health from the state of his beard. Often his mouth looks ready to smile but his eyes forbid it, the camera being a serious business. Sometimes he looks like a clerk in his wing collar, or an elder of the church, though I know severity sat unsteadily on him. At other times the head pushes forward a little, daring the photographer. Occasionally he looks round-shouldered and resigned. These pictures mean as much to me as any book: and I can see that they describe an arc, just about.

Chekhov was born in Taganrog on the Black Sea, a town

> so poor that only the Mayor and a couple of Greek merchants were permitted the luxury of a chamber-pot.

The sturdy fourteen-year-old, known at school as 'Bombhead', juts his chin with boyish pomposity, standing up very straight, and, not knowing what to do with his hand, puts it meaninglessly across his chest. The whole family is there. Standing to his left are two elder brothers, Nikolai (Kolya), sixteen, and Alexander, nineteen, black sheep both: the first a gifted artist on the way to his tubercular death (aggravated by alcohol) at just thirty-one, the other to a longer life plagued off and on by the same addiction. Alexander is making the same Napoleonic gesture as Anton, but it looks even sillier: between them, Kolya, shorter, is much more natural, hooking his arm affectionately over Anton's shoulder, his hands lightly clasped. Enraged by the orthodoxies of their father (but also needing to avoid military service by getting into university), the older two are preparing to leave for Moscow, beginning the rapid unravelling of this tightly-framed group. A year after that their bankrupted father will avoid debtors' prison by slipping away to Moscow himself, almost immediately followed by their mother, by Masha and Misha, and a year after by Ivan, the final brother. Still a schoolboy, Anton, completely alone, then becomes the family head in exile. He occupies the Taganrog home as a tenant, since it has been bought by Gavriil Selivanov, an associate of the family, as an ambiguous act of friendship. Chekhov thus joins a group of writers predisposed by paternal failure – Dickens, Shaw, Ibsen, Strindberg – who want, in Arthur Miller's words, to make 'a new cosmology [...] a new order of perception, that would make the world all new, as seen through their eyes'.[1] While his discredited, unemployable father continues to deliver him moral lectures by letter, Anton tries to stave off the Taganrog creditors by selling the family furniture and tutoring in his spare time.

His own departure for Moscow to enrol as a medical student at nineteen is part of a wretched need for self-determination – a comical idea in view of the flailing family's efforts to keep him in his *de facto* paternal role – but he looks confident and blessed nevertheless. Unsurprisingly, contemporaries describe a big physical change at this time, but it is more like an assembling of his character. Just under six foot (my height), he has brown eyes flecked with blue, he is brown-haired, long-faced and fair-skinned. In Moscow, his face and body waver and settle under the strain of five years' medical training and the struggle to keep the family afloat by selling stories to the weekly journals – under a variety of pseudonyms, so that he can supply a variety of publications. In 1881 the young bohemian leans against a desk (or piano) watching Kolya sketch, a portfolio with his initials scratched on it at his feet. Anton looks pudgy, almost epicene, with full hair, like a more tight-lipped young Oscar Wilde, and nothing at all like Kolya, who always had a slightly Asiatic look. Around this time Chekhov seems to have written a five-hour play and sent it off to the actress Maria Yermolova: when she rejected it he, so to speak, threw it in a drawer, where it was found fifteen years after his death, and now has a fingerhold in the repertoire as *Platonov*. The most skilful adaptations – and there have been several – can hardly conceal the fact that, though drawn in energetic primary colours, it was ever too long for its own good, its narrative pulse barely sustaining the long disquisitions. However, it does introduce us to the 'friend' who buys the estate, as Selivanov had at Taganrog, who would turn into Lopahin in *The Cherry Orchard*, as well as other Chekhovian leitmotifs such as the doctor who likes a drink.

1. Arthur Miller, *Timebends*, Methuen 1987.

As Chekhov passes out of university in 1884, there is still some puppy-fat, but the eyes are darkened a little by experience or fatigue, so he looks rather sexy, the mouth quite loose, full and sensual. His hair falls from a central parting and is swept back; the shoulders look slight, certainly under such a high buttoned jacket; there is a light fluff of beard, as if acknowledging graduation. For the next few years there's nothing nearly as good to look at as a rhapsodic description by the writer Vladimir Korolenko – the man whose autobiographical novel about his Siberian exile, by the way, started Chekhov thinking about Sakhalin. According to Korolenko this was the family's happiest time, as if some point of balance had been reached – mother at the samovar, the affectionate sister and brothers, the infectious flair of their hero. Korolenko describes the young writer's eyes as sparkling and deep-set, shining with a swift intelligence but the ingenuousness of a child. However, this is not evident in the few pictures of the time, which are dead-eyed and posed. On the verge of literary *réclame*, Chekhov seems to see the camera as the eye of the public, and becomes solemnly self-important.

He comes alive again in January 1889, a few days after his twenty-ninth birthday, on the day of the Petersburg premiere of *Ivanov*. If *Platonov* is discounted, *Ivanov* becomes Chekhov's first major play, a challenge the young man-about-Moscow took up almost by accident. As a critic, he had derided a production at the independent theatre run by Fyodor Korsh: let alone the play, Chekhov described the building as looking like a mixed salad. Korsh's inventive retaliation was to suggest that Chekhov write his own play, to show how it should be done. Korsh's actors encouraged Chekhov too, on the basis that he knew well enough how to get up people's noses. He sat down and wrote *Ivanov* in ten days, having promised four acts (dramatists were commonly paid by the act, two per cent of the gross), each of which would end with a punch on the nose (it does). Ivanov is the most common of Russian names, so it was a bit like calling a play *Smith* – not so much an act of silliness as of satire, since Ivanov was to represent a type of educated man disillusioned by the repressions that followed the assassination of the reforming Alexander II in 1881. Through this new Everyman Chekhov inspects the intelligentsia's inability to cope with the present and tendency to dream of the past.

The Moscow first night, in late 1887, had been quite an event: signing his letter Schiller Shakespearovich Goethe, Chekhov had described it to Alexander as a 'triumph of talent and virtue'. He was ever a wayward witness: in fact the actors had spoken few of his lines and Ivan Kiselevsky, playing Shabyelsky, had been 'drunk as a cobbler' by the last act. There was a punch-up in the bar, the police were called, Chekhov's sister almost fainted, one friend, Mikhail Dyukovsky, rushed out of the theatre with palpitations of the heart, and another, Alexei Kiselev, clutched his head with his hands and for some reason cried,

'Now what am I going to do?' *Ivanov* played only three performances, and Chekhov was so shocked that he announced the first of his many retirements from the theatre. However, the 'dramatic miscarriage' obviously bothered him, especially as he had been so convinced of his flair, and he now worked hard at a revision for the Petersburg Alexandrinsky. In the interim he had a success with *The Bear*, and both *Swan Song* and *The Proposal* came easily ('one-act plays ooze out of me like oil out of the Baku earth'), which perhaps accounts for a little missionary zeal. Apart from cutting some jokes about Anna's Jewishness from *Ivanov*, he strengthened its theme to avoid misunderstanding, at one point drawing for Suvorin a fever-chart of Ivanov's clinical depression. So he was already applying to his playwriting the objectivity of a scientist, the moral impartiality that confused audiences for so long. In the event, the revised play was a hit with the public, though friends and acquaintances weren't quite so sure: it made him a thousand roubles, nearly a tenth of what he would pay to buy Melikhovo.

Whether or not he understood the fever-chart, Alexei Suvorin, publisher and friend – some would say evil angel – had collaborated a little in the process, and he is there in the picture, together with two actors whose relationship must have been interesting in itself. Pavel Svobodin was a great Petersburg star, but he was to play Shabyelsky; Ivanov was to be Vladimir Davydov, for whom Chekhov had written the part (as well as *Swan Song*) and who had therefore played it in Moscow. Davydov is a tubby cherub with his arm (companionably? proprietorially?) through Anton's: but the truth is that Chekhov had had to sit up with him night after night persuading him that the new version of the play was better than the old, only just convincing him to stay with the production. No doubt Davydov, too, hesitated to abandon the idea of heroes and villains, and his intelligence seems to have been coterminous with his friendship with Chekhov. At the Alexandrinsky in 1910, he would be seen incorporating a Cossack dance into Chebutykin's drunk scene in *Three Sisters* and winning a round of applause for it.

Svobodin, meanwhile, was a new friend, and a surer one. Consumptive like Chekhov and rather similar in temperament, he would urge him towards his next play, *The Wood Demon*, and remain close until his own death three years later. Whatever troubles preceded the opening are surely past. Anton looks younger than ever, very handsome and clear-eyed. The four men seem to be standing on the stage set, with arches and columns behind and a painted rug in front. You can almost hear their interrupted conversation echoing: as you might expect in the theatrical context, the atmosphere is congenial and relaxed, though in another way the merriment is surprising since it is the day of the first night.

Facing the unknown, whether a play premiere or a journey across Siberia, seems to bring the best out of Chekhov. There is great good humour again on his face the next spring, back in Moscow with his family before leaving for Sakhalin. This is on the porch of the house on Sadovaya Kudrinskaya (where the Chekhov Museum now stands). Some wooden chairs have been pushed to one side for a hasty grouping that includes an unnamed friend or two, mysterious accompanists of history. The improvisation of it seems to amuse the company and distract them from posing – even the forbidding father, holding his hard hat at the apex of the picture, seems content with the noisy, ad hoc atmosphere. The rest wear dark clothes, but Chekhov's pin-stripes are offset by his light jacket, and he leans a little towards his brother Misha, who looks as if he is acting the part of a tax inspector, which in fact is what he became. Chekhov is the star of the family, leading from the front, his open face trained on Siberia and beyond. He may be helping Misha restrain the small dog crouching between them, something like a Cairn terrier.

Turn the page. It is June of 1892, the Chekhovs' first summer at Melikhovo, soon after the miracle of the horse. Pavel Svobodin is here, balder and heavier now, sitting on a bench with Chekhov, who wears a light collarless tunic and a hard-peaked cap like a station-master's. The picture hasn't survived very well – and you can also read too much into such a thing – but there seems to be sadness in the hang of Chekhov's shoulders: despite his doctoral reassurances and Svobodin's burly dissimulation for the camera, they know that the actor has advanced tuberculosis. Chekhov says that Svobodin at this time was 'astonishingly meek and calm, with a morbid hatred for the theatre – perhaps a man preparing to die can no longer love it'. He has told Anton that he is now working only to pay his debts to tailors, butchers, innkeepers and money-lenders: 'Tell me, dear sir, what is a man to do with three children?' Soon after returning to Moscow from this visit, he will die in the middle of a performance. Chekhov, typically, will avoid the funeral: he detested them; and, like Kolya, Svobodin had gone at an even younger age than Chekhov would himself.

With the inescapable diagnosis of 1897, a poisonous inner disarray begins to seep through the pores of this strikingly good-looking man. There is a very upsetting shot of him spreadeagled on the sofa at Melikhovo, looking like death; but a month later he rallies for the picture with Quinine. My favourite photograph of all dates from this year, Chekhov's inner grace chiming with style and self-possession: he wears a thick coat, standing at the foot of the stairs leading up to the *Seagull* summer-house. There are rampant climbing plants behind him, and his face has an open, friendly neutrality: the moustache rather overgrown on one side, his gaze level and attentive, both welcoming and unforthcoming. But put a hand over its lower half, and see only the veiled eyes: I fancy there is something there older than thirty-seven. The next year, about to leave Melikhovo, he sits in a jaunty black and white check, looking away from us, for once slightly self-conscious – the colour in his cheeks is high, the hoods are descending at the corner of his eyes, the beard is full and straggly, and you would describe the general look as kindly. This is the kind of shot you see in the programmes of English theatre productions.

In fact this is the beginning of his relationship with the Moscow Art Theatre, who set up a couple of photographs of him with the actors. One purports to be of the *Seagull* read-through, but in fact it is a celebratory shot done the following spring. It all feels rather oppressive, overcrowded in the Russian way. Chekhov reads the play demurely from a small book, while the actors assume highly contrived listening postures. He looks fairly natural, but perhaps it is easier for him as all he has to do is look down and read. In the other photograph, the actors behave as if they are in a very pre-Chekhovian comedy, with Chekhov doing his best to ham it up as well – but he still looks like the civilian he is. Nemirovich-Danchenko leans over him, self-consciously making some point, while next to him Olga Knipper edges as close as she can – he has begun to woo her on this visit, presenting her with a signed photograph of Melikhovo and an invitation to stay.

Throughout the portfolio, of course, you look for evidence of what Chekhov was feeling about women. From five years before this there is a contrived study (it became known among them as 'The Temptation of St Anthony') of the handsome young writer, apparently playing hell with two rather plain girls: as he sits with his legs outstretched from his chair, holding what might be a small cigar, the poetess Tatyana Schepkina-Kupernik and the actress Lydia Yavorskaya adoringly make up to him. Ever the zoomorphist, he used to call these girls his 'two white seagulls' – and Yavorskaya sounds not much different from the Arkadina he would eventually create. Why are these women always so dowdy, you might wonder, and he so handsome? The story is in any case not quite what it seems: Tatyana and Lydia were themselves scandalous lovers. It seems likely that Chekhov had been drawn into a *ménage à trois* by sleeping with Lydia – a rather daunting enterprise since she was also the mistress of Fyodor Korsh. Apparently he found this rackety arrangement too much for him, and quite soon got out of it. Who would have thought such erotics could exist beneath the musty cloth and great rouches of linen?

Next the young man sits on a bench in his garden with the actress Darya Musina-Pushkina – he is friendly enough, but his body language gives him away. Darya gallantly flirted with Chekhov, trying to break into his charmed circle, but he really wanted very little to do with her. Significantly, he is in his coat again in May, as with Quinine. On the same bench, on another day, sits Lika Mizinova, the lifelong friend he might have done well to marry rather than to surrender to Levitan and Potapenko. The trouble with Lika, a young teacher and, like Nina, an aspiring actress, was that she was a fan turned friend: her welcome in the Chekhovs' home as 'a swan princess from a fairy tale' had been the result of an admiring letter from her, which is a shaky basis for romance. Chekhov once told her she had a crocodile inside her and he was wise to flee from her; but in fact, if he had wanted it, she would have stayed with him devotedly, not run off to act in plays in Moscow. She was consumptive as well, which is only good in so far as she would have recognised the arsenic injections and all the horrible discomforts that accompanied the exaggerated tubercular libido. In fact, something about this illness may explain Chekhov's come-on, get-off attitude to women – not to mention the freely acknowledged fact that he suffered most of his life from bad, bad haemorrhoids.

In addition to Potapenko, her lost child and Levitan, Lika also had to endure the quite poisonous attacks of Olga Knipper, who obviously knew a rival when she saw one: later she would cruelly audition Lika for the Moscow Art Theatre and reject her as a pale imitation of herself, suggesting that she might play a small part or perhaps open a hat shop. In the end Lika got a job as an unpaid theatre secretary. Poor golden girl: at the time of the picture, Chekhov has also started an affair with the writer Elena Shavrova and he is turned resolutely away, as far as politeness will permit, the shoulder nearest to hers arched up defensively. Lika meanwhile has no idea how to pose. Her hands grip the bench on either side of her and she looks round at him with a dogged concern.

Olga Knipper described Lika as 'terribly fat: enormous, garish, all swishing about', but she's not so slim herself at this point, and has a general tendency to look tight-lipped – the mouth and teeth small and ferrety. But Chekhov certainly achieved love with her. They were married in 1901 by the priest who had buried his father; looking at the shot taken at Aksyonovo on their honeymoon, Chekhov improvised:

> You look like a nice little German wife, generous, tender, married to a poor doctor.

In February 1902, they are joined for the camera in Yalta by Chekhov's mother Evgenia and his sister Masha, for a delightful high-spirited picture in which all the tensions – Olga and Masha, Evgenia and Olga – seem to have relaxed. Only Evgenia seems a little solemn, as befits her generation. She had been reluctant to move back south to Yalta – she was afraid of drowning – even though in Melikhovo she was afflicted with loneliness 'whenever the samovar hisses or the stove whines or a dog barks'. When Chekhov finally married Olga, he sent a telegram to her, blankly informing her of the news but stating that everything would stay the same. After this cowardly message, he continued, in the dreary way of such things, to duck and weave and do his best, generally leaving the three women to slug it out. The absence of a moderator naturally aggravated their distrust. Evgenia sometimes withheld the customary blessings when Olga left the house for a journey, and Olga, with splendid inappropriateness, occasionally sent a diet list for the mother to operate while she, the wife, was away acting:

> You should cook him kidney and mushrooms in sour cream. A fish
> soup, not too many meatballs – and the breakfast eggs must be fresh.

Three months later, alone with Olga, Chekhov is defiant and rueful all at once, her chin on his shoulder, as if he were delighted by her ease with him but about to pull a sheepish face. But still his hand is clenched in his lap, and he leans very slightly away from her. He looks more sixty-two than forty-two, and no tidier for his marriage, though his unbrushed hair does add to the look of marital concord.

Chekhov routinely called Olga his 'dog', his 'puppy', his 'pony' and his 'horse' – that's love for you. But there are cicadas, toads, spiders, otters, hedgehogs, cockerels, whales and cockroaches in the menagerie as well. This tendency to turn your familiars into animals is very Russian – but then Russian names, particularly those of peasants, have always had Biblical or at least character overtones, and I have a friend whose name, Barashka, means 'little lamb'. And of course Chekhov himself was crocodile to the artist Levitan. Sitting with him one night in Yalta in the winter of 1899, the painter dashed off an impromptu study, *Haystacks In Moonlight*. It was immediately set into the chimney piece. Perhaps because of a lack of light, there are so many candles in the subsequent photograph that the scene is almost ecclesiastical – certainly the best print I've seen is so underexposed that Chekhov's eyes seem to be popping. The fireplace is of crude brick, and there are pencils in a pot on the table. In his coat, Chekhov is struggling for once – his relaxed pose is unconvincing, his weight dispersed oddly and heavily, and he looks a little bloated in the face. In a second shot he has moved across the fireplace to the corner of the room, between a small desk and a garish-looking wardrobe. It might be only a few seconds later – he is dressed the same, though there has been some re-ordering of the furniture. All I can think of is the mayhem inside his clothes.

It is from this point that things go downhill, the unfolding story not so much his as that of the canker within him. The cheeks become prominent and shadowed, he seems short-sighted without his pince-nez, and in the melancholy late images he prods the ground with his cane, kindly and enfeebled and slow, inspecting a tame crane in his garden. There is one lovely picture left, from 1900: the skin is too parchment-like round the eyes, like that of a lifelong smoker, but the striped suit (grey?) suggests the country doctor, and the characteristic slight tilt of his head, to one side and upwards as if in a state of continual interest, emphasises his gentleness. This is the one I need for companionship and encouragement, the one to take with me to the unwelcoming venues I can imagine for my show – the show I'm now obviously going to do.

The main engine of *Anton Chekhov* – working title, never to be improved on – will be my own conviction, of course, rather than the reorganisation of face and body. Still, to catch the angle of Chekhov's head and his characteristic look in the right light could make the audience jump, as if they'd seen in a crowd the face of someone they know to be dead. I remember at Tolstoy's house his famous blue smock hanging well-worn in his cupboard and the chair pushed aside from his desk as if he had come to answer the door to me. What if you looked up to see approaching the stooping, broad-browed Chekhov, stroking his goatee, his eyes alight and his footsteps audible? Then he starts to talk, and he sounds just as you always knew he would.

I feel a little like the white man stealing his subject's soul by means of the camera. If I mix these impressions together and peer through half-closed eyes, I'll be looking at the strangest composite from my own time, not his: some combination of a couple of rock stars (Eric Clapton and Robbie Robertson of The Band), an actor (Richard E Grant) and the director Adrian Noble. But what, after all, do you think of when you conjure up that famous face? The goatee and pince-nez mainly, though he came to both of them only after a time. The main benefit of these speculations is that, having been bewildered by all the frozen figures – what were they saying just before the shutter went, what was the smell they tolerated around them? – I can now hear whisperings and ticking clocks and sense some traffic to and fro, feel their sudden high spirits and their thoughtful Russian regard.

Beyond that, what have I got? From *The Island of Sakhalin* the scientist, the angry liberal, the gossip, the homesick diarist and the fiction writer. From *The Seagull* the paradoxes of his anatomised craft. And from these civilian photographs, something else – a doctor and countryman, an undeceived lifelong loner of considerable personal charm who finds it difficult to love though he is often the object of love, dark, complex and highly original. Until I get closer, any alias is welcome: and in fact, the face beginning to peer out could easily be that of Astrov in *Uncle Vanya*.

THE INSPECTOR OF ACTRESSES

> Gorky thinks I've invented a new form of dramatic art. He says everything up to now has been written with a log, not a pen.
>
> — Anton Chekhov on *Uncle Vanya*

Astrov is a doctor, and presumably a good enough one, though, in common with Chebutykin in *Three Sisters*, he has recently had a patient die during an operation – these mortalities are cautions issued by Chekhov to his fictional colleagues. If Dr Dorn in *The Seagull* is cynical, Astrov is far more refinedly so; it is hard to imagine Dorn being subject to nightmares, and so he has no need for the self-defence of Astrov's articulacy. But this new doctor is full of the enthusiasms that cause a man pain. He feels a passion for Russia's declining wildlife and its threatened forests, together with a certainty that provincial life destroys men of culture; and he has little expectation of the future except 'sweet dreams in the grave' – negatives expressed so firmly that they become like articles of faith. His sense of struggle, of principle at war with self-denigration, makes him very attractive to the women in the play: Professor Serebryakov's young wife Yeliena, saying goodbye and admitting her attraction, calls him an 'original'. Perhaps as a consequence, Astrov has the freedom of the house: although he lives nearly twenty miles away, in a place nobody seems to know much about, he is on permanent call at the Serebryakovs, and in fact has a work-table in the room of the Professor's brother-in-law and estate manager, Voinitsky (Vanya), where he relaxes by painting and bringing up to date his maps of the district. Like Trigorin in *The Seagull*, he loves beauty, he loves life – but not this parochial Russian life, or his disappointing private arrangements. He is convinced that the last decade has ruined everyone, and prefers the forests both to the peasants, who are crude, and to the intelligentsia, who are 'just stupid' – these are the sort of people who can only account for his eccentricity by calling him a psychopath. He is very 'green', and a vegetarian; but his love of nature is matched by a love of vodka, and of women as well, though only in the roughest terms. By his own admission, Astrov becomes arrogant and impertinent when drunk, but believes (despite the recent mortality) that he is still capable of executing difficult surgery, and so of advancing humanity's destiny. Whenever he starts to speak finely, Chekhov counterpoints it by making him either drink or become coarse. In the first Act a workman interrupts his great discourse about climate and the forests – just as he is expressing his joy at seeing a birch-tree he has planted swaying in the wind – by delivering him a glass of vodka, bang in the middle of a sentence, and he never completes his train of thought. In his long second Act scene with Sonya, his passionate volubility is matched by her determination to stop him refilling his glass; and finally trying to get Yeliena to meet him in the fields, he uses his redeeming love of nature as a decoy – it would be better for her to have intercourse with him there, in God's pasture, than with some stranger in Kharkov or Kursk. Altogether, this is far and away the most complex stage character Chekhov has achieved so far, preparing the ground for Andrei (frustrated hopes) and Vershinin (philosophising) in the next play, *Three Sisters.*

As reluctant as most authors to be thought autobiographical, Chekhov used to warn the curious not to look for beer when he was offering them coffee, but his relationship to Astrov is both circumstantial and intimate. As with Trigorin, there are plenty of false trails: Chekhov, distressed by his alcoholic elder brothers, was a very moderate drinker. But Astrov is the same age as Chekhov was as he wrote (if, as is thought, this was around the time of *The Seagull*), from his own profession, with a similar passion for the country and much of his contradictoriness.

Astrov's literary origin, meanwhile, is a stroke of inspiration. In 1889, the year of the second *Ivanov*, Chekhov had produced *The Wood Demon.* It was not a success. Refused by the Alexandrinsky, *Ivanov* notwithstanding, it was heartily booed on its first night at the Abramov Theatre in Moscow and achieved just three performances. But as with *Ivanov*, initial failure nagged at Chekhov, and at some point he took hold of it and began turning it into the masterpiece of *Uncle Vanya.* The Wood Demon of the title had been Mikhail Khrushchev, whose enthusiasm for forestry and invective against human wastefulness was marked by a certain preachiness (Chekhov was not entirely free of the influence of Tolstoy at the time). He coexisted in the play with the impossibly rakish eccentric Fyodor Orlovsky, who at one point boasts that he has had goldfish soup. The contrast of character is certainly striking. Chekhov's insight now is to see that a contradiction within one man is more interesting than between two exemplary types, and so he combines the two men. The goldfish soup goes, and so does the sermonising. Cooked in the same pot, Khrushchev humanises Orlovsky, who roughens him in return, and the blend is called Astrov.

In fact, *The Wood Demon* had always had a bad seed inside it – so much so that Chekhov broke off several times in the writing to start improbable dramas about Holofernes and Judith, King Solomon and Napoleon instead. And peculiar as it may be to imagine a playwriting collaboration with the distinctly reactionary Alexei Suvorin, so it had briefly been on this, as with the revival of *Ivanov.* The partnership was odd in practice as well as principle: their letters suggest that each would be in charge of certain characters in the play, as if they were assembling a joint exhibition. At one point Chekhov compliments Suvorin for having realised the character of Blagosvetlov:

> If the audience listens to him for a couple of minutes they'll think, 'Oh, do shut up'…he's a cross between an old moaner and some boring piece of music…

The original plan had been to work on Sonya, Blagosvetlov's daughter, together, to do separate sections each of Mikhail Khrushchev, and for Suvorin to work on Yegor Voinitsky to Chekhov's prescription: 'arrogant…drinks mineral water…shouts…isn't afraid of generals'. This piecemeal business smacks of the one-act farceur; perhaps Chekhov felt that if the right idiosyncratic characters were assembled, the plot might even generate itself. In the event, Suvorin's only contribution was to be Blagosvetlov, re-christened as Serebryakov.

For the work of transformation into *Uncle Vanya* Chekhov was on his own, and he worked in relative secrecy: he usually corresponded quite freely about what he was doing, but there is no running commentary this time, perhaps because he hesitated to confide in a collaborator who had cried off. So nobody quite knows whether it was done straight away, in which case *Vanya* lay unperformed for the years leading up to *The Seagull*, or, more likely, between the writing of the latter and its disastrous premiere. Now, if you wish – and in a way that would no doubt displease the author – you can sit with the two plays in front of you and try to muscle in on Chekhov's thinking, noting where he crossed out and re-dipped his pen – moving across the paper in that distinctive hand, its fluent clarity suggesting both a writer's open-heartedness and a doctor's exactitude.

The *Vanya* version of *The Wood Demon*'s Serebryakov is perceptibly nastier. Chekhov obviously liked Ilya Dyadin ('Waffles'), but to turn him into Telegin, the down-at-heel local landowner, he reduced the part quite a lot, as he did Voinitsky's mother – sketchy enough to start with, she becomes in *Vanya* perhaps the only weak characterisation the mature Chekhov did. Clearly the author felt, and rightly, that Yegor Voinitsky had been a success, especially in the sheer vigour of his invective against the Professor – 'I pity the paper he writes on' – and he becomes Ivan Voinitsky: the new first name is slightly more commonplace, with less of an old-fashioned peasant feel. Astrov loses his position as the titular character to him; but Ivan has, significantly, been given his diminutive name, Vanya, the soubriquet that his niece Sonya would naturally use. In other words, the play's title is now a measure of her affection, and softens our response to his bitter personality, so that it is possible to feel for him despite his unrelievedly negative tone of voice.

Around this time, Chekhov wrote to the actor and director Vsevelod Meyerhold:

> Every civilised person feels the most annoyance in his home, in his family – that's where conflict between the past and present is mainly felt.

He could have been speaking of the *Vanya* group, the tensest and most intricate family he had yet written. This is, by virtue of his first marriage to Vanya's sister Vera, Serebryakov's estate (or, as Vanya will argue, their daughter Sonya's), which he hates since he'd rather be near the capital, as befits a vain academic. He has brought his urban habits with him, particularly that of getting up at noon, much discomposing the orderly household: everyone finds themselves drinking cold tea and eating at six in the evening, and the disastrous business meeting in Act Three happens when they should be having their lunch. The underwritten Mrs Voinitsky, the head of the family and an intellectual snob, seems more attached to this son-in-law than to her surviving child, Vanya. The dead Vera haunts the play largely because of Vanya's continuing grief at her loss, a nostalgia shared only by the nurse Marina: however, in one of Chekhov's sly clues, there is a hint of some great wrong done to her and not quite forgotten – something more than her husband's exhausting hypochondria. Serebryakov has now married the much younger Yeliena, who has become Sonya's step-mother though of the same generation: she is uneasily placed in this group in a way she is never allowed to forget.

Vanya argues that this is not Serebryakov's estate at all, but belongs on his side of the family. His father, now dead, bought it as a dowry for Vera. (At 95,000 roubles for eighty acres, it must have been a good one, or very overpriced – Chekhov's Melikhovo was seven and a half times bigger but cost seven and a half times less.) The former owner was a completely untraceable figure, the uncle of Telegin. Old Voinitsky paid all but 25,000 on the nail; Vanya has helped out by giving up his inheritance, and has then slaved to pay off the outstanding balance. He believes that now Vera is dead Sonya owns the estate in law, but Serebryakov thinks he is still in a position to sell it by virtue of the new marriage. The rights and wrongs of this are never settled, since Serebryakov, under the most violent pressure from Vanya, back-tracks, protesting that he is selling for Sonya's benefit not his own, then offering Vanya the estate outright. Abandoning his plan altogether, he ends up going to Kharkov (which sounds more and more like a Chekhov joke for not fulfilling your dreams), rather than to some cottage over the Finnish border from Petersburg, as he would prefer.

So, as for some English Restoration plays, the audience has to keep a good business head to appreciate the feelings of the characters. The overall point is that the links holding them together are an encumbrance. They are struggling in out-of-date bargains, and their antipathies create remorseless claustrophobia. Chekhov is extending a point he made in *The Seagull* – these people have to rub along as best they can, fearful of solitude but disliking the company they are keeping, and Vanya's torrential complaints are recognised by everyone as unhelpful.

Another argument for the new work having been done in the wake of *The Seagull* is that *Vanya* is even more experimental. Though the soliloquy convention doggedly persists, there is a still bolder use of diminuendo at the end of each act, even after the gunshot in the third; and the final moments almost move into music, with this pattern played out over a very few minutes of text:

> *Harness bells are heard.*
>
> Astrov: They've gone.
>
> > [He goes on to comment that the Professor and Yeliena won't be coming back soon.]
>
> Marina: (*Coming in.*) They've gone.
>
> > [She sits down to knit.]
>
> Sonya: (*Coming in.*) They've gone.
>
> > [Wiping her eyes, she encourages Vanya to work.]
>
> Mrs Voinitsky: (*Coming in slowly.*) They've gone.
>
> > [She sits and reads. Sonya and Vanya start to work. Marina feels like bed. Astrov comments on the cosiness of it all.]
>
> *Harness bells are heard.*
>
> > [The servant brings Astrov his bag, he accepts some vodka, chats a little more and leaves.]
>
> *Harness bells are heard.*
>
> Marina: He's gone.
>
> Sonya: (*Coming back with a candle.*) He's gone.*

The other great originality is Vanya's outburst at the end of Act Three. Roused by Serebryakov's plan to sell, he vents all his frustrations. It is not only that for the last twenty-five years he has been paid next to nothing for making the great scholar's life possible here, but the process has soured his idealistic view of intellectual life. He loses this lucidity when he then gets a gun in his hand, and his assault on the Professor, apart from bringing real danger into the room, triggers an hilariously human outburst – 'I could have been a Schopenhauer, a Dostoyevsky!' The attack is as passionately motivated as

* Square brackets in this extract indicate my summary.

Konstantin's suicide, but ridiculous: 'Bash!' Vanya shouts as he fires from point blank range and misses. This remarkable incident takes the place of Voinitsky's successful attempt at suicide in the penultimate Act of *The Wood Demon*, and jolts the new play away not only from that but from most other antecedents. In fact, we seem to have been catapulted into a later form of theatre. Chekhov, replacing the principles of melodrama with those of life, significantly referred to such moments as 'accidents, not dramas'; this one makes Vanya a sort of modern hero. His protest leaves him in a ludicrous position, with a misfired gun and an overspill of self-reproach, but it revitalises our relationship with him.

This mix of tragic effort and laughable failure was hinted at from the start:

> Enter Vanya. He has been having a siesta and looks dishevelled. He sits down and
> straightens his showy tie.
>
> Vanya: Yes. (Pause.) Yes.
>
> Astrov: Sleep well?
>
> Vanya: Very, yes. (He yawns.)

Why in the world is his tie showy, *shchegol'skoy*? In one way it is for the same reason that Lopahin, destroyer of the cherry orchard, will have delicate hands and the soul of an artist. More immediately we see that Vanya has made a great effort today and then spoiled it by going to sleep. This is a man permanently at odds with himself, straightening his clothes before stepping onto his own banana skin.

Sluggishly turning over like a cold engine, he now begins his play-long denunciation of the Professor, deeply felt but absurdly obsessive. He claims that it would be more principled for Yeliena to betray her old husband than to waste her own potential. This very much upsets Telegin, who has the abundant good nature that makes everyone else in the play look petty, and who replies by telling the story of his own marriage. The day after the wedding, his bride, unable to accept his 'unprepossessing appearance', ran away with another man: but Telegin still loves her, is still faithful, and has spent all his money on the education of her children by her new lover. She is ageing now and no longer beautiful, and the man is dead – Telegin poses the question: who is the loser?

> I've lost my happiness, but I still have my pride. What does she have?

There is not very much of Telegin, but as in *The Seagull*, small parts hold big clues. His stoicism winds discreetly through the play in counterpoint to Vanya's bitterness; his good faith contrasts with the indifference of Yeliena, and his resolute passion rebukes Astrov's idle attempts at intrigue. There is even a trace of his stamina in the play's marvellous ending, when Sonya and Vanya shoulder their burdens and think of the future at last.

Astrov would say that the real reason for all the discomfort in the house is Yeliena – this virus of beautiful lassitude that devastates everyone around her as surely as canker-rot does the forests. Chekhov won't quite have that. Yeliena is certainly indolent, and her moral responses can be flaccid – as when she treats Vanya like a servant after he finds her kissing Astrov, or ineptly tests the doctor about his feelings for Sonya, using his passion for his maps as an alibi to be alone with him. Oddly enough, though, she can be as self-aware as he is, so that the attraction that flickers between them is exciting to watch, far more so than Vanya's blundering and resentful infatuation, which seems to come from the same epicentre as his hatred for the Professor. Much of the play's unhappy wisdom rests in Yeliena – she is far from the 'secondary character' she calls herself. Despite all temptations she will stand by her husband with a loyalty born of conscience, but she is clear-sighted and spares herself nothing. She spares Sonya nothing either:

> you thought I married your father for money, but I swear I married
> him for love… I found him fascinating…it wasn't love though, it
> was something artificial – but I thought it was real…

Sonya has to listen to this only moments after Astrov, to whom she is devoted, has admitted that Yeliena could turn his head in a day, even though that would hardly be love either.

Yeliena's candour is bracing. It is she who sees, in words that could be Astrov's, that 'in Russia a brilliant man can't be a saint'. She reserves her fiercest criticism for Vanya – even accusing him, with some justice, of what Astrov has attributed to her:

> people like you are destroyers; because of you there'll soon be no
> innocence or self-sacrifice left in the world…you've no pity for the
> forests, for the birds, for yourselves

– and later she tells him:

> the end of the world won't come with fire and mayhem, it'll come
> with all these petty squabbles… your task should be to make peace,
> not to keep moaning…

It is not just that she is, as Astrov finally admits, 'a good, warm-hearted creature'; next to Vanya's self-absorption and Astrov's misogyny she can look positively heroic.

The intense self-contradiction of Astrov and Yeliena, and the juxtaposition of hostility, frustrated yearning and self-hatred in Vanya, are set against a certain stasis elsewhere – as if, rather than being reconstructed from *The Wood Demon*, the other characters had been filled out on the same simple lines, albeit to great effect. Serebryakov seems to be one of Chekhov's rare antipathies, the harmless verbosity of Blagosvetlov now laced with casual unpleasantness. He is capable of calling Sonya deaf when she understandably mistakes his pills, which are so various that Astrov wonders if there's a town in Russia he has not plagued with his gout. He patronises everyone and sourly deprives them of their sleep. However, he has his purpose; to parody Vanya's despair and Astrov's contempt for provincial life in more snobbish terms. And Chekhov would hardly leave him without some redeeming feature, so there is real pain in his knowledge that he has worked all his life only to find that nobody wants to hear a word he says. Sonya's self-awareness, meanwhile, is more attractive. She knows that it is only when a woman is as plain as she is that her hair or her eyes are complimented. But neither of them, or Telegin, could be called particularly complex.

As the emotions swirl, stillness is very much needed in the play; and Marina, the nanny whose children are all grown-ups, is one of Chekhov's great old ladies, steady as a deep, quiet breath. Significantly, and alone, there is no equivalent for her in *The Wood Demon*, and her role here is to mediate where she can, providing strategic common sense like a spring of water. When, in the first moments, Astrov becomes disorganised, complaining about his oddity, his stupid moustache and his blunt feelings all at once, she has the answer:

> Perhaps you want a bite to eat…

But it is not just soothing normality that she represents, or the desire for lunchtime to return to its right place. She has power; knowing that the 'old are like little children', she is the one who takes over the unmanageable Serebryakov, finding an old person's common cause with him:

> My legs hurt too…it's your old trouble, isn't it?

In fact she has been smart enough to see that what he is really complaining about in everyone else is their youthfulness. After the explosions of the third act, she has the strength to dismiss 'these cackling geese', proposing raspberry tea and taking such care of Sonya that the tumultuous episode ends with the girl quietly repeating:

> Nanny…nanny…

When the action then re-starts with the household breaking up, she comforts Telegin and insists on life's small rituals; she knows even better than Astrov does himself that he needs vodka before his long journey home. It is not just that she is a nice old girl, warm and human. Her immovability balances the play as it swings between vertigo and merciless continuation, wasteful neurosis and the cycles of ordinary life.

> The theatre is an importunate mistress – sophisticated, yes, but noisy
> and irksome. When I watch a play I've written, I always think someone
> in the gallery is about to shout: 'Fire!'

As a result of Chekhov's various hesitancies, *Uncle Vanya* took a long time to reach the stage, or at least the Moscow Art stage, being published first and then playing the Russian provinces. He briefly offered it to the Moscow Maly in early 1899 and even to the Petersburg Alexandrinsky, where Komisarzhevskaya would have played Sonya and Davydov Vanya. This was a surprising idea in view of *The Seagull*'s fortunes there. The snag for Chekhov was that, isolated in the south, he had not yet seen the Moscow Art Theatre's revelations for himself, and he remained suspicious of Stanislavsky. Meanwhile, the Maly had to jump the usual hurdles. There were two university professors on the Imperial Theatres Committee at the time, and they objected to the idea that an 'enlightened' person like Vanya might fire a gun at the holder of a university chair. They would hardly have liked the characterisation of his victim either. Such professors belonged to the highest grade of the Russian civil service and were to be addressed as Your Excellency – indeed a student had been flogged for attacking one not so long ago. These gentlemen also found themselves bored by Astrov's speeches about forestry and objected to the amount of drinking Vanya and Astrov got through. Chekhov withdrew the play at the moment they rejected it. However the committee of four had included Nemirovich-Danchenko, who was quietly in favour. In a piece of neat footwork, he resigned before the vote, which therefore went against, and he was able to secure the play for the Art Theatre, who were of course not subject to the Committee's attentions.

Having at last seen *The Seagull* at a performance specially arranged for him, Chekhov let the company start work on *Vanya*; and it opened in October 1899, after being in print for two years. The reception was quite good, but not as good as for *The Seagull*: Serebryakov caused some of the same affront in his audience as he had in the Committee, and Knipper as Yeliena had a particularly bad first night – as anybody can, though the consequences for a new play are alarming. Tolstoy was there, complaining that it was impossible to create tragedy with guitars and the sound of crickets, and personally reproaching Stanislavsky over Astrov's sexual hunting of Yeliena, as if it was being done by the actor not the character. He praised two things only, the very items that he thought had kept the play earthbound: Telegin's guitar-playing and the imitation of a cricket chirruping that Alexander Vishnevsky, who played Vanya, had painstakingly prepared.

Feeling differently from Tolstoy about the sound effects, Chekhov had continued his assault:

> I told them: 'In my next play the hero will come on and say, "What wonderful quiet! No birds, no cuckoos, no owls, clocks, no sleigh bells, no crickets." '

It was a losing battle. All directors pay sharp attention to sound, and so they should. In any case Chekhov is disingenuous: just as he specifically demanded the wind sighing through the trees and howling in the chimney in *The Seagull*, he asks for a flat-out storm in the second Act of *Vanya*. Stanislavsky always claimed that he supplied such things in profusion not in order to impress the audience but to help the actors feel their roles – the same presumably applied to the more questionable swatting of invisible mosquitoes in the first Act (where Chekhov asks for muggy weather) and the real chickens that Marina shooed away.

There had been a casting shuffle (at least it was done by the directors, not the Alexandrinsky stars), as a result of which Chekhov's childhood friend Vishnevsky and Stanislavsky had exchanged roles, and once again Chekhov was alarmed by the latter:

> He wants to weep. That's wrong – Astrov should whistle. Stanislavsky thinks Astrov is passionately in love with Yeliena at the end, but the fact is he kisses her to pass the time, and talks in the same tone as when he discusses the heat in Africa. 'My horse is lame – I must get him reshod. It must be very hot in Africa. Well, let me kiss you. Yes, very nice. Goodbye.'

Chekhov gave little advice, but it is gold-dust for the actor, and miles ahead of its time.

Most of his strictures were reactions from afar to what his cordial ally Olga Knipper was reporting from rehearsals. Chekhov finally saw the play the following spring, when the company made a Crimean tour, first playing Sevastopol nearby and then Yalta – at last he witnessed them performing Chekhov before a paying audience. The visit gave rise to much festivity, but it had a practical purpose. The Art Theatre were finding that only Chekhov's plays were filling the house, and running up a deficit. If the author, whom they were now referring to as 'the Inspector of Actresses', liked *Vanya* – and liked seeing Knipper in it – perhaps he would give them another play. Chekhov became very excited for weeks ahead, whether at one prospect or the other, dreading that every time the telephone rang it would be news that the visit was cancelled. He got Masha to ship all manner of delicacies to him from Moscow for the company's entertainment. Olga arrived a few days early to spend time alone with him – as alone as they could be with his mother in the house. It sounds like an idyllic week, except that for the first time Olga witnessed Chekhov's alarming haemorrhages. Trailed by a police spy, Gorky turned up too, and was ordered by his friend to entertain the guests with stories of life on the Russian road. Chekhov enjoyed the initial Sevastopol performance of *Vanya*, but liked even more the companion production of *Lonely Lives* by Gerhart Hauptmann, whom he considered a real playwright – 'Listen: I'm a doctor.' When the company moved to Yalta for a ten-day stay he kept open house – a documented episode that has attracted subsequent writers looking for a way of dramatising his relations, both affectionate and critical, with his theatre.

On his home patch he watched *Uncle Vanya* again, at a sort of gala premiere, despite feeling agonies of embarrassment that his mother, who was not normally interested in his work, was sitting in a box in an ancient silk dress, and despite the misplaced music supplied during the action by a band from the local park. Having denied the actors any vainglory by forbidding individual curtain calls and a published cast list (something else I might have had a word with him about in Romanov's) he now gave each of them a gold medallion in the form of a book with his or her name and role engraved in it. In return they presented him with the bench and swing from the set of *Vanya*. Olga and the company went back to Moscow relieved. Their next collaboration was assured.

And then Chekhov was alone again, in this place in which he felt 'like a transplanted tree, not knowing whether to take root or wither away'; but he reacted with characteristic energy. Within a few days he rushed off to Moscow to see Olga once more and paid a last visit to the dying Levitan:

> His heart doesn't beat, it puffs and blows... I think the women have worn him out... If I were a landscape painter I'd have intercourse only once a year and eat once a day. May the Heavenly Kingdom be his. May his memory last for ever.

Then he dashed away to the Caucasus with Gorky – bumping into Olga and her mother en route on the train, in a coincidence he would have spurned in a play. He finally spent the summer with Olga in Yalta, consummating their relationship. Life, if you are quick to reinvent yourself, usually throws out a line: rather than staring at the sea and missing his friends, Chekhov had packed his bags and found a future. Trying to determine what it is about him that is most realisable on the stage, I am impressed by this. Resilience is a great theatrical virtue: look at Hamlet.

Meanwhile Vanya remains forever the man pointlessly holding a bunch of flowers while his inamorata, the ray of sunlight falling into the dark well of his spirit, kisses someone else who doesn't really care about her, and, well, everyone can understand that. Just as the gloomy waves of Sakhalin had once threatened to turn Chekhov, looking towards America, into a sorrowing statue with not even a bird for company, Vanya and Sonya will stay locked into their fastness, a beautiful image of immobility to strike dismay into us all. One Doctor Kurkin, a member of the play's Moscow audience, wrote memorably to the author of

> the tragic way in which ordinary routines fall back into their place, and imprison your people forever…the unending routine of crickets, abacuses, and so on…I felt unwell, as if I too had been left by everyone and was sitting doing my accounts…

What he has seen is that (for the first time) Chekhov has achieved a true tragedy in which nobody dies – in which indeed the idea of sudden death becomes ridiculous. Vanya's failure to turn the play into a melodrama has led to far deeper feelings than his success ever could. His attacks on himself are no luckier than his attempt on the Professor, and therefore as moving. He cannot even hold onto the phial of morphine he steals from Astrov, but meekly gives it back, and is left with the empty-handed misery of continuing to live; his repetitive work at his abacus perfectly implies a long, circular future.

The insights of *Uncle Vanya* almost obliterate Chekhov's past and reveal a future of awesome range. He has turned his familiar co-ordinates to a new purpose. The superficial comforts of Sorin's house by the lake with the seagulls overhead have been replaced by a sense of blunt confinement. Serebryakov's smug desire for a cottage near Petersburg is a feebly derisory version of the longing for flight of *Three Sisters*, where the dullness of the town will at least be relieved by some interplay with an outside group, the military. There is no such comfort in this stifling household of contested ownership in the middle of nowhere. And from now on, bound to their wheels of cold fire, few of his characters will be allowed a full stop. The play itself has ended at a remarkable point of balance, kept going by contradictory motions – Vanya's downward swing spun upright, just about, by the new force of Sonya. Sonya, whose career has been marked by inadvertent small conspiracies from which no good has come; who felt happiness at the prospect of music to dance by with her new friend Yeliena, but was immediately crushed by her father's prohibition. From her position of weakness it was she who bluntly insisted to everyone on the value of work to counter boredom and introspection; she was the only one tough-minded enough to see that the 'ordinary' thing about Astrov was his drinking, and even got him to stop. What a wife she would have been – but she was so plain, she would lament, whereupon the gorgeous Yeliena always seemed to enter. But then Sonya would bring out the apathetic one's better nature and stimulate a feeling of guilt in her; and she was powerful enough to persuade Vanya to hand back his morphine. She has turned out to be the play's salvation, while the more 'interesting' characters have ridden home to their forestry maps or accompanied their old husbands to Petersburg. This is a new kind of work that, stubbornly believing in what Nina called 'her faith' – the ability simply to keep going – reposed its final authority not in the dramatic flight of a seagull-turned-actress but in one of its least self-advertising, most easily overlooked characters.

> Olga Vasilieva wants to translate my work into English. But I think I'm
> of so little interest to the English public that I really don't care about
> it.

There have been very few cinematic versions of Chekhov's plays, though there are many of the stories, and one quite remarkable film which is the best Chekhov you could hope to see, though it is not by Chekhov at all. Nikita Mikhalkov's 1976 *Unfinished Piece for Mechanical Piano* takes *Platonov* as a loose starting point, but cuts and adapts it, interlacing it with references to the other plays: thus a doctor ignores his patients, an Irina rhapsodises on the joy of work, a Chebutykin's ornament is dropped. A do-gooding 'man of the eighties' like Gaev wants to give away his suits to the peasants ('Just imagine them mowing the hay in tail coats,' mocks Platonov) – and the ghosts of both Astrov and Vanya flicker around Alexander Kaliagin's interpretation of the despairing hero. This man furiously denounces the company at dinner before charging into the countryside, mixing up Platonov and Vanya in a great lament (at thirty-five he is older than Lermontov when he died and he isn't a general like Napoleon) before jumping into a lake which turns out to be only a few inches deep, like Charlie Chaplin in *The Gold Rush*. Meanwhile the husband he has cuckolded, having tried to flee likewise, goes to sleep in his carriage as he waits for horses to be supplied. A house party sends out for a pig, for a joke, only to abuse the servants when they finally bring it, and a mischievous central image crystallises the political unease: a peasant appears to be playing a piano, but of course a peasant isn't capable of doing such a thing, so he gets up and leaves the player piano to continue on its own, to the delight of the aristocrats.

The film is so arresting – the rackety estate, the dark corners of the house – and so beautifully acted by an ensemble as familiar with Chekhov, blood and bone, as we might be with Shakespeare, that one can live with the shortage of more direct versions of the plays. There is one *Seagull* that I can think of, with James Mason and Simone Signoret, a *Three Sisters* which is adapted from a National Theatre production, and a recent *Cherry Orchard* directed by Michael Cacoyannis; but most of what films there are are of *Vanya*, though two of these transplant the action, and the characters' names therefore, to Wales and Australia. However, the version made in 1971 by Mikhalkov's brother Andrei Konchalovsky is nothing if not authentic, creating the play's claustrophobia by means of an almost complete lack of animation. As you would expect in what is a fully realised movie and not a filmed stage show, large swathes of the play are cleared away – anything resembling a soliloquy, Waffles' background, much of Vanya's wooing of Yeliena, Yeliena's and Sonya's attempts to celebrate their reconciliation – and in their place sits an acreage of oppressive silence in which time passes infinitesimally slowly. Innokenti Smoktunovsky as Vanya is forever fiddling with some small object, and the ordinary lassitude is so sickening, so ever-threatening to them all, that the sight of Astrov briefly becoming excited in the first Act creates a wild delirium in everyone. The film moves in and out of monochrome, and occasionally directorial inventions fill the empty spaces – such as Astrov riding home through a landscape of almost nuclear devastation, Vanya waking from a nightmare or eavesdropping through his wall on Serebryakov and Yeliena, nosily reading the Professor's papers, or wildly playing the piano in the middle of the night. The camera dwells lovingly on the drips from a leaky roof filling an empty glass on a billiards table – it is like something from the work of Andrei Tarkovsky, for whose *Andrei Rublev*, indeed, Konchalovsky had co-written the screenplay. Waste and failure stalk the house like a distinct character. The most provocative interpretation is of Yeliena, who is both outrageously beautiful and sexually needy, welcoming not only Astrov's attentions but Vanya's as well; when the latter kisses her in Act Two, her line 'Where's the Doctor?' unmistakably suggests that she hopes he is out of the way so that she and Vanya can continue. She is a flirt who nevertheless suffers extremely from guilt: it makes sense, even if Yeliena becomes less the virus of apathy than an agitated sprite. Her frustration with Serebryakov is not so much because he is an impossibility, but because he ought to be all right – quite personable, quite elegant, unassuming even: having heard Vanya's denunciations (whispered in his ear rather than announced to the company), he has the courage to laugh uproariously at his attacker's pretensions, and stands calmly in front of a mirror adjusting his clothes while Vanya misses him and fires on a table lamp. Sergei Bondarchuk as Astrov slightly betrays his background as an heroic classicist (a remarkable figure, he also directed a five-hour *War and Peace* and, later on, spaghetti Westerns); but the great benefit of the film is to see Smoktunovsky at work. A big hairy baby in a woolly cardigan, he gives a performance he would repeat many times on the stage: there is a story that on the eve of the May Day Parade in 1985 Mikhail Gorbachev came to visit the Moscow Art Theatre's director Oleg Yefremov, his heart broken by Smoktunovsky's Vanya, just wanting to 'talk theatre'.

You could never accuse this film of the vitality and joy of *Mechanical Piano*: it is Chekhov as he might have been conceived by Michelangelo Antonioni, though Chekhov would not have found quite the apathy he required in Astrov's thorough kissing of Yeliena and inspection of the map of Africa. But it certainly casts a spell. On the other hand, what is odd, given such authority, is its anxious editorialising: the snowy wastes of Russia, montages of starving children and wretched peasants and the urban gentry insist on your attention in a way that would attract criticism if the film were English or American, since the audience would feel its intelligence insulted. However, it was shot in 1971, so its aim at Russian audiences was slightly deflected by its need for Soviet approval.

Where Konchalovsky's version, with its lived-in linen jackets, its bad teeth and its squealing furniture, could be called the real Slavic thing, *Vanya on 42nd Street*, made in 1994 by Louis Malle with a group of actors working on David Mamet's version of the play, starts at a hot dog stall, with Wallace Shawn despondently watching the world go by. It turns out he is on his way to work, appropriately enough to play Uncle Vanya in a public rehearsal at the half-ruined New Amsterdam Theatre in New York. During an extended opening sequence, a collage of 42nd Street life plays through under Joshua Redman's jazz score and the other actors converge, the Sonya and Yeliena narrowly missing being run over as they cross the road. Larry Pine – who if we did but know it is to play Astrov – takes a look at a pair of legs in hot pants on the way by; and at one moment a Russian babushka from real life flits past. These details we may or may not remember later. Some guests are going to watch a run-through, which gives the actors the chance to explain that the theatre was once the home of the Ziegfeld Follies. (Subsequently it will be renovated by Walt Disney and occupied by *The Lion King*, but at this moment its condition is such that nets are hung out to catch the falling plaster and the cast have to work in what look like the orchestra pit, foyer and corridors.) There is much of this light preparatory talk – some of it, I am sure, dubbed on afterwards – and then Shawn, taking a step towards his Vanya identity, declares he is exhausted today and lies down to sleep. The overworked

Dr Astrov-to-be complains that he is obliged to wake at dawn to learn rewrites and run all over town rehearsing different theatre projects. The actor of Waffles tinkers with a guitar. If all this sounds like a contrivance, it is, for a good purpose, since the segue into the opening lines of the play is achieved without an interrupted breath in the middle of a camera movement; and the action goes forward on the same conversational plane, except that the actors seem more at home in their Chekhovian characters than in their slightly forced versions of themselves. The purpose of Malle's work is clear enough – to bring an audience into the heart of this play without any sense of attending an event. The few shots of the invited guests watching with worried raptness have the effect only of underlining Chekhov's astonishing ability to dive well beneath an audience's guard and to tackle its deepest concerns.

What has happened is that the director André Gregory has over the past five years brought together a group to rehearse *Vanya,* though not with any plan to show it to the public. These actors, by the way, are busy and distinguished rather than hopefuls, and it is hard to imagine their English equivalents doing quite the same thing. By now the work proceeds with an intimacy and sureness ideal for the camera, which after all can examine two or three reactions to a speaker's words with great intentness, and allows Astrov to register his sudden memory of the patient who has died in his care by the merest, but most deeply felt, inclination of the head. There is some cunning involved – police sirens, distantly overlaid, gently remind you of where you are, and the sound of a lone saxophone from 42nd Street is allowed to sit behind Vanya's soliloquy in Act Two, and I doubt if that's by chance. David Mamet's version allows the American actors to be completely at home, as it should:

You've bilked us…are you up for it?… What should I tell you?

Most references to Russia, together with the complexities of the Russian names, are taken out; you can often glimpse in the action a police barrier fencing off the dangerous parts of the dilapidated building. There is certainly no map of Africa for Astrov to refer to, and at the height of his passion against Serebryakov Vanya drinks his water from a plastic I LOVE NY cup.

What emerges most strongly is the impossibility of anybody sleeping in the house because of the extraordinary distraction produced by Yeliena and Serebryakov. As Astrov says, one could really imagine some great catastrophe if they'd stayed longer. The film even improves on the play in respect of Vanya's mother, who becomes a foolish parasite on the Professor and has a couple of blazing rows with her son. Brooke Smith's Sonya is incomparably good, the more heartbreaking for her toughness. Her reunion with Yeliena is so guarded and prone to relapse that the kissing that even the tough Mamet specifies in his text is cut. Larry Pine's Astrov proves that you can be a handsome devil and still have a passion for forestry and what life will be like for those coming a hundred years later. Wallace Shawn and Julianne Moore achieve performances of miraculous complexity as Vanya and Yeliena: Shawn so possessed with malice that his sweet and joyless smile is more devastating than his frown, which tends to be composed of self-mockery rather than anger. He pretends to be like a turkey or a lapdog in front of Yeliena, opens his mouth to speak well and spits venom instead, feels his memories of his sister creep up on him not with sentiment but with a sort of terror ('it's not good...it's not good...') – and when at the end, under Sonya's nursing, his laughter becomes a true and accepting thing, it is extremely moving. Meanwhile Moore, like Irina Miroshnichenko not so much lethargic as displaced, uses laughter as a weapon against everything – to forestall yet lead on Vanya, to assess Astrov, to keep Serebryakov at bay, even to purge the women's disappointment when he won't let them play their music; and she suggests an inexplicable tangle of emotions in relation to all three men and to Sonya.

Gregory may, as he said, have set about *Vanya* as a spiritual exercise, an enquiry into how the balked process of communication reveals the light and dark of human character. But despite his insistence on its non-theatricality, his version comes across as a hymn to the theatre, or rather to acting, or rather to the company of actors, since what you see through Louis Malle's lens is a group of fine colleagues rehearsing their hearts out, with no expectation, at least until this point, of their work reaching the light of day. The fact that the setting is so filmically reassuring – Times Square, the coffee shops and so on – and that the actors wear rehearsal clothes, doesn't altogether explain the popularity of this film, which may have something to do with the fact that you could never believe you were in nineteenth-century Russia; what matters – the characters' transactions – is wonderfully done, stewed in several years' absorption, as if it were the work of Stanislavsky's company without the dogma.

Meanwhile, for many people old enough, Laurence Olivier's stage production, which opened at Chichester in 1962 and has become available on video, remains the golden memory among English *Uncle Vanyas*. It is unlikely to win over a new audience at this stage, as Malle's film may have done, but in its time it marked a coming of age, a final agreement in England that these were tough-minded plays about their own tough subjects, and not serenades or vague acts of solidarity with a wartime ally. Constance Garnett's text, considered out of date now, has real insights, and is the only one that I know of that refers to 'moralising' rather than the conventional 'philosophising'. The screen version is the stage production photographed, neither more nor less. You see an empty theatre, pan to the lighting rig, then back to the packed auditorium, and each Act ends with a theatrical fade. Allowances have to be made for its origin – these were the days when television thought it worthwhile to record outstanding theatre productions in situ, without adaptation. There is a fair amount of looking into the middle distance and a number of swooping theatrical moves that don't look good on film, while the general tone is rather rhetorical, with an overall evenness of pace. There is, in fact, plenty to be irritated by, including the opening caption that announces that we are on an estate in Russia in 1900 – at least four years after the play's composition – as if a less round date would confuse us. There are also some remarkable cuts in the text, as if repetition – Vanya's complaints and Astrov's forestry arias – were a dangerous thing rather than part of the play's warp and woof. Further cuts give you the queasy feeling that some characters are being taken more seriously than others. Serebryakov's academic background is gone, as is Waffles' account of his marriage (the centre of his part), and so is much of Marina's complaint about the house's disorganisation. The Moscow Art Theatre had visited Britain three years before with a repertoire that included *Vanya*, and audiences had been astonished at the fact that stars in one play could be seen in tiny parts in others: I have an impression that this sort of thinking made little impact on the planning of Olivier's production.

The film, like the stage show before it, depends heavily on Michael Redgrave's stupendous performance as Vanya, described by a critic at the time as 'a giant built for action but let down by his body…a refined intelligence going to ruinous waste'. Not for the first time you can observe the great benefit of physical size in a male actor if he has a delicacy as well – Albert Finney, Michael Gambon, Richard Griffiths. Redgrave's performance is informed by his own mix of working intelligence and ungovernable passion. Observing the offhandedness of Vanya's first entrance, he adds to the effect by briefly picking his nose; and his silly giggles embarrass him as he imagines himself married to Yeliena and comforting her on a stormy night. Like Wallace Shawn, he finds that a vital part of Vanya's personality is the ability to infuriate himself long before he reaches for a revolver.

The men together (Olivier is Astrov) are wonderful, especially when drunk; the women (Joan Plowright is Sonya and Rosemary Harris Yeliena) only a degree less so because they are not quite so well directed. It is a hard thing to say, since both are consummate actresses, but their performances seem to belong a little more to their period than do the men's. On the other hand, Olivier, self-hating in his cups, and Redgrave, in a performance that could have been filmed yesterday, plumb the depths of the play, and there are stabs of insight, as when Vanya is transported by Yeliena's kiss at the end but Astrov isn't. What is rather striking now is the production's general confidence and lack of introspection – like a no-nonsense Shakespeare of the time: and this is English Chekhov to be sure, virtuoso single performances rather than a symphony. The questioning Russian is seen as offering Great Parts for Great Actors, and if there is strong support, all the better: the Great Actors are needed for their idiosyncratic take on these distant figures, for their gratifying psychological insights. The fact is, though, that something is lost in this highbrow proceeding, since Chekhov's people live with a shared knowledge of the time they are in and what it has done to them; in the theatre they must operate as a team, and a dominant star can be as destructive to the fabric as Arkadina is to Konstantin's play in *The Seagull.*

I was in the midst of my ideological tribulations at Cambridge when the Great Actor *Uncle Vanya* came to the Old Vic in London the year after its Chichester success. I went to see it with Carey Harrison, a fellow student who was Rex's son and Olivier's godson. Carey was incensed by the ending, complaining that Chekhov's polyphony – Telegin on his guitar, Nanny muttering over her wool, mother rustling her pamphlets, the workman knocking outside – had been betrayed (the word seemed not too strong) by having Sonya and Vanya at their abacus picked out by a single spotlight while everything else faded away. I think he was probably right. He rose from his seat and resolved to go round immediately to see his godfather and register his disapproval, a mission I didn't join him on – I couldn't rely on a family tie to save me from professional suicide before I'd even started. In many ways Carey was justified in his distrust of Olivier. A few years later (the National Theatre, 1967) he would introduce into an otherwise good version of *Three Sisters* (he is a wonderful Chebutykin) a dream sequence of the Prozorovs getting to Moscow – travelling in carriages, going to the balls and so on – to the dismay of Josef Svoboda, his Czech designer, and all other good people. His touch as a director in Chekhov was less sure than as an actor, and as a general witness he is certainly outstripped by John Gielgud.

It is specially striking as I look at the film now, my own purposes in mind, but even in 1961 I could see that Olivier had made sure that his Astrov would look like Chekhov – goatee, pince-nez, the floppy hair. He had already played the part in 1945, with Ralph Richardson as Vanya, when he seems to have been too dandyish (*shchegol'skoy*, in fact) and confident, the very faults Chekhov found in Stanislavsky. His 1961 Astrov was both coarser and more vulnerable, though strictly speaking he was by now a bit old for the part. (It is always a shock, which I relish less with the passing years, to remember the young ages of Chekhov's characters and to recall their different life expectancy.) Olivier cut the reference to Astrov's age, and for all the physical likeness, veered away again from Chekhov's instructions. This Astrov knew quite well that Sonya loved him, and clearly wanted more from Yeliena than a casual kiss.

Like all good plays, *Uncle Vanya* adapts itself to its interpreters. With his maps, Olivier gives Yeliena a cheery one-to-one tutorial which also affords him the opportunity to come quite close to her to explain his points. Larry Pine does the same speech very fast for Gregory and Malle, enthused and fluent as if he were used to lecturing people conversant with his point of view. Yeliena simply has no chance and her 'I understand so little of it' could be our own reaction. His charts are big and unmanageable, unlike Sergei Bondarchuk's, which fold up very small, like English Ordnance Survey maps. Konchalovsky shoots most of this scene in a neutral midshot, until close-ups of starving Russia take over, the haunted faces making Yeliena look particularly bad as she leads Astrov on. Rosemary Harris' boredom with Olivier, meanwhile, is obvious – or rather her infatuation with his mellifluous voice takes her into a daydream, easily interpreted as indifference to the subject. Where Pine and Bondarchuk readily survive their disappointment at this, Olivier's face thickens with resentment and he admits his attraction to Yeliena with a certain vengefulness, whereupon she gives in to him quite fully. You could say that the Russian director is above all interested in where Astrov's environmental feelings stop short; that Malle and Gregory understand well the intimate politics whereby an expert male will make few concessions for a susceptible woman; and that Olivier is mainly interested in the sex, frankly acknowledged. As for me, I'm beginning to think of another option.

BUILDING BLOCKS

> I have a disease — autobiographobia. And when people start talking
> about me, I have an impulse to climb under the table.

> — Anton Chekhov

At some point or other in *Anton Chekhov* matters should grind to a halt for
a moment. Chekhov is talked out and seems to be giving up. He looks
balefully at us, imitates the ticking of his clock, relapses into silence. Then he
has an idea:

> I know what I can show you. (*Digging out a collection of maps.*) This is a
> special pleasure I allow myself about once a month, not more. I
> entertain myself with these for an hour or so, and then I become
> warm and peaceful and the crickets chirp…

What was Astrov in *Uncle Vanya* complaining to Yeliena about the despoliation
of the countryside is now the author confronting his audience:

> This is a map I've made of our district as it was fifty years ago. The
> green is forest, about half the whole area…

Some will be enthralled by this ecological question, some minds may wander,
and as Chekhov waxes indignant some will dislike being got at, especially by
a man whose geniality they have come to prize. God knows, some may be as
bored as Yeliena. At the end, Chekhov will stare out candidly, not reproachful
but disappointed, and say, like Astrov,

> But I can see from your faces this doesn't interest you at all

to which I might add

> Perhaps you don't have such problems

and hold a steady look. What will happen next? Feeling that he shouldn't
have lectured us, Chekhov apologises briefly and hints at something we know
even better than he did:

> But this Russia of ours is such an absurd, clumsy country that one day
> events will take us unawares, like sleeping fairies…

Having peered into contemporary Britain for a moment, he has invited us
home with him. It's the first real idea I've had for the show, and it will never
change.

After my Siberian journey, I managed to keep busy, mostly with the Royal Shakespeare Company, for five years. So it was quite easy to continue curling the lip at Lucien Stryk's suggestion to me; slightly less easy when, having done Hamlet in 1980 and left the company, I fell into one of those odd professional troughs that afflict even Hamlets, or perhaps especially Hamlets. My career went to sleep for a while, and the need to originate something of my own pressed hard. Still mulishly evading Lucien's point, I began to think about writing a play for three characters: Leo Tolstoy, Chekhov and Maxim Gorky. In 1900 Tolstoy was seventy-two, Chekhov forty and Gorky thirty-two. The relationship between the paterfamilias, the prematurely-old humanist and the burgeoning socialist – generally conducted in conversation between two of them on the subject of the third and then reported by one or the other to the absent party – is a beguiling mixture of high regard and petty irritation. It is also of course full of ideas about how to write and how to live, and what should become of Russia and the world. Bickering but bound together as on a Chekhovian estate, all three keep defying their stereotypes. Tolstoy, rebel against Church and Government, sometimes reveals a personal conservatism. Gorky, champion of the outlaw, often grovels like an acolyte. Meanwhile the unostentatious Chekhov – fundraiser, unsalaried doctor, road-builder and sponsor of schools – keeps emerging as the true revolutionary.

I'm quite afraid of Tolstoy. He's a colossus – though I can't help feeling there's more love of humanity in electricity and steam than in chastity and the refusal to eat meat.

– Chekhov on Tolstoy

Ah, what a dear, beautiful man he is: modest and quiet, just like a girl. And he walks like a girl! He's simply wonderful!

– Tolstoy on Chekhov

In a way hard to imagine now, all Russian writers of the time had to define themselves by their relationship to Leo Tolstoy. Though an encounter with the great doyen was an inevitable rite of passage for an emerging star, Chekhov delayed and delayed it – once indeed, hearing that Tolstoy was in a bath-house in Moscow that he planned to enter, he ran away. Eventually, in August 1895, he broke off from writing *The Seagull* in Melikhovo and faced the music at Yasnaya Polyana, Tolstoy's estate seventy-five miles to the south. The meeting left him with the toothache, Chekhov records, but it started promisingly, with a swim in the lake. Unlike his guest, Tolstoy clearly viewed the encounter with the utmost insouciance: he had gone for a dip when Chekhov arrived and he invited the younger man to join him. Chekhov undressed and waded in. So one may imagine the two famous heads, their beards floating on the water, doing the courtesies. Then they went for a walk along the highway towards Tula so that Tolstoy could show Chekhov the district's young people making use of a great new invention – the bicycle. That evening, Tolstoy read to his assembled company of disciples and womenfolk some selections from *Resurrection*, which was in draft. There was one demurral: listening to what is in part an assault on Russian criminal justice, the young veteran of Sakhalin ventured to correct a point of detail, observing that the heroine's sentence for conspiracy to murder was too light to be believable.

It would be interesting to freeze the frame at this moment. As far as we know, the suggestion was welcomed, but I don't know how warmly at such a public gathering, and certainly the two men's priorities would have been briefly on show. Tolstoy could be approximate on matters that half-interested him – for all his good public works, he was a little hit-and-miss about man's physical welfare, being preoccupied with his spiritual health. He was also inclined to scorn the medical profession. Chekhov, on the other hand, treated peasants like those in Tolstoy's story night and day, and had a passion for detail in both literature and science. To him, helping the poor was not just a matter of 'putting on bark shoes and sleeping next to the workman on the stove'; and, though his own work had been touched by Tolstoy's doctrines as recently as *The Wood Demon*, he had since tired of the older man's pronouncements on such subjects as syphilis, foundling homes and women's repugnance to sex. In fact, he declared them to be those of an ignorant man who has never taken the trouble to read two or three specialist books.

The most revealing outcome of Chekhov's thirty-six hours at Yasnaya Polyana was his astute and beautiful observation of Tolstoy's nature, characteristically based not on the old man's demeanour but on that of his two daughters:

> ...they adore him, they ardently believe in him...daughters are wise birds – they can't be caught with chaff. In a lover's eyes, a donkey may pass for a wise man, but daughters are another matter.

In fact, the elder girl, Tatyana, conceived something of a passion for Chekhov – never a good idea with this flirtatious magpie. A couple of years later she was dismayed to relive Lika's and Levitan's experience with 'The Grasshopper', recognising herself in Chekhov's 'Darling', a beautiful story about a woman too credulous with men but with such a need to love someone that she ends up looking after an abandoned child. Tatyana's father quite misunderstood this story, interpreting it as a satire on the 'new woman' which Chekhov had been unable to pull off because of the instinctive lyricism of his nature. In spite of this backhander, he also had plenty to say about its good qualities:

'It is like lace, made by a young girl. There were lace-makers like that in the old days: they used to weave all their innocent, uncertain love, their lives, their dreams, into the lace.' Tolstoy was speaking agitatedly, and there were tears in his eyes. It happened that Chekhov's temperature was high that day. He sat there with colour on his cheeks, his head lowered, carefully wiping his spectacles. For a long time he said nothing, but then sighed deeply and said in a low, hesitant voice, 'There are too many misprints in it.'

For this account we have to thank Maxim Gorky, who now joins the charmed circle, and is probably our best insight – sometimes sentimental, sometimes exaggerating the small detail, but always as zealously affectionate as Boswell – into what Chekhov and Tolstoy might have been like to meet.

Gorky has a nose like a duck – it's only unhappy, unkind men who have noses like that.

—Tolstoy on Gorky

Tolstoy is like a great steeple whose bell is heard around the world, with cringing little dogs scurrying about its base trying to make an impression.

– Gorky on Tolstoy

Gorky had escaped from a terrifying childhood into a vagabond life – barman, baker's assistant, dishwasher on the Volga steamers, railway worker, woodcutter and errand boy. He had an insatiable appetite for culture: he had also attempted suicide at twenty-one, an act which had the one advantage of keeping him out of the army. When he first visited Tolstoy, Tolstoy's wife thought he was a tramp and invited him into the kitchen for a glass of tea and a roll. The self-created Gorky disliked the Tolstoys' self-conscious domesticity in any case, and from Tolstoy's point of view there was a lot wrong with Gorky too – he complained to Chekhov that the young writer described things he had not felt. He then contradicted himself by admitting that Gorky knew life and seemed to have been born an adult. At this time, Gorky was a true man of the people, and knew a great deal more than Tolstoy about Russia's shoeless ones, his own bark sandals having tramped all over the country. I would guess that in each other's presence, Gorky felt intellectually outclassed but Tolstoy a little transparent. Accompanying the old man on his walks, Gorky thought he resembled some provincial governor, readier to judge men than to love them, and he watched his hyperbolical behaviour sceptically – Tolstoy would leap over ditches and throw himself down to smell the earth, compare *War and Peace* to *The Iliad*, pronounce that Chekhov would write better if he were not a doctor, and wish that he, Tolstoy, suffered more and felt less happy. Gorky often felt he was being treated as a curio, concluding:

> It is a trial to be with Tolstoy too often…his surroundings are like a desert, which he has scorched like a smouldering sun.

At other times, as equivocal as Chekhov, he felt Tolstoy was a master of the earth, of every flower and stone in it, his limbs knotted into 'some deep and powerful roots beneath the ground'.

> He is like a spectator in the theatre who expresses his feelings so loudly that he prevents himself and others from listening.
>
> – Chekhov on Gorky

> He disliked deep conversations about how we Russians live, forgetting how ridiculous it is, how unamusing, to argue about velvet clothes in the future when one doesn't have a decent pair of trousers.
>
> – Gorky on Chekhov

Three years after meeting Tolstoy, with the old man pretty much on his side, Chekhov had a letter, or rather a salvo of words, from the thirty-year-old Gorky, who had seen a performance of *Uncle Vanya* at Nizhny Novgorod, his home town. This was 1898, long before it was done at the Moscow Art Theatre, at a time when Chekhov was still smarting at his dramatic failures. Gorky had wept like a woman at *Vanya*, he said, and he elaborated typically. Its effect had been to make him feel like 'a garden from childhood being dug up by a great pig'. In fact, he seems to have made quite an exhibition of himself: 'I howled as I watched. It was as if I was being sawn in half by a dull saw – its teeth go straight to the heart.' Act Four in particular was like a hammer beating its audience's head – presumably concussed, it is unsurprising that they didn't seem to him to understand the play. 'Will the people be cured by it?' he fretted.

Chekhov of all people would not have cared for the tone of this, but in other ways the praise was timely – he was in a state of some tension as he waited for the Art Theatre's revival of *The Seagull* to open just a few weeks later. Somewhat overwhelmed, he wrote back. He had read some of Gorky's early stories and praised the plasticity of the writing – 'when you describe something, I can see it, almost touch it with my hands' – before moving on to his reservations. He warned the younger writer against 'rapture', reminding him that grace depends on expending the least possible movement on an action, before signing off apologetically:

> If I speak about the weaknesses of a tree in an orchard, it may not be a matter of the tree but of the tastes of the observer.

The next spring the two met in Yalta – probably under police surveillance: Gorky was an undesirable, even banned from visiting Moscow. Facing Chekhov dressed like a peasant, Gorky apologised for his excessiveness with more, describing himself as being 'as stupid as a train without rails'. Listening to Chekhov's plans to build a TB sanatorium and his disgust at Russia's treatment of its teachers, Gorky warmed personally to his hero.

In all the extant pictures of the two alone, Chekhov is obviously pleased with Gorky as well. In one, as if in a Chekhovian half-light, he seems on his way to a greeting, with the enquiring look of someone caught a little off-guard, while Gorky, like a great hippy, towers confidently over him. The friendship was to be lifelong, at least for Chekhov's life, and more sincere than that of either with Tolstoy. In 1902 Gorky was elected to the Academy of Sciences, but the Government immediately annulled the appointment of such a dangerous thinker. Even though he disliked (or feared) gestures of this kind, Chekhov resigned from the Academy. He then tried to persuade Tolstoy to do the same, but Tolstoy made an excuse and stuck his nose back in a book. Conversely, Gorky worked hard in 1901 to release Chekhov, never a good businessman, from a bad contract with a publisher inappropriately named Marx, who had offered him the equivalent of £8000 for all his rights. It was a complete buy-out with no further royalties, and Chekhov was obliged to supply copies of everything he had ever written, which he said was like making a list of every fish he had caught. Gorky's embarrassing zeal continued to characterise their friendship – believing that all kinds of people brought honey to him ('even if the honey isn't clean') he once made Chekhov a gift of an ex-prostitute because he thought her an interesting character for study; and years later, when he read 'Lady With a Little Dog', he declared that he wanted to trade in his wife for a new one. Still, whereas Tolstoy exhausted Chekhov in the clinic after the Moscow haemorrhage, Gorky was quietly there at the end, for the Art Theatre's celebration of his final birthday in 1904 – the very frail Chekhov declaring that the two consumptive writers had enjoyed 'an interesting cough together'.

Clearly, what I was assembling was not the solo show Lucien had suggested, but a two-handed piece with a significant absentee, and it seemed logical that there should be a central scene in which the three men met, especially as there is sufficient historical basis. In the autumn of 1901, Tolstoy arrived in Chekhov's Crimea in a private railway carriage to recuperate at a great mock-Scottish castle after a bout of malaria, while Gorky was renting a dacha nearby. Chekhov and Gorky spent the most time together. By this stage, if ever Gorky went out he would evade the policeman outside the house, who would then telephone Chekhov to find out where he had gone. Then the writers would visit Tolstoy. The photographs of these meetings have clearly been doctored. In one of them, Gorky stands behind the seated Chekhov and Tolstoy; in another version of the same shot, he has ominously been removed (a lasting Russian skill, this), as the Government of the day would no doubt have preferred. (Paradoxically, this picture joined the archive of Sovfoto, who would have liked to have the Great Socialist Gorky in there with the other heroes.) Tolstoy looks self-consciously unliterary in a great white Panama hat, peasant blouse and high boots; and Chekhov, who always worried long and hard about what to wear when visiting him, has this time settled on a rather formal dark suit and felt hat. His hands clasp his knees tightly and he is not altogether at ease – but more so than in a second study, at breakfast on the balcony, where he looks thoroughly miserable, hunched forward while Tolstoy gestures at him with what might be a teaspoon. Between them in this one is Tolstoy's big wife Sofia, a daunting woman who never liked Chekhov: she thought he 'sneered', which I suppose is what you would think if you were unsure of him. The Tolstoy daughters are also hanging around. But in another version of the shot, all the women have been efficiently brushed out, leaving two great writers apparently in private intellectual colloquy rather than at a ramshackle family occasion. For this reason perhaps, Chekhov now seems to be scrutinising something on the table with respectful attention to his animated host.

Since there is no actual knowing, I must imagine this scene going forward – the old man sounding off about the detested Shakespeare, while Chekhov spots the real problem:

> Shakespeare exasperates Tolstoy because he is an adult, and doesn't write like Tolstoy.

At this, Tolstoy rounds on Chekhov – he considers his plays even worse than Shakespeare's, and as for his fiction, the radical protest of 'Peasants' is 'a sin against the Russian people'. Is Chekhov an atheist, he demands, and did he screw around much as a young man? For lack of any other answer than a mumble, Tolstoy turns to the (reinstated) Gorky, warning him that man can endure anything but 'the tragedy of the bedroom'. While Tolstoy goes for a pee, Chekhov argues against Gorky's plan for a 'people's theatre', and for a moment his liberalism clashes with Gorky's Marxist zeal:

> Gogol should not be lowered to the level of the people, but the people raised to Gogol's level.

And so on and so on. You can see what I mean, and where the rub was. Too many desks and deckchairs, the air thick with bon-mots – not to mention 'Good morning Gorky, have you met Tolstoy?' They did all say these interesting things to each other, at different times, but it is thin satisfaction to come out of a show marvelling that it was all, after all, true. Pretty clearly Chekhov, the author's favourite, would emerge as the best part, followed by Tolstoy, made rather sillier than he was, with Gorky trailing behind, calling himself all sorts of bombastic names.

I had failed to animate the thing, though I had become rather interested in the police spy standing outside Chekhov's house. So from time to idle time I returned to the single voice of the good doctor, which I was hearing a little more clearly now that I had poked around in his lumber-room and interviewed his contemporaries. To get any further I needed to be still better acquainted. What in the world would it have been like to meet Chekhov? Gorky observed that in his presence everyone felt an involuntary desire to be simpler, more themselves:

> When Chekhov laughed, his eyes were very fine: they were tender, soft like a woman's – they caressed you. And his laugh was almost silent, it was so unusual… I've never known anyone who laughed in – so to speak – such a spiritual way…

And what would he have been prepared to say to an English actor – how large or small the talk, and in what unlikely setting? Chekhov's gregariousness is reported and so is his unapproachability. So I felt sure that the meeting would be all right in the end, as long as he felt well and not too cornered. Best not to rush him: oysters, champagne and Viennese neckties would be a better start than querying his friendship with the conservative Suvorin. And as for any awkwardness, I dare say he would be as gracious as Samuel Beckett is said to have been to a fan who, having secured an interview at last, became so tongue-tied that he had to flee from the restaurant. Beckett immediately sent him the manuscript of a new play no-one else had yet seen.

Next I encounter the writer Vladimir Korolenko asking the young Chekhov how he chooses his subjects. Chekhov chuckles and picks up an ashtray, declaring that the next day he'll have a story named after it – his eyes sparkle with merriment as the possibilities swarm through him. So I imagine myself, or an interested theatre audience, asking the same question. After an initial wariness, we would observe the speed of mind, the mix of self-deprecation and confidence:

> Everything's a subject: you dig them up by the spadeful. For instance, look at this wall – at first sight it seems to hold no interest at all, does it? (*Looks at the wall of the theatre and waits.*) But if you look really closely, you'll see something unusual about it, something nobody else has noticed, and then a really good story can come out of it.

As with Astrov and his maps, the trick will be to wait, and wait, until they really do think about it – and if the wall of a particular theatre is too interesting, it can be the worn carpet instead, a cracked light-fitting or the exit door, or even a pair of shoes in the front row.

Having turned his audience into talented writers like this, Chekhov declares that the effect of reading a good story should be instantaneous, like swallowing a glass of vodka. So far so pleasant, but he knows that the question of how he proceeds can't be shrugged off. He once explained it to his brother Alexander:

> In nature, you should go for the tiny details, and group them together so that you can then close your eyes and see a whole picture. Detail in psychology as well: don't describe the characters' psyches – it should be clear from what they do.

Trying to pinpoint examples of this for the audience makes Chekhov uneasy, and he ventures into metaphor, hesitantly, his voice not quite his own:

> You might see a monk, going from place to place, begging a bell for his monastery. There's something tragic about that black monk against the pale background of the dawn.

In fact this monk rings another kind of bell. When Chekhov crossed the Straits of Tartary to Sakhalin it seemed to him that the water was knocking on the lids of coffins on the sea-bed, that the figures he saw on the barges were petrified by an endless sorrow:

> Three reefs rise from the white spray of the breakers at the entrance to the port: they're called The Three Brothers, but they look like three great black monks.

This is the second time on his Siberian journey that a black monk has appeared. Near Tomsk he had noticed, trudging along the road, a man who seemed

> …like a holy black monk, terribly grave and emaciated.

Three years later, during his family's second summer in Melikhovo, Chekhov was still labouring at *The Island of Sakhalin*. One day he had a nightmare during the siesta hour: it brought him running out into the garden, rubbing his head. He had seen the figure of a black monk go 'whistling across the fields'. The ominous dream shortly became a story. The editor of *Russian Thought* found 'The Black Monk' watery and unreal, but since Chekhov was a big name by now, he published it anyway. Tolstoy inexplicably thought the story 'quite charming', which only proves that there is a kind of praise you don't need: 'The Black Monk' is closer to Dostoyevsky than anything else in Chekhov.

Its protagonist, Kovrin, an overworked academic, is spending an idyllic summer in the country with an old friend, a horticulturalist called Pesotsky. He becomes obsessed with a strange legend he's heard, or perhaps read, or dreamed, about a black-robed monk who was seen a thousand years ago, walking in the Sahara Desert. At the same moment, it is said, a group of fishermen a few miles away saw another black monk moving slowly across the surface of a lake. Kovrin believes that these mirages have multiplied until the monk's image 'has been endlessly transferred from one layer of the earth's atmosphere to another'. The point of the story seems to be that exactly a thousand years after this, the monk is expected to return to earth, and that time is approaching. Sure enough, walking in the fields one day, Kovrin sees such a figure flying towards him like a whirlwind. He just has time to plunge into a patch of rye. But the alarming apparition seems affable enough:

> What a white, fearfully white, thin face. He nodded to me, in a friendly way.

The next day, to the accompaniment of singers and fiddlers in the distance, the monk steps out from behind a pine tree and starts a conversation with Kovrin. He assures him that he is among the chosen people of God, and that he should be glad to sacrifice his health and life to great ideas – what could be better than that?

Kovrin is so euphoric that he immediately proposes to his host's daughter Tanya and marries her. To her bewilderment, however, he continues his exalting conversations with the ghostly visitor, who encourages him to think of himself as above the common herd, and Kovrin becomes wantonly cruel to her. Withdrawn and misanthropic, he eventually develops tuberculosis, a disease that in those days was sometimes associated with hallucination and delusions of grandeur. He leaves Tanya, takes up with another woman and travels with her to the Crimea. There, insomniac, he tries to get something done, as Chekhov used to do in Yalta:

> I sat at my desk and started writing... What a price life exacts from man in return for its commonplace rewards. To come this far I had had to work fifteen years day and night, endure a solitary life, and do a

number of stupid and unnecessary things that are best forgotten. I
saw clearly that I was a mediocrity, and I was glad, seeing that everyone
should be satisfied with what he is…

He is distracted by a light wind blowing in from the sea. The bay beneath his
window stares back at him with the dark blue of vitriol, with turquoise and
fiery red eyes; the barometer rises. Sure enough, the monk is returning. He
arrives in the room, but Kovrin is unable to speak as blood is pouring from
his mouth. He calls to his wife, and dies euphorically, her name on his lips.

The story is an odd mixture of melodrama and jokiness; and you might
say that Chekhov's interest in pathology and his instinct for a ghost story are
slightly at odds. But the impression of Kovrin's psychosis was so convincing
to Chekhov's friends that he had to dispel some fears:

I'm quite sane, even if I'm not specially keen on living… I wrote it
out of cold deliberation… I just felt like describing megalomania.

The setting of 'The Black Monk', with its fruit trees, fine saplings, its
nightingales and kingfishers, could be Chekhov's Melikhovo, and Pesotsky
the gardening side of the author. The fields of rye where Kovrin sees the
monk are reminiscent of paintings by Levitan such as *Country Road*; and the
last part of the story is set just where Chekhov would eventually be forced to
live himself. As for Kovrin's fifteen years of hard work, it was near enough
that long before writing the story that Chekhov had arrived in Moscow and
begun a literary career of sorts. The meetings between Kovrin and the monk
teeter between foreboding and a tongue-in-cheek guignol which I can imagine
Chekhov relishing speaking aloud. It may be that I could put parts of 'The
Black Monk' – the beginning and the end in particular – into Chekhov's own
mouth and bookend the show with them. It also pleases me to know that this
was the first of his stories to be translated into English, though few people
will realise that.

It is not often that he deals with mental derangement like this, or with the
consumption that stalked both him and Kovrin; and to my mind, the recurring
black monk is the creative element in Chekhov's great effort at evasion.
Covering up was as normal for him as putting his clothes on in the morning,
and it is a Chekhovian irony that he was on so many days dealing with his
own symptoms in others. The spectre that stared out of his patients' eyes into
his had also, of course, stared out of his brother Kolya's. Alexander Tikhonov,
a literary journalist, found himself spending a weekend with Chekhov in
1902 on the estate of Savva Morozov, a benefactor of the Moscow Art Theatre.
Tikhonov's account is convincing enough, though sometimes spoiled by such
little expediencies as Chekhov commenting, like Trigorin, 'There must be a

lot of fish in that lake.' The author was very morose during the days, fidgety and critical, and during one night there was a thunderstorm: between the claps of thunder Tikhonov, sleeping in the next room, heard coughing and groaning and an ominous gurgling. He rushed in to find Chekhov in the midst of a convulsion, blood pouring from his mouth into a blue enamel spittoon, but his tone was kindly where it had been surly before:

> By the light of the candle I saw his eyes without his pince-nez for the first time, large and vulnerable and blurred by tears. He spoke with difficulty: 'I'm terribly sorry...I'm disturbing you...excuse me, dear friend.'

This horrible disease has its own melodramatics, and is thus a little bit of a theatrical cliché. In the playing, you can't forget about it, but neither do you want to keep drawing attention to it. Chekhov's infinite skills in concealing his symptoms – he used to carry little paper cones in his pocket, spit blood into them and discreetly dispose of the evidence – are much in my interests, and leave me with the chance to engineer one moment in the show that parallels Tikhonov's painful discovery. One reason why Chekhov would have disliked public speeches, especially play-length ones like mine, must have been fear of a coughing fit (for him, both literature and speech were better when terse); so a breakdown during our performance would mortify him as much as it did with Tikhonov. Such a thing might come at a moment of stress, as yet unidentified, and he would surely say again, this time to the public, 'I'm terribly sorry.' The apology should be so simple and direct that the audience thinks that the actor has swallowed a fly.

In 'The Black Monk', the countryside grows supernaturally dark, the rye rustles with foreboding and the trees whisper. For the artist Levitan too, Russian nature can be as ominous as idyllic. Behind his luminosity you can glimpse the grumbling chaos of Russian life, a life of carelessness, unfinished thoughts and incomplete dreams. Kovrin's story could easily be played out against the backdrop of *Vladimirka*, a picture Chekhov probably knew (though it was painted during the friends' estrangement), with its single dark figure trudging along a rutted path, tiny under a wide sky. It is hard to tell whether it is approaching or receding, and what the white object is that stands out against the black clothes. Were it not for what looks like a dovecote or a postbox standing near to it in ridiculous isolation, you might miss the figure altogether.

But Chekhov came from the south, where Levitan spent less time, and I also need to recall *Mountains in the Crimea* and *The Village of Savvino*, with their warm browns and rocky dryness, their broken down *izbas*, piles of logs and benevolent chaos, bringing a less mysterious landscape to life. This is Chekhov's spiritual home, and the logical setting for his first unequivocal success. In early 1888 he wrote a long story, 'The Steppe', drawing extensively on childhood memories. Although the effort left him tired and fed up (wanting to do nothing but 'lie in bed and spit at the ceiling'), the work was a sensation and won him the Pushkin Prize. Interestingly, this recognition sent him on another journey into his past, and he spent the spring and summer not writing at all but travelling, first in the Ukraine, then in the Crimea, then the Caucasus. The result, in September, he typically described as 'a wretched little subject'; but in fact 'Beauties' is an exquisite account of a boy's journey to Rostov-on-Don with his grandfather, narrated with the wistful regard of the grown man. Rostov is only about thirty miles from Taganrog, his home town, and at seventeen Chekhov had indeed travelled to an Armenian village, Bolshiye Saly, which surfaces in the story as Bakhchi-Salakh. Reading 'Beauties', a cousin of Chekhov's had no difficulty in recognising the grandfather as Yegor, their own; his coachman's name, Karpo, is unchanged in the story; and the fictional Armenian at whose house they rest, Avet Nazarovich, is pretty clearly related to the Armenian Nazarov who was an associate of old Yegor.

Nostalgia, natural beauty and the oblique turn taken by physical attraction characterise 'Beauties'. The narrator remembers stopping at Bakhchi-Salakh and glimpsing Nazarovich's daughter, a girl so lovely that he felt

> not desire, nor joy, nor pleasure, but a kind of painful pleasant sadness, vague and hazy as a dream…for some reason I felt sorry for myself, sorry for grandfather and the Armenian, even sorry for the girl herself: I felt as if the four of us had lost something important and necessary in life that we'd never find again.

Linking her inexplicability to nature, he compares it to a sunset, when

> one cloud becomes like a monk, another like a fish, another a Turk in his turban… Everyone who looks at it – the boy out herding his cows, the surveyor on the mill dam, the fine gentleman out for a walk – all gaze at it and find it beautiful. But wherein its beauty lies, no-one knows, no-one can say.

Having seen the girl, neither of the visitors is able to speak. She gives the narrator tea, and he feels as if a fresh breeze has blown over him. His grandfather stops talking about sheep and gazes tenderly at her. The groom overseeing the threshing follows her around with his eyes. No one any longer notices the dust, the flies and the dreary steppe. It is only when the horse has been bathed and hitched up and the boy and his grandfather set out again – in silence, as if they were angry with each other – that their driver, infuriated by his own sensibility, breaks the silence:

'She's a fine girl, that Armenian's daughter.' And he whipped the horse.

The refrain of al fresco love is proving irresistible to me: it begins even before 'Beauties' and 'The Steppe', with 'The Huntsman', written on a friend's estate in Babkino when Chekhov was twenty-five. Loaded with the usual disclaimers – it was just one of those things he'd done 'in a flash, in less than a day, in the bath-house, in fact' – this was the work that caused Suvorin to sign him up for *New Times* and begin to pay him properly. It was also spotted by an old novelist, now forgotten but at the time an *eminence grise*, Dmitri Grigorovich, who wrote him a fan letter mixed with wise counsel. Grigorovich noted the false modesty with which Chekhov hid behind his pseudonym, and urged him to take his talent seriously. Chekhov answered, it must be said, in a most grovelling manner, like a drama student responding to praise from Laurence Olivier. He apologised for still being more than a journalist but less than a writer, and promised to take the literary veil.

So 'The Huntsman' was the turning-point that made 'The Steppe' and many other things possible. Turgenev had died the previous year, and in some ways Chekhov's story, with its tremendous sense of high summer, is a homage: to it he adds his own depth of sympathy and a shrewdly unsentimental eye, and as always he writes far less intricately. It also, with its sustained dialogue, gives me an opportunity on the stage. I've an idea that it could be set up in the show by a return to the nagging question of what constitutes good writing. Chekhov is forthright about what does not – his cure for insomnia is anything written by Dostoyevsky:

> I went home and fell asleep trying to read The Brothers Karamazov. So long-winded and indelicate. Oh dear, oh dear.

Gogol fares little better:

> Think of a man in a field of rye on a sunny day. Now, Gogol would write: 'A tall, narrow-chested man who had a short red beard sat down on the green grass, already trampled by passers-by, sat down noiselessly, timidly, fearfully glancing about him...' I'd write: 'The man sat on the grass.'

The public generally likes professional bitchiness, especially if the names are big. Encouraged by their laughter Chekhov will warm to his subject and begin to demonstrate his own methods at last:

> Little details. The sun rises. The birds sing. It's a hot and sultry afternoon... The forest is quiet and still, looking out from its treetops as if it were waiting for something.

Our lighting gently warms up. Chekhov is improvising, and it turns out to be 'The Huntsman'. For characters, he will need – what? – a pale-faced peasant girl, about thirty, with a sickle in her hand, and there she is, Pelageya; she will need someone to accost, and he becomes Yegor, crossing the fields with, let's say, a hunting-bag on his shoulder and a crumpled woodcock hanging out of it:

> With his eyes screwed up he watches his scraggy old dog, who's running ahead and smelling at the bushes. Everything is quiet...not a sound...every live creature is hidden away from this heat.

Now Chekhov sets the two of them going. Pelageya persuades Yegor to sit down for a moment. She timidly complains that she has not seen him since that day in Holy Week when he arrived at her house drunk, beat her and left; for all that, she entreats him to visit again. Yegor resists – he has a good job now, providing game for the local Count, for which he gets a good bed, good tea and good conversation, whereas in Pelageya's village there's only poverty and dirt. Pelageya is scornful. This life he takes such pride in doesn't sound respectable to her. Yegor, stung, insists that he is the best shot in the district – written about in a magazine, even – and that once the free spirit's entered a man it can't be got out again; but to his annoyance Pelageya is crying now, and we get a clue:

> I'm not crying...it's just that it's wrong, Yegor Vlasych. It's been twelve years since I married you, and we've had no love, no love...

There's the story. The Count was so jealous of Yegor's prowess with the gun that he got him drunk and married him off to Pelageya, to keep him in his place: Yegor has evaded his wife ever since, but they're stuck with it. The conversation limps on, the two of them blanketed in midsummer heat. Narrating, Chekhov too comes to a halt every so often. What next? He can fill in with exquisite grace notes:

> Silence. Wild ducks fly over the scrub. Yegor watches them till they drop down below the forest, three tiny white dots...

How does Pelageya get by then, asks Yegor, then regrets the question – she earns a rouble and a half for taking a baby from the orphanage and feeding him from the bottle.

> Silence again. From a strip of land that's been harvested comes a quiet song, but it stops as soon as it starts. It's too hot for singing...

Pelageya lets slip that she knows Yegor is building a house for a new woman. Being a man, he abruptly avoids the point and sees a way out. He's been sitting here too long and has to get to Boltovo by nightfall. He gives her a rouble – she stares blankly at it. Then she watches him as he trudges on his way, and her feelings re-form:

> …her gaze runs over her husband's tall figure, touching him, cherishing him… He walks along the road: it is long and straight as a leather belt… Then the red of his shirt mixes in with his dark trousers, she can no longer see his steps, she can no longer tell which is his dog and which are his boots…
>
> – Goodbye Yegor Vlasych, Pelageya whispers, and stands on tiptoe, trying to get a last view of that little white cap.

Chekhov has performed this story for us off the cuff, just as he might conjure up something on the subject of an ashtray; and I suppose the sense of his becoming an actor may be interesting too. He has forgotten his surroundings, as if he were sitting on the ground with Yegor and Pelageya, warmly edging them forward. It will be dull for him to come back from the field of rye to an empty stage – to a property glass of tea, to books and a guttering candle. Storytelling being what it is, he may also need a break:

> *The clock starts ticking again. Silence. Chekhov strolls to his desk, looks through some papers, surveys us. He takes a sip of tea, but it is cold, and he recoils slightly. He looks at us again, a little uncertainly, and makes his excuses.*

Just going to have some tea.

> *He wanders off into the depth of the room.*

'The Huntsman' has created a point of balance in our evening, as in Chekhov's career. He has broken through as a writer and also earned our second half, so the interval will be well-placed here.

What else do I have? Various reminiscences and implications but little way in or out of them; Astrov as a mouthpiece, 'The Black Monk' as a confession and 'Beauties' as a memory, a few comments about writing as linking material. The surprise has been to find Chekhov completely accessible through his fiction – this is where his big voice is heard, while at other times he is intimately deprecating, sometimes blunt and sometimes delicate; companionable enough for the audience to feel they could ask him the question they always wanted answered, but reserving the right to withdraw. It might not be strictly true to say that I was pondering this on a day when the telephone rang – or that I had, the moment before, flung down my pen in despair. But what happened was certainly odd. The call was from Granada Television, asking if I would care to play Anton Chekhov in a new play about his life by Anne Allen. It was early 1982.

A Wife Like the Moon, which would have given Chekhov extreme autobiographophobia, dealt mainly with his relations with the Moscow Art Theatre and with his courtship of and marriage to Olga Knipper. Allen had been understandably drawn to the six-year period between his first meeting with Olga at rehearsals for *The Seagull* and his sad, sad death beside her at the Hotel Sommer in Badenweiler, in the summer of 1904. The Chekhov-Knipper letters are often pulled out of Chekhov's correspondence as a volume on their own, and they do indeed make one of the great love stories, poignant in the extreme. Partly this is because of the pair's frequent separations and partly because it was so clearly a relationship of equals. You don't feel the familiar disappointment of looking into the life of a great artist only to find that he was foul to his women.

The story is also thick with ambiguities, its theatrical context being both congenial and uneasy for Chekhov. The flow of feeling between the lovers is skewed by the fact that Olga lived and worked in Moscow, giving life to Chekhov's heroines, while he remained under doctor's orders in the south. He was, of course, constantly enraged by Stanislavsky and by the shortcomings of the actors as well; but he also knew how devoted they were and he loved their company when he visited, sitting in dressing-rooms gossiping and watching his enchanted stage being set up – part doll's house full of childish nooks and crannies, part industrial plant. I certainly believe him when, back in his wilderness, he writes to Olga with acute nostalgia: the companionship of such colleagues is hard to replace, even if you're not sick and far away.

The couple spent as much time writing to as seeing each other, and to the embarrassment of their ghosts, we have most of the letters – moving, passionate, workaday, intimately jejune. In all his endearments, the only animal Chekhov does not call Olga is a crocodile, though he does once warn her not to become like one. The central paradox lies in Chekhov's attitude to the relationship – to which Knipper did her best to adjust – counterpointed by his life's loudly ticking clock. The title of Allen's play is drawn from a letter he wrote to Suvorin in 1895, protesting that while he would be a good husband, it would be best to have a wife who, like the moon, would not appear in his sky every day. Something in his character dreaded the kind of happiness that lasts from one day to the next, he said; and he finally agreed to tie the knot in 1901 on the proviso that 'everything should go on as before', with Olga in Moscow and him in Yalta, that none of his family be told about it, and if possible not

Olga's either, because he was 'terribly nervous of standing around holding a glass of champagne and talking to relatives'. Chekhov may not have been a cruel man, but his disposition caused an awful lot of discomfiture, especially to his sister, who was thus not informed of the wedding, and whose own chances of marriage Chekhov had blighted by accepting her lifelong dedication. She now, naturally enough, formed the third corner of an explosive triangle.

Olga was sometimes absent from Chekhov's sky, even after they were married, for months at a time; and as illness closed in on him he found it increasingly difficult to lie on the bed he had made. Truly in love at last, he would undertake ill-advised journeys to Moscow, and she to him. Should Olga have sacrificed herself and spent more time in the south? (Yes, say the traditional male critics, to a man.) Chekhov used to complain that if he married an actress he would have 'an orang-utan or a porcupine' for a son, but in 1902 Olga became pregnant in Yalta and then took the 700-mile journey back to work. Because of that, and possibly too many parties after she got home, she miscarried. Should she have returned to rehearsals so soon after conceiving? (No, cry the same critics.) But why did Chekhov so often, within a sentence, long to see her in Yalta but advise her not to travel? Did he or did he not want her there? Why did she not override him? When she does become importunate (there are a couple of cracking rows) he tells her meaninglessly that she is not to worry, as he is drinking tea three times a day and is only sorry that there are too many toads and crocodiles in his garden:

> I bow low to you, so low that my forehead is touching the bottom of my well, which has now reached a depth of fifty-six feet...

As so often, his elegance barely masks a hurtful withdrawal.

It is easy to see that the whole story – as elusive, touching and riveting as if he had written it – could make a two-hander on the stage, presumably under a title such as *Chekhov in Love*, one of those lectern dramas like that of Bernard Shaw and Mrs Pat Campbell, though not one I would particularly want to see. Allen's play at least allowed for a bit of movement. It made little attempt to explain Chekhov's other drives, and I got as far as a rather warm and sympathetic performance, bordering on the impish, which left the question of his genius open. Isabelle Amyes played Masha, Prunella Scales was Olga, and Julian Amyes, one of the father-figures of television drama, directed. Indeed, in its studio presentation it greatly resembled a 1960s production, the kind my generation get sentimental about. Its technology seemed quite advanced at the time, since we sometimes used the 'blue screen' technique, in which the camera refused to photograph anything blue and substituted a programmed image of Russian forests, in which I would then be sitting fishing.

It was all charmingly pre-digital, with little fuzzy borders on the superimposed picture that gave the game away. Today's audience would laugh, but at least it made it unnecessary to go on location. Best of all, because the play marked the stages of Chekhov's declining health, I was able to catch that well. Julie Jackson, Granada's make-up supervisor, and I identified six or seven physical states for him, and because the short scenes were then shot out of sequence, we dotted to and fro between them on any given day. Although not really resembling Chekhov, I became an expert on his skin and bone, his hairline, his body temperature and his attitude to his beard.

It is hard to imagine in these impoverished days getting such an abstruse subject onto British television at all. Running at ninety minutes at peak viewing time on the commercial channel, *A Wife Like the Moon* was taken very seriously. In a full-length review of a kind that no TV drama receives now, Peter Fiddick of the *Guardian* commented that he would have liked to see the same performances less constrained by pen, ink and the electric telegraph. Pretty clearly, what had been wrong with my Tolstoy-Gorky-Chekhov outline was also what hampered this: nobody really spoke to each other. Two characters would be shot in close-up, angled as if they were conversing when in fact they were reciting letters written from far apart at different times. People rarely speak as they write – but this being a time before tape recordings, the only alternative would have been to make it all up, interposing a writer's sensibility between the audience and the subject. Privately I sensed that I was finding a third possibility in my own work – to construct an alibi by which Chekhov uses his fiction to tell the truth about his life, even presenting himself as one of his own characters.

Another thing I knew – I wanted little or nothing of Olga in my show, and became quite wilful about it, accepting that the result would be that there wouldn't be much about theatre life either. I think Chekhov might have approved. The two themes are very familiar to anyone interested in him, and there are many other things he would prefer to discuss. One quote on each subject, slightly cobbled up, should be enough:

> My wife doesn't look after me. (*Knowingly.*) She's an actress. I go about in torn socks. I say to her: 'Look here, darling, the big toe on my right foot's sticking out.' 'Wear it on the left foot,' she says. I can't live like this

– and as for the Art Theatre:

> As you may know, I have sinned in the dramatic line, but not much, because I don't like the theatre and I can't stand the actors. What nonsense they talk. When they're young they scrape their feet and

neigh like donkeys; when they're old their voices become so hoarse
with drinking you can't hear what they're saying.

I tinkered on, breaking off to do a TV version of Bulgakov's *The White Guard*,
but *A Wife Like the Moon* had intruded. In early 1983 the phone rang again: it
was John Drummond, then director of the Edinburgh Festival, inviting me to
premiere *Anton Chekhov*, which he had somehow heard about, there in the
autumn. Could I possibly be ready by then? Why not – I agreed. The prospect
concentrated the mind wonderfully, but then I got stuck again and cancelled
at rather shorter notice than I should have. Drummond was princely about it.
I couldn't quite understand why my nerve had failed, unless I was hoping to
have my eye caught by something else: some tasks, however delightful, are
of a kind you long to be disturbed in. The instinct turned out to be right
enough. Had I not ducked out of Edinburgh I would not have been free for
another, most interesting, interruption and the beginning, for me, of a
remarkable year.

PART TWO

PART TWO

LYUBIMOV AT THE LYRIC

Writers like Dostoyevsky think we should be solving great questions, like God and pessimism. But for the most part, people have dinner, that's all they do, they have dinner, yet during this time their happiness is established or their lives are falling apart.

      – Anton Chekhov

Moscow, 18 June 1983

The famous statue of Yuri Gagarin, an angelic Superman in flight – his arms like wings, body like a rocket – looms out of the early morning light on Lenin Prospect. The pervasive smell of gasoline and the thump of tractors seep through the windows of the Sevastopol Hotel on the southern edge of the city – a building, like the Soviet Union itself, with a handsome enough façade but work still to be done at the back. On the sixteenth floor of Block Two (queasy title for a hotel annexe), Masha from Intourist is insisting that, whatever I have heard, there is no housing shortage in the city. No, I know: no *shortage*, but the official norm that makes that possible, the one determining how much space a person needs to live in: nine square metres, is it, these days? We look each other in the eye, much as I used to with Sergei, the KGB representative passing himself off as a friend on the Trans-Siberian, when he told me I would be bored by taking a walk outside at the station stops.

Anton Chekhov has been shelved again, for its own good and mine, by an invitation to play Raskolnikov in Yuri Lyubimov's production of Dostoyevsky's *Crime and Punishment*, due in London this autumn. Lyubimov is by any account one of the great Russian directors (closer to Meyerhold than Stanislavsky) and there should really be a Moscow statue of him in flight as well. He is profoundly of his country but halfway out of it, a supernova moving easily through world theatre but grounded by his need to jab thorns into the Soviet side. He abandoned an acting career and formed the Taganka Company on the site of a former prison on Shakespeare's birthday in 1964, and he has been pushing ever since at the limits of the politically permissible. When I arrived in Moscow from Siberia in 1975 the Taganka were not one of the theatre options proposed by Intourist, the Soviet Union's official travel operators: in fact, their existence was barely acknowledged. I was, the guides felt, much better off queueing for the Bolshoi. At the time I duly noted the company merely as 'a good radical theatre that experiments with the classics', which only proves that Intourist had done its egregious work well on me, for the Taganka and its inspiring director are a great deal more than that.

It used to be said that to miss one of Lyubimov's productions would be like not reading the newspaper – quickly, I suppose, before the newspaper was banned. The name Taganka is similar to a word for a tripod placed over hot coals for cooking – a trivet, in fact – and Yuri is fond of pointing out the very Russian truth that theatre is like a warm fire in a cold house: everyone wants to sit near it. His repertoire – Shakespeare, Pushkin, Bulgakov and Dostoyevsky – looks conservative, but his way is to abandon scene-by-scene narrative, instead editorialising and encoding the works so that they become subtle calls to arms for a demoralised audience. If he were working in England, the hoary old debate about whether revered texts should be dealt with in this way would immediately flare up – did Shakespeare intend *Henry V* to feel like the Falklands War? – but in the Soviet Union the argument is curiously irrelevant. Here, the present calls urgently for explanations from the past, and the loss of freedom is a common denominator to both.

It is at this point that the low-grade politics, disingenuous postures and shifty accommodations between the artist and his minders are transacted. For Lyubimov, it is a kind of blind man's buff, and his sense of hearing is correspondingly sharp. In the old days, ignoring the *chinovniki* – an old Russian word for civil servants that he likes to use (it is certainly not out of date) – he relied a little on an acquaintanceship with President Brezhnev, who, knowing the value of a safety valve, would sometimes override his own censors and let the intelligentsia get on with it. To some extent his luck held with Brezhnev's successor, Yuri Andropov, who felt personally grateful to him for discouraging his son and daughter from being actors (actually he turned them down at their auditions without knowing who they were). As Andropov became ill and Konstantin Chernenko and his hardliners loomed, so the water froze over, and Lyubimov's last three productions have been banned. You can see why. In his adaptation of Pushkin's *Boris Godunov* he had the boyar who upbraids the cheated Russian people – 'Why do you remain silent?' – patrol the audience, out of costume, asking them the question with an emphasis on the 'you' – so that was the end of that one. A satirical play called *Alive* and a tribute show to the legendary singer Vladimir Vysotsky (who played Hamlet for him) were stopped as well. But official standards are dizzyingly paradoxical. The other end of the push-me-pull-you bargain is that the *chinovniki* continually pester him for tickets to enjoy his thrilling work. The whole painful business has had the ridiculous effect of making Lyubimov an *enfant terrible* at sixty-five.

The Taganka has never played in London as a complete unit. In the 1960s, the much-missed producer of the World Theatre seasons, Peter Daubeny, fought to bring them to the Aldwych, but the idea was too much for the Soviets. Now, after years of negotiation, Peter James, director of the hardy Lyric Theatre in Hammersmith, has secured Lyubimov alone, to recreate his version of *Crime and Punishment* with English actors. For the Russian, the moment is infuriatingly critical. He has made forty-two required changes to *Boris Godunov* in Moscow, but the show has remained closed. He has offered his resignation to Andropov but had no reply, and he is coming to London not only to work with us but to start a stalking game with the Kremlin, hoping to win better terms by shaming them noisily from the West. He will soon be suggesting to the English press that he might be thrown off the balcony of the Lyric or assassinated in some other way, as Meyerhold was by Stalin.

Lyubimov's *Crime and Punishment* got past the censors back in 1979, and has been in the Taganka repertoire ever since. This is a little surprising, for it was obvious what he was up to. The Soviets have always been uncertain about this great novel, as were Dostoyevsky's original critics. Then, it was seen variously as an unjust attack on progressive students, as a protest against housing conditions in Petersburg, and as a warning against a Russian tendency to take every philosophical idea to an unacceptable conclusion; while for a modern audience Dostoyevsky lays surgically bare the delicate Russian question of ends and means. Is Raskolnikov, the story's anti-hero, in any way justified in murdering with an axe an old money-lender for the cash to rescue his sister from a sacrificial marriage to the rich but loathsome Luzhin? If he then hides his plunder and never uses it, where does that leave him morally? What is the meaning of the complex character of Svidrigaylov, a figure from de Sade who is also a benefactor? The novel was belatedly placed on school syllabuses in 1969, its Christian message dumbed down and Raskolnikov officially reinterpreted as a Soviet hero before his time, doing his bit by murdering the Tsarist exploiter. Lyubimov will have none of this simplification, since murder is murder, he is a Christian and takes Dostoyevsky to be one. He shows Raskolnikov as a nightmarish predator who even steps forward at the end of the production to read the official view from a school textbook: 'Raskolnikov was right to kill the old woman – too bad he got caught.' For every performance at the Taganka of this extremely adult production, a group of schoolchildren was invited, so he was undermining the revisionism at its roots.

I was keen to do the English version of this show from the moment I heard about it, and, unlike some of my peers, cheerfully submitted to auditioning for the Russian director, who among our fraternity seemed only to have heard of John Gielgud. I read the novel fast, got hold of a roneo-ed script, climbed onto the Lyric stage and snarled at Lyubimov:

> He who can spit furthest makes the law…a real Napoleon is permitted everything… How disgusting men are! You have to be brave enough to take a step over…you have to dare. As I dared…

There was a cry from the stalls:

> Ha! *Kelt*, da?

I admitted I was indeed not really English, but Scottish on one side and valley Welsh on the other. So perhaps I have my parentage to thank for my first stage work since Hamlet two years before, a job that was to be as much of a defining moment for me as that had been. Three of us were called back a few days later, not for further auditions but to be sat down and allotted our parts in person (no discreet calls to the agent for Yuri). For the one television star among the three, this treatment was the last straw and he staged his own defection, but Nicholas Farrell (Razumikhin) and I were delighted with our fate.

A few weeks later, a strong and intrepid cast had been assembled, and I had organised a small working party to go to Moscow to see the Russian production before our rehearsals began. Yuri's generation was not encouraged to learn languages and it was a bit late for him to start; he had a little French and Italian, but in English nothing beyond 'Let's go, please,' so the more we understood of our prospects the better. I'd coerced Veronica Roberts, who was to play Sonya; Louisa Bell, then Peter James' secretary at the Lyric; Annie Dyson, who was to be Raskolnikov's victim (she did not know yet that the script only started after the murder), and one civilian, Leigh Malone, friend and designer. Intourist couldn't quite see why we were there: they were acknowledging now that the Taganka were 'interesting people', but still pretended amazement that we would not, having come all that way, prefer the folk-dancing. We had cover, having hooked up with a group of doctors attending a convention on nuclear disarmament – Intourist had their hands full with these politicised medics, who did the theatre party a still greater service when, halfway through the visit, its instigator sustained a case of haemorrhoids on the great Chekhovian scale.

Having touched down in Moscow at four in the morning, one of these unfortunate doctors was shortly awakened by a misrouted telephone message: the English actors were to be at the Taganka forthwith for the performance specially called for their benefit, its time now advanced by a few hours. Unannounced and now rescheduled, word of it had got out to the street all the same, and we could barely get near the place for the throng. Welcoming us,

Yuri seemed to think I had come with my harem. Much more at ease on his own patch, he displayed a relaxed energy not far from joy – the theatre can make quite elderly men almost indecently young – and a passable resemblance to a great Teddy, except that this bear had teeth. After tea and jam, vodka, pickled cucumber, black bread and caviar, he proudly walked us through his foyer, where portraits of Brecht and Vakhtangov hung in uneasy truce with Meyerhold and Stanislavsky: his actors' pictures were on the walls as well, and he offered comments on the talents of each – 'fifty-fifty', most of them. For some reason this didn't make me apprehensive.

The bodies of Raskolnikov's two victims, the money-lender and her sister, lie in this foyer, and a mirror hanging over them invites the audience to observe its own reactions. In the deep black void inside, Raskolnikov's lodgings seem suspended on one side of the stage while on the other a beehive of doors, their paint chipped, candles flickering behind their cracked glazing, is the home of the consumptive Katerina Ivanovna, wife of the drunkard Marmeladov. The recurring props are waterjugs and basins, brandished newspapers, rusted axe and candles; the music harsh stabs of gypsy fiddle, circus drum and kazoo and Russian choirs. The light strikes in rods and rectangles, the lamps often held by the actors and brutally directed like searchlights at each other. At other times the cast clusters into candle-lit processions, blindfolded or gagged, freezing in a slash of light into shocked family groups. Often a pencil-thin beam lies across the face of the divided Raskolnikov, seeming to slice it in two as he contemplates what he has done. Most of the show is an hallucinatory recapitulation of his crime. There being no attempt to re-enact the murder, some of the most terrifying few pages in fiction, a dazzling theatrical equivalent takes its place – a free-standing blood-spattered door which swings open on its hinges and moves, apparently under its own volition, around the stage in strobe lighting. This very concise idea arises from the hair-raising fact that Raskolnikov left the front door open as he murdered the women: presumably his nightmares are now full of self-willed furniture. As he wakes from one of these, the door turns once again on its axis, a child (himself?) in a nightdress comes round it and a maid throws red paint at it. Or is it soup? 'That's bad blood acting up in you,' she says, with awful humour. Later it inclines to become a bed and a bier; as Svidrigaylov takes his leave at the end – 'If anyone wants me, tell them the gentleman has left for America' – you see not his suicide but the door collapsing to the floor and opening upwards to reveal a yawning trap down which he seems to descend to hell. At other times, when you most expect it to participate – at Marmeladov's funeral dinner, when a candle is lit, a glass of vodka placed for him, and he's addressed as if he were there – the door does nothing, just stands there and watches. Throughout the performance, a torchlight flashes from the back of the auditorium. This is Yuri, guiding the actors' performances according to his own sophisticated semaphore – nothing so simple as Faster and Louder, but More Plastic, More Intellectual, A Degree More Neurosis.

Back in Block Two of the Sevastopol Hotel, Masha of Intourist has taken to calling me Raskolnikov – approvingly, of course. She has been appeased into this joke by our agreeing to a routine tourist trip to Kolomenskoye, where Peter the Great had a weekend cabin – though how a man approaching seven foot can have managed in a hut I get a humped back in, I'm not sure. Here she claims that Intourist are not allowed into the beautiful Church of the Assumption; this being a society of unprovable alternatives, it may just be their way of not acknowledging the faithful. My colleagues look at her impartially, I with practised cynicism – I want her to remember that I have been here before. Over the next few days we get sick in Moscow's main Georgian restaurant, recuperate in Zagorsk Monastery and take unskilled photographs that nevertheless, Russian landscapes being what they are, could have been painted by Shishkin or Levitan. We also return to the Taganka for Yuri's celebrated version of Bulgakov's *The Master and Margarita* – and for his *Three Sisters* as well, for it will surely be fascinating to see him head-on with Anton Chekhov.

And so it was, in a way scandalous to a Westerner and essential for his audience. Early on, as Masha declared

> You must believe in something, know why you're living, or life is empty

the theatre's side wall slid open to reveal the wide view of Moscow which it happens to command, so that we could see the reality of what the girls were yearning for; against the silhouette of the Church of St Martin the Confessor a military band stood playing a march, but of course they were lit by neon and tonight's traffic was roaring. One dying regime, you might say, confronted another. The wall closed and turned out to be reflective, like the mirror above the bodies in *Crime and Punishment* – the audience was left staring at their own faces. This image of lost hope gained its original force from the fact that the show opened the Taganka's new auditorium in 1981, and no-one had any idea the wall could do such a thing. As the evening moved forward, the cast sometimes stopped to stare at us as if asking, as in *Boris Godunov*, why we remained silent. When Irina spoke of the necessity of work, she stood on a little interior stage, somewhat as Nina might in Konstantin's play in *The Seagull*, and intoned the lines as if they were Soviet propaganda. In the last Act, Anfisa, with her official living quarters at the school, had clearly become a contented Soviet before her time. The philosophising military, a more or less humanising influence in the original, were extremely aggressive, overwhelming the sisters' world. Military marches broke in on their ruminations, and an iconostasis suggesting a monastery was set inside a miniature barracks. The abstract score by Edison Denisov battled with Tchaikovsky. Conventional Chekhovian props were stacked disrespectfully in a corner. Occasionally tape recordings of old Moscow Art performances of the play could be heard: this mocking effect concealed a serious purpose, to offer not just Chekhov's *Three Sisters* but by implication its whole history, which is, near enough, that of the Russian century. There's that point again: our English creed of respecting the author's intentions is not so holy here, and there was little point in being precious about it. Chekhov, protective as he was of the plays, would have understood it well, recognising in Lyubimov's clamorous provocations a theatrical necessity, even if for his fans from the West it was a little tiring, like watching wood cut across the grain.

Intent on our research, we climbed onto the Red Arrow, the overnight train to Leningrad, where I was glad to be once more – after the Trans-Siberian I spent two days there but was sick, lying trembling on a hotel floor looking at the bug in the ceiling. My companions were now as delirious at what they were doing as I was when I first stepped off *MS Baikal* in 1975. Suddenly helpful – Intourist knew the value of the unexpected, even of placatory jests about the KGB – Masha had arranged a tour not usually available to visitors, through the city's poorest areas. More through neglect than historical respect, the Haymarket looks much as it did a hundred years ago, perched between the canals like a collapsed Venice, a honeycomb of taverns, brothels and dusty back lanes running off its central market. Dostoyevsky, Griboyedov and Gogol all lived here at various times, and just as Gogol describes a particular house in *Diary of a Madman*, for *Crime and Punishment* Dostoyevsky near enough identifies Sonya's and Svidrigaylov's lodgings as 73 Griboyedov Canal. Raskolnikov's address meanwhile is at the junction of Stolyarny Lane and Grazhdansky Lane, and it is possible to walk in his footsteps down the thirteen stairs from his flat, as he crept with his axe, carefully, inaudibly, like a cat, towards the old woman's rooms at 104 Griboyedov Canal. The whole district would stamp itself on my memory for the run of the show, its smells and sounds forming a nervous current: under every line I spoke would be some association from these days. I now remembered that hunger is a part of Raskolnikov's compulsion, and quietly embarked on a diet designed to lose me two stone. The only ill-effect of this would be a continuity problem in a television film, *Freud*, for which I still had to do a few exterior sequences before our rehearsals started – as if suffering from agoraphobia, Carl Gustav Jung would appear on the screen as a man stout and healthy within doors who shrank fearfully into his clothes on stepping outside, regaining confidence once in his rooms again.

London, 25 July 1983

Will the English understand the, well, the 'Russianness' of *Crime and Punishment*, asks a fretful actor on the first day of rehearsals. There is a small pause, thick with embarrassed enthusiasm. Well, says Yuri, there is a story (I've never heard it before or since, by the way): when Stanislavsky persuaded Edward Gordon Craig to change his *Hamlet* to suit Moscow audiences, it was such a catastrophe that Craig ran from the theatre naked into the snow and out of the country. But then, comments Yuri, his return visa allowed him to do that, after all. The mordant jest glitters in the air, a half-answer that makes everybody half-laugh. At least Yuri has his wife Katalin with him, and their four-year-old son Petya. Katalin is Hungarian, a journalist. She doesn't much benefit from being associated with Yuri – in fact she has been fired from her Budapest post because of his notoriety – whereas an advantage for him is that he can drive her car, which has a foreign number plate, thus gaining some immunity from the Moscow cops, who also fear Katya as a journalist. (If ever he is stopped Yuri pretends to speak no Russian.) Being allowed to travel with his family puts him in a significantly better position than that of his designer David Borovsky, who – in a recurrence of one of the Soviets' foulest standing contracts – is only allowed to work abroad if he leaves his wife and children behind. Not so much better though, since Petya Lyubimov is confused and keeps asking to go home, and if the doors close behind them Yuri and Katalin will be cut off from their own families.

In the 'pausa' after the read-through Yuri moves lightly across the floor to join me in a corner. He is happy and relaxed, studiously courteous, not quite humble but gifted with a child-like grin, his bulk resolving at the feet into rather delicate espadrilles. He is worried at my new thinness – 'Energiya, Mikhail?' – but assumes I know what I'm doing. We talk briefly about earning power, this truly great man of the theatre and I, and I am immediately embarrassed. At the Taganka Yuri earns 300 roubles a month, while the director of the Bolshoi gets 900. Comparisons with the West are hard, but you can see the differential. The money would be enough, sort of, for a single man, but not for the three of them; they have a three-roomed flat in Moscow, but certainly no country dacha, unlike the average Intourist guide.

The noisy and dilapidated Clarendon ballroom at Hammersmith roundabout where we rehearse (this at least is like Moscow) has a lighting rig in it, with tapes and sound equipment and operators at the ready, since Yuri believes in having all this in place from the start. There is also, and will always be, a battery of interpreters and observers – and, by the director's side, a Russian-American academic who has done the (not very good) English translation. He is an example of who shouldn't be let into the rehearsal room.

Apparently convinced by working beside Yuri that actors are best treated rudely, he immediately loses our confidence – except of course that he does speak Russian. Most of the other lieutenants will last a couple of days only, before having a shouting match with the maestro (I now know some good street Russian) and storming away.

In between his own set-pieces – impersonations of Brezhnev and Stalin in particular – Yuri describes Dostoyevsky as the man from underground: you don't know what opening his head will suddenly look through. In an increasingly extreme world, he says, this writer keeps nosing in. Someone suggests, echoing the views of the 'reasonable man' Razumikhin, that Raskolnikov's crime is the result of crushing environmental factors. Yuri points out that Razumikhin endures the same thing but doesn't become a criminal. Paola Dionisotti, who is to play Katerina Ivanovna, believes that the confrontational attitude towards the audience of some characters, especially mine, might be too hostile, and Yuri's answer is significant. Raskolnikov's aggression is all intellectual, a fierce means of insisting on our human involvement with each other. Otherwise we might end up as what the author most feared – citizens adrift from conscience and community who shrink from arresting such a man. Yuri believes passionately that Dostoyevsky foresaw our century's catastrophic glorification of the individual and prefigured it in Raskolnikov's Napoleon Complex. It is a bracing hint that he speaks with an urgent morality far removed from any liberal aesthetics. This is a disillusioned socialist and, more importantly, a Christian – he fears on behalf of his author that there may be atheists in the cast, a serious matter for him since a blind person cannot see colour.

Accustomed to rehearsing for months – he says bitterly that nobody minds how long the Taganka rehearse, as long as they don't actually open – he will find these six weeks a serious pressure, and what with the language barrier as well, certain things follow. Observing the technical *faits accomplis*, some of the actors immediately shy away, sensing that something complete will soon be required of them too. The cast is full of fine performers, one of whom, Gary Waldhorn, I have been largely responsible for bringing in to play Svidrigaylov. Gary is quite a wary man, no less so for hearing Yuri bluntly tell him that if he only mimics him, Yuri, in the part, he'll be fine. Paola Dionisotti is like a cat hesitating before entering a room, sensing the territory – it is her nature, and a full-blooded commitment will follow shortly. I can see that this job will be more than a matter of playing Raskolnikov. Since I've worked with several of the cast before, and because Yuri trusts me, there will be some mediating to do – reassuring him by day that the English actors will let rip in the end, and taking phone calls in the evenings from those enraged by his blunt methods. But that's the deal: anyone hesitating to dive will have a tough time, and it has little to do with talent. And how, after all, is Yuri to communicate, unless by demonstration? He is an extremely expressive actor, and though apparently dictatorial, very observant. On my diet I have become the physical polar opposite to him, but he not only does a natty impersonation of me but makes his suggestions through its filter, as if he were himself a very thin man.

Lyubimov has described his job as the director of this intellectual thriller as being that of someone letting loose fierce animals into a battle arena. Rodion Raskolnikov is tautly suspended between two competing figures – the detective Porfiry who waits to entrap him and Sonya Marmeladov, Katerina Ivanovna's daughter, who has been forced into prostitution by her family's poverty. Shuttling obsessively, he pitches his arguments into the face of the salvation she offers while being drawn to Porfiry like a moth to a candle. Like me, Veronica Roberts has been deeply affected by the things she saw in Moscow and Leningrad: the memory is a bond between us, like the hidden connection between Raskolnikov and Sonya. Sonya is generally seen as Dostoyevsky's first Christian hero – meek, humourless, quietly determined on Raskolnikov's regeneration. Her first reaction when he confesses to her is pious fear of what he has done to *himself*: she begs him to abandon his theorising, to respond to Christ with his heart and to accept punishment, while he calls her a great sinner who has likewise destroyed her life. Lyubimov's reinvention is to intensify Sonya's passionate reasoning but to deny that it can succeed. At the furious climax of our first half, Sonya in vain berates Raskolnikov with the story of Lazarus, and he violently washes her feet, drags her around and hurls water in her face. This humiliation of her seems to be a refusal of Lyubimov's own beliefs and certainly involves an adjustment to Dostoyevsky's ending, but he has his purposes: Veronica and I are loyal, and Raskolnikov remains unsaved.

The detective Porfiry, played by Bill Paterson, is the murderer's secular nemesis, strong enough to let Raskolnikov go because he knows he cannot do without him and will return as if homesick. The training of Soviet police has included some of Porfiry's interrogative techniques – quite a subtle variety of chit-chat leading to the killer punch – and Yuri's response is to make him a sort of sinister clown. A powerful affection has grown up between Bill and him. They share a physical inventiveness and a taste for threatening comedy, so that the rope Porfiry takes to carrying is used now as a noose offered to Raskolnikov, now as a skipping-rope for himself and even as a magnifying glass. Dressed as Raskolnikov's hero Napoleon but sometimes sporting a Hitlerian moustache, Bill's Porfiry comes to me in the logic of a dream and once again offers me the axe: his enquiries, part skylarking and part savagely knowing, are accompanied by the unmistakable discomfort of haemorrhoids.

Assessing the 'pale angel' he is stalking, Porfiry refers to his

> bookish dreams, his heart aggravated by theories…he forgot to close
> the front door but murdered two people for the sake of a theory. He
> murdered them, but didn't have the sense to take the money, and
> what he did take, he hid under a stone.

Like Albert Camus' Outsider, Raskolnikov is exhausted by the effort of redefining himself after a half-understood crime. Mersault wants to go to sleep during his trial and is then surprised by an inadvertent longing for life; the self-oppressed Raskolnikov is likewise plagued by fatigue. His very name is a pun, derived from 'to split away'. The *raskolniki* were schismatics who first broke with the Russian church in the seventeenth century, preferring to retain the old rituals at a time of doctrinal reform – it was one of these Old Believers who had killed two old women in Moscow with an axe in 1865. (By extraordinary chance, as the first section of the novel was being prepared for publication, a further murder was committed by a student in Moscow of a pawnbroker and his maid. Neither event can have influenced the other, but Dostoyevsky, with the artist's amoralism, must have rejoiced.) Like all heretics, Raskolnikov greatly fears the possibility of God; and the Russian word has an obvious psychological application as well. He commits his crime partly to redeem the world from the usurer and to help himself into useful work, as the Soviet reading insists: but on the other side of his *raskol* he is arrogant, misanthropic, individualistic, hoping to prove himself a superman above the 'pygmies, lice, slaves, trash' – a vicious version of Kovrin in Chekhov's 'Black Monk'. Oddly enough, both of his stances are less emotional than experimental.

In the midst of his agitated dialectic, even as he demands that the audience consider murder as a philosophical act, Raskolnikov will relapse into apathy and surly observation. Adding petty detail to his grand polemics might seem difficult, but Yuri, a clowning metaphysician, senses the particularity as well as the big movement: and I remember how his Taganka actors seemed simultaneously casual and declamatory. He points out to me one day that a man who cuts himself off from life may find it revenges itself by reversing its most minute laws in the privacy of his room. He takes my cap and hurls it down onto a stool, but badly, so that it falls off – and then again, and then a third time, in panic: always it falls off. This is quite tricky to do technically, but completely worth it – Raskolnikov is not only a terrifying philosopher who struts around with an axe, but as pitiful as you and me when we kick a cupboard door that won't close properly.

September 1983

The show, running to capacity for six weeks, was a sensation: *The New York Times* flew in and described it as 'one of the most sustained nightmares ever put on a stage…makes the Dostoyevskian atmosphere a theatrical fact, giving the inhabitants of the crowded streets and fetid rooms the dimensions of Lear on his heath.' The London press called it 'modern theatre at its very peak of achievement…an awe-inspiring theatrical landmark', referring to 'acting on an ennobling scale – a miracle'. According to one critic, the stalking door symbolised a 'change of state, from one form of knowledge to another, one argument to its opposite, damnation to salvation' and on reflection I suppose it did: it certainly scared the hell out of everybody. Inwardly somewhat lit up, I myself looked like hell by now – critics, wondering what had happened to a not unbecoming Hamlet, reached into their reticules to find an El Greco Christ, a feverish bag of bones, and a pale razor-like scarecrow sucked dry by his arrogant convictions. Yuri's expressionist panache and full-blooded debate annoyed a few but electrified most; and the idea that he might be choosing this moment to join the ranks of defecting Soviet stars – Nureyev, Makarova, Rostropovich – was much relished: under such circumstances, even without his talent, the Western press would have lapped him up as they had Solzhenitsyn. In return, he proved himself a dab hand with them. Announcing that 'every time I go abroad it is a complex, tense and humiliating situation', he celebrated the opening night with a momentously well-timed interview in *The Times*, denouncing the Soviet authorities: there was renewed talk of a KGB kidnap, and Yuri lay low at a secret address. It was heady stuff.

Inside the profession, a few sneered that all this was just 1920s European expressionism, missing the subtler point that for a Russian to work in that style at all was a substantial protest against orthodoxy – Meyerhold was executed for less. The view was expressed at an RSC directors' meeting that the show was 'just typical Moscow theatre'. This sort of thing infuriated me, and I took to lacing my press interviews with powder trails of outrage. How xenophobic had we become, in our view that we were the brightest and best – we, who had once hosted Daubeny's glorious World Theatre Seasons? Could any of us imagine, as we sat in our theatrical shopping arcade, having to work with no budget at all, developing our virtuosity with two sticks and a candle – or staging a harvesting scene, brilliantly but also necessarily, with beams of torchlight instead of scythes? Could we guess what it was like to be approached just before the first night, as Yuri had been by a Soviet Embassy official, and informed in front of many guests that this was the crime, and the punishment would follow?

Trade rituals were duly enacted. Commercial producers sniffed around the show before throwing up their hands at the size of the cast and the cost of re-rehearsal. Sounding a little like Intourist, one declared that this 'interesting' production was 'not really being talked about in West End circles'. We then set about trying to film it; but Channel Four, the obvious means, opined that Lyubimov's work represented '1940s expressionism of the worst kind' – 1940s? – and so that was that. We did get an hour-long *South Bank Show* out of it, on ITV: the very extensive excerpts in that programme are the production's only record. In some ways, of course, all this was a relief, like knowing the world was still turning.

Crime and Punishment's season at the Lyric has acquired the status of a minor legend – if you weren't there you can imagine the best of it. In the last week John Gielgud gallantly came round for a chat, sitting among the breeze blocks with a plastic cup of wine. It was entertaining to imagine the great Englishman, nothing if not game, in such a show, and I bet Yuri asked for him to be approached. Gielgud described his own Raskolnikov (1946, in a more conventional adaptation by Rodney Ackland) as starting out full of 'gulps and snorts', but, as he persevered, becoming one of his most underrated performances, perhaps second only to his Hamlet. He too was fascinated by the character: the production had transferred to New York, but despite his bringing in Theodore Komisarjevsky to re-direct it, it had flopped, and remained the failure that mattered more to him than many successes. I cheered up about the West End, and started reading Chekhov's short stories again.

Seven hundred and fifty calories a day had proved just enough to keep up the 'energiya' as well as creating the feral look. Light-headed but efficient, I had been short of sleep throughout but open to astonishing dreams, in which Charles Manson stepped into the witness box to defend Raskolnikov, Shirley MacLaine came to tea, Yuri proved that he spoke perfect English by lying down on a cricket pitch speaking the lines of Richard II, while I discussed the Cyrillic alphabet with Trevor Nunn. Everyone in our constituency seemed worried about me, even my agent: it was most gratifying. While the thin gruel upstairs at the Lyric propelled me forward, my son Mark, just seventeen and working as an usher, was being accused downstairs of stealing the ice-cream money, if not quite of murdering the vendor. Faced by this and having in those days something of the temperament of a Raskolnikov himself, he, shall we say, resigned. I never managed ice cream, but later in the run I took to making gingerbread for everyone, proving the theatre fact that the grimmer the job, the greater the need for silly comforts; however, I was outdone on the last night by the Lyric staff, who created a magnificent chocolate cake topped with marzipan models of a miniature Petersburg, complete with tiny door, axe and buckets of blood.

Rituals like this are the English actor's way of coming in to land. I wished Yuri had been there – I don't think he encouraged this sort of festivity at the Taganka – but he was hiding away still, and I would visit him secretly during the few weeks before he left for Milan to direct Moussorgsky's *Khovanshchina*. He was looking at offers from all over the world, but really wanted to stay here, and he was bewildered by the lack of interest. For all our commiserations, most English doors, like Raskolnikov's, seemed to have closed on him. He was new to the politics of echoing silence that we do so well: as effectively excluded as in Moscow, his friends in England remained two – Peter James and myself, to be joined later by Pierre Audi, who would manage to bring him back to the Almeida in 1985 for Dostoyevsky's *The Possessed*, which he had never managed to get on in Moscow. In the interim, like substantial driftwood, he was to be swept this way and that by the tides of Soviet policy, living for months in anonymous flats as he shuttled about Europe on temporary visas. The next year he would be fired from the Taganka for 'failing to return'; soon after, he would hear on the BBC World Service that he'd been expelled from the Party, to which, like many idealists of his generation, he still belonged. Then he would be stripped of his citizenship.

Well, he shrugs, there's a Russian novel in which one character says, 'The Party has two wings, you know,' to which another replies, 'Yes, and I wish it would take off on them and fly to hell.' Yuri smiles sweetly at me, his soft silver hair flopping over his eyes. His lower face, like that of many fairly fleshy men of his age, shows a soft femininity where the jawline has begun to give. I recall that this malleable actor's mask was ever stuck onto a spirit so obstreperous that he found it difficult to deal with helpfulness. He had functioned best if he thought that everyone – the fire authorities, stage management, even the patient Peter James – was against him: it was a way of making it all feel like home. If I had ever wondered what a life of humiliation does to a Soviet artist, I only had to observe Yuri at one of the Russian gatherings for which his presence was a rallying-point. His paranoia determined that all fellow countrymen in London were suspect, with the result that he became preposterously convinced that Irina Brown – a Leningrader living here with her English husband, and much his most helpful assistant – had been working for the KGB. Thus an exaggerated gallantry to important Brits was matched by haughty stand-offs towards everyone else – even someone as gentle and tolerant as the great Andrei Tarkovsky, who had perhaps suffered more (seven major films only, in the teeth of tremendous official obstruction) and who was here, already stricken with cancer, to cast his last film, *The Sacrifice*. To look at Yuri, you would think a lifetime's enemy had been invited to his birthday party.

Meanwhile, Tarkovsky was a man who would quite literally be interested in watching paint dry. He used to tell a story of having spent an afternoon watching water dripping onto his verandah floor and forming a puddle, then the sun reducing the puddle to a stain, then to a shadow, until the wooden planks were finally restored to themselves. The anecdote reminds me of Chekhov, who, according to the writer Ivan Bunin, would sit with his head cocked, turning something over in his mind for an hour at a time. For a 'highbrow' director, Tarkovsky was also rather homely, referring to his washing machine as *kuzya* ('the big tummy') and the vacuum cleaner as *lolik* ('lazy silly thing') – a variant of the Russian trait of calling your friends animals. In this too he was a little like Chekhov, and very unlike Lyubimov, in whom professional extremity had aggravated an inherent defensiveness, like a nail on glass. The result was a Napoleon Complex not so unlike Raskolnikov's: detesting totalitarianism, Yuri was himself a sort of Tsar.

Listening to him for the last time, I have to admit that I've grown a little tired of the myth of the great auteur, fashioning and shaping us all. In his more grandiose interviews Yuri has been declaring that he 'pulled Michael onto his hand like a glove'. I don't know if this is a compliment or not, but I do know the luck has been mutual. He has certainly depended on advice – to abandon his torch semaphore during performances, and to see that for Raskolnikov to pick a civilian out of the audience, drag her onto the stage and push her about might be all right in Moscow, but here could lead to legal action. His view now is that my predecessor, the Taganka's Alexander Trofimov, whom I thought quite terrifying, was not hateful enough in the part. Christ. Misinterpreting my dismay, he swiftly compliments me on economy, intellectual force and a generally unyielding quality – or rather on catching the character's anger with himself at any moment of yielding. Overall though, he thinks I tend to go soft, as Trofimov did, 'repenting all evening'. That's all right – propaganda theatre has its limits, and I know for sure that the English cast has given his ideas more nuance and line than he expected.

In parting, he acknowledges the chronic problem of translation: and in fact I've put him in touch with Michael Glenny, who has rendered many Russian classics into English and might perhaps work on *The Master and Margarita* for him. Excited now, Yuri becomes implausible, suggesting I do a Taganka *Hamlet* in English. I'm not sure how I would compare with Vladimir Vysotsky, a folk-hero on such a scale that his funeral brought Moscow to a standstill, like Chekhov's. I can see that at this moment, for all his pride, Yuri thrives on dreams, and so I talk to him about my show, which I have kept secret until now – perhaps he could get over to direct it. I don't really mean this, in fact it could be a disaster, but it gets him going. He thinks the real trigger for 'The Black Monk' was that a huge moth got into Chekhov's study and flew in panic around. He would stage this, I'm sure, in some marvellous way, and I refrain from pointing out that he's confusing this moth with the one that flew into the hotel room moments after Chekhov died. After all, I might not like him correcting my Shakespeare. Yuri once met Olga Knipper, but found her uncongenial; he also knew Chekhov's nephew Mikhail, a good Moscow Art Theatre actor but a drunk, he says, who married Olga Knipper's niece. Mikhail ended up teaching Stanislavsky in Hollywood while his estranged wife became a Nazi and as a result was able to save the Yalta house from destruction. Actually, I thought this was achieved by Masha Chekhova. He also thinks that Anton Pavlovich believed his brother Misha would have been the better writer, which sounds very unlikely. All in all, I don't think Chekhov interests Yuri that much: he seems not to be from the same gene pool. Everything slides into apocrypha, goodwill, bear hugs, heartfelt salutations in doorways: it will be fifteen years before we fall into each other's arms again. The hard work has been a homage to a director I thought truly great, worth every minute, and at the time I would have lain in front of a Soviet tractor for him, though he would hardly have done the same for me.

The show gently slid from sight. The only person not pleased with it all was my mother, furious with me for the starving business, though my father certainly got the idea. They had endured the production, holding hands tightly in the dress circle and wondering if it was for this that they had first taken me to the Old Vic for some Shakespeare in 1956. Worse, within a couple of months they were huddled together still tighter at the National Theatre, watching their only son being castrated, broken and flayed in another part of the Russian Empire:

> There were about a hundred horses in the field. A piebald gelding stood by himself in a corner, licking a wooden post with his eyes half-closed…who knows what flavour he found in it but his expression was serious and thoughtful… Like a living ruin he stood there, in the middle of the dewy meadow.

My next part, obviously.

WALKING THE COURSE

> To hell with the philosophy of all the great men of this life: it's not
> worth a single filly in *Strider*...
>
> — Anton Chekhov

Tolstoy loved horses: he once reckoned he had spent an aggregate of seven
years of his life in the saddle. Turgenev describes watching the great man
talking to a mangy old nag on his farm:

> He was stroking it and whispering to it – the horse listened attentively.
> Then he told us what the animal was feeling. He had taken me right
> into the soul of that poor beast. I said – I couldn't stop myself: 'Lev
> Nikolayevich, I believe you must once have been a horse yourself...'

Strider – The Story of a Horse is based on an incident at the turn of the last
century in which a disregarded piebald won a great race in Moscow, achieving
the then remarkable speed of twenty-five miles an hour: but not being the
official dappled grey of the Orel breed it was gelded. Tolstoy started his story
in 1863, but only finished it in 1885; although the work's development is not
documented, it is easy enough to see how far he travelled in between. From
the earlier, benign phase of writing a certain anthropomorphising mawkishness
survives, as if a children's story was in hand: the fillies on the stud farm are
described as 'a merry crowd of virgins', pining for love with a passionate
neighing and playing skittish pranks on the old horse. Rather often, too, the
defeated writer observes of his protagonist: 'God knows what he was thinking.'
A quarter of a century later, Tolstoy, disillusioned that the Emancipation had
not eased the life of the peasant more, used Strider's life story as a thinly-
disguised polemic on the rights of the enslaved and the interdependence of
all beings. Observing this denunciation of Tolstoy's own class as idle and
destructive, Lenin was to call the writer himself a piebald.

The iconic figure of *Strider* (*Kholstomer* in Russian – the word is derived
from *kholst*, meaning linen, and suggests the arm's-lengths by which an old-
fashioned draper measures material) emerges from this contradictory process
as a great character, once a sporting hero but now 'no stranger to insults,
humiliation and grief', both endearing and reproachful. At this end of his life

> his expression was patient and severe, thoughtful and full of sorrow.
> But you always paused as you passed him... An expert would say he
> must have been a fine horse in his day...

127

As he quietly tries to go about his business in the paddock, flicking his bedraggled tail and standing crookedly on his scraggy legs, the rest of the herd bully him mercilessly, until he can stand no more of it; he answers back by telling them the awesome story of his life in five nightly episodes:

> The new moon rose: its narrow crescent lit up Strider in the middle
> of the paddock...there the tall stern figure of the gelding stood,
> wearing a high saddle with its peak at the front...

He reveals his secret: that he is in fact the famous racer whom the experts are still looking for, a legend unmatched in all Russia because of his long, sweeping strides. As a young horse he was bought by an officer of the hussars, Prince Serpukhovskoy, and shown off as a champion in a harness so beautifully and elaborately wrought that it was hard to say where it ended and the horse began; but after one spectacular victory the Prince overworked Strider in a wild chase to recapture a fleeing mistress. Damaged for good, the horse's chest began to sink in and his hoofs to come off. Now he has gone abjectly from hand to hand – sold to an old woman, a peasant and then a gypsy in exchange for some small commodity. Fate has brought him back to the farm where he was born, and he is preparing to die unknown. The horses are deeply impressed, struck by their common fate at the hand of man:

> They were all silent. A light rain began to fall.

As Turgenev would have expected, the beauty of the story lies in Tolstoy's penetration of the soul of the animal, both sensually and, so to speak, philosophically – it is in these moments that the fable hits its own stride. Strider's pleasures nowadays are simple. He loves the smell of his groom's pipe in the dewy morning because it reminds him of pleasant things gone by; he has his own special scissors for the cutting of his whiskers; he is careful to drink long and patiently through his torn lips before eating, for he knows from experience it is better so; and when a flogged coachman comes into his stall and cries, he learns that tears 'have a pleasant, salty taste'. He both understands and is profoundly puzzled by men. He wonders why they call 'forward' at him, as if he was thinking of galloping backwards; he senses the vanity of his groom, who likes to ride him side-saddle but would never dare to if anyone was watching; and, interestingly, he feels a helpless love for his handsome officer precisely because the man is cold-hearted and without love himself.

He is specially struck by the way men call him 'my horse', when he belongs only to God: it seems as strange as if they were to say 'my earth, my air, my water'. But then:

> There are people who say the land is theirs even though they've
> never trod on it...there are people who say other people are theirs,
> but they've never seen them...

On the day when Strider is finally put down, despised and superfluous, the
returning herd sees crows and dogs and even a peasant making off with his
bones, while a she-wolf and her cubs feed on his carcass. So he is of some use
even now – unlike Serpukhovskoy, who for twenty years has just 'walked
round the earth eating and drinking'; whose swollen body will finally be
dressed in uniform, put in a lead coffin with tassels on the corners, have an
expensive Mass sung over it and, decomposing in its clothes, be covered with
earth. Neither his skin nor his flesh nor his bones will be used for anything.

Taking the fairly delicate point and happy to broaden it somewhat for
Soviet audiences, Mark Rozovsky adapted *Strider* in 1975 for the Gorky
Theatre in Leningrad, in a treatment that combined mime, dance and narrative;
it was directed by Georgi Tovstonogov, and became a success at European
Festivals and on Broadway. Now Peter Tegel has done an English adaptation
for the National Theatre. Where Lyubimov radically reinterprets Dostoyevsky,
Rozovsky's simplification extends Tolstoy's didacticism. The aristocrats are
sketchy, and the moral points hammered home in song. As the chorus beat
Strider, chanting like Houyhnhnms, a stage direction emphasises that

> It is no longer clear whether he is being beaten by animals or humans.

However the moralising resolves rather beautifully in a final chorus when
Strider has been destroyed:

> No beast there is more ravenous than man;
> He drinks the ocean; devours the mountain.
> He feasts till into the pit he falls
> And his mouth is filled with earth.

In the theatre the story gains greatly from being told mainly in the first
person. Since Strider is now the narrator he is able, more vividly than even
Tolstoy could, to guide the audience through the world he looks out on and
into the workings of his own mind. The odd effect is to make him both
intimate and more strange. Stalled by the limits of his imagination, his insights
are pungent but incomplete. His joy in the small things of life is accompanied
by a tentative curiosity, which he often expresses with a descriptive falling-
away, like the melancholy flick of a tail:

> I was sold to a dealer who fed me on carrots and something else

or:

> the peasant sold me to a gypsy in exchange for something...

Meanwhile, the staging possibilities were exhilarating, the training and racing of the young horse in particular. And its gelding: in the original this has a eugenic point (he is a piebald at large), but in the play it is frankly punitive, following Strider's innocent attempt to mount a filly. The result is a great equine *accidie*:

> I stopped neighing, for good. I became what I am now. Nothing mattered… Sometimes it occurred to me to gallop, but then the question: Why? What for? My neighing sounded sad, ridiculous, meaningless…

But soon Strider reinvents himself, and the play resounds with his joy as he demonstrates a great winter ride on the Kuznetsky Bridge in Moscow, feathered plumes waving, all tinkling with bells, his sleigh ('so elegant and perfect') of plaited cane with velvet cushions. His harness has silver buckles, and his reins are made of silk. This gives way to despair during his dreadful chase after the faithless Mathieu, when for the first time he loses his step. He is ashamed – the whip cuts into him. He hits his foot against the iron front of the sleigh. Never again will Strider be the horse he's been.

Tolstoy ends his story with a rather lengthy scene in which the bloated old hussar sits up with the farm-owner the night before Strider is killed, bragging about horses and women, asphyxiated by wine and cigars. In the play this is simplified so that the decrepit Strider, tied to a post, listens while his unwitting ex-owner sings his praises, claiming this has been not a horse but a friend. In our production Strider gently laid his head against Serpukhovskoy's arm in appreciation, but the man didn't recognise him and shoved him off disgustedly. Strider remained philosophical:

> He didn't recognise me. How could he have?

He is near his end now, and as his throat is cut the narrative is taken up antiphonally by the company:

> It hurt. He shuddered. Kicked. Waited to see what would happen. A warm mass flowed down his chest. He sighed, sighed deeply, and felt better. Now they've cured me, he thought… He closed his eyes. He lowered his head… He quivered… Not afraid. Surprised. Moved forward to rear. Fell, to the left. Tried to rise. Fell. The whole burden of his life was being eased.

By this time I was almost expected to go around in a *shapka* and Russian boots, and I set about the gentle figure of Strider with something of

Raskolnikov's implacability. People smile if you say you're going to play a horse, and you know the sort of thing they're imagining: the whole enterprise was going to be an exercise in judiciousness. Tolstoy refers to the terrible union in Strider between 'repulsive decrepitude' and the traces of his earlier beauty and strength, so I had to find a way, without leaving the stage, to be by turns the foal, then the young racer with its delicate skin and deep black eyes, and finally the scarred old beast with its bald haunches, the veins of its neck like knots twitching when a fly touches them. I also had to decide in what grave, meditative tones he would speak. I went to Somerset to visit breeders, I stood in stables at night with the horses – well, I would, wouldn't I. I watched them shiver through the shoulders and back, a little like Kathakali dancers, and saw how the cagey eyes focus over the nose. I consulted with the great choreographer David Toguri, learning how to do steps like the *pas de cheval* before turning them into something heavier and non-balletic. Moving into a dance studio in the National Theatre at eight o'clock most mornings, I tried to reproduce the animal's weight and balance – head and shoulders twisting together in imitation of the looping inclination of its neck, the chest cage high, wide and forward; and to develop some version of the canter that belonged more to me than to pantomime. An imitation of a horse at speed could look like no more than a fast strut: the trick was to keep pushing smoothly through this jarring action, with a prayer for my knees. Strider's pedigree name is Muzhik, peasant, so at any given moment he might be horse or man, and what an audience made of him should depend on which eye they were looking through. The designer, Chris Dyer, and I chose ambiguous materials and colours. I nagged the NT not to give me any old boots but to make a pair of ballet shoes with the uppers of peasant boots hinged in two parts over them, so that I could get up on point to be the spindly, splay-legged foal.

Next we needed to strike a deal – essentially playful – with the audience. At the opening the actors would stand in a circle, with Strider in the middle, holding a switch of horse hair. He studies this tail: the audience does the same, not noticing him move his weight forward over his knees. The tail swishes gently. Over to the side of the stage is a bucket of water. Strider sees it and a thought dawns – slowly, slowly, as if the idea was coming from his chin or the back of his head. He decides, and begins to move towards the bucket, very gently, rolling forward from his lower vertebrae. He finally gets to the water and we to the first crux – what will this actor playing a horse do now? What he has to – bend down and gently lift the bucket in both hands, then lower his horse's head to it. The ambiguities continue: what, after all, is the difference between a horse whose lips are pulled by the twitch and an old fellow chewing tobacco and spitting from the corner of his mouth? Or between a young racer bounding over the Kuznetsky Bridge and an athlete breasting the tape? Or between a gelded animal testing out its frail legs, wondering whether they still work and why, and a man launching himself with apprehensive curiosity from a hospital bed?

The action of the water-drinking must have taken a couple of minutes of silence, and the reordering of time was part of the bargain too. While much of the play moved in conventional theatre tempo, it sometimes waited patiently on the heartbeat of the old beast. So with luck the audience became hypnotised, slowing down to keep him company. Why not? In Tarkovsky's *Nostalgia* a man takes ten minutes to cross a deserted thermal pool with a flickering candle, and you don't get tired of that. One of the central tenets of Stanislavsky's teaching is that if the actor is thinking, really thinking of what he wants, the spectator is unlikely to get bored.

I also had to get very fit, fit enough to show Strider's great accelerando. At a flick of the reins, his muscles would quiver and his gallop begin, wider and wider, the muddy snow flying from his hoofs. What we settled on was quite dangerous. Strider was tied to a central post by a long rope, which he pulled outwards against to describe three wild circuits round the very edge of the Cottesloe stage; then he stopped dead, and, since there was a narrative jump, had to speak, at length, without any breathlessness. In this, as in the rest, I found I was trying to do what the horse himself was proud of:

> I developed exactness in myself...as soon as one foot touched the ground the other lifted at once and no effort was lost, everything carried me forward...

At least this time I was free from any disabling sense of mission on behalf of the director. Michael Bogdanov (Ukrainian father, Welsh mother – another *Kelt, da?*) hardly needed my championing – and I had worked with him before, on Sean O'Casey's *The Shadow of a Gunman* in 1980. Indeed, the time was not far in the future when we would sit in a coffee bar, perhaps hoping to seem a little like Stanislavsky and Nemirovich in the Slavyansky Bazaar, dreaming up the English Shakespeare Company, which however did not last as long as the Moscow Art Theatre. I missed the sense of occasion, though. *Crime and Punishment* had been, without doubt, an Event – hand-picked cast, special circumstances all round; *Strider* had plenty of good actors in it, but I was a guest in the existing National Theatre ensemble. Companies who know each other well can get a little routine, and I made few friends, chafing at what I saw as casualness. After all, who wants to come and see *Strider – The Sort of Story of a Sort of Horse, Sort Of*? I cajoled and insisted: since making the animal real depends on how he's treated by his grooms and riders, please handle me as if I was several times my own weight – yes, lean your shoulders in and shove, feeling for the moment when his bulk slowly begins to move. In fact, when you look at me please imagine something of quite a different shape. Please shut up in the wings.

All day on the opening I shivered with cold, though the weather was fine. This was a new kind of fear: I was off my patch, wondering what dancers do to control nerves, which threaten their balance even more than an actor's breathing. We played the first night the best we would ever do it. For ten minutes at the end Strider was tethered to his post, his pulse beating gently: a little girl watching from her seat only four feet away whispered to her mother that she was going to lean out and touch him. Strider cocked his back leg in warning, as horses do when they might kick. I remember the girl's intake of breath and her mother's chuckle – it was our secret.

Käthe Kollwitz's father once told her: 'Be what you have chosen to be with all your heart.' It is hard to talk about my job in the right register, without pretension or mock-naiveté; but this long hermetic winter, with Chekhov still standing by, I did seem to be getting to the bottom of what I could do. To put it no higher, the bruises from Raskolnikov's door and the weight of Strider's harness were real enough; I used to rejoice at surviving another night's damage. And was duly rewarded. Just as it may not be strategic to go into all the workings, I suppose modesty about the result is becoming, but I don't really see why. If ever I wanted to be remembered for a piece of work, this was the one. I'd been called many things by the press over the years, but not miraculous or awesome: it was the same for Michael Bogdanov's production, which the *Daily Mail*'s Jack Tinker described as 'a miracle of suspended disbelief which leaves you feeling you have been in direct touch with the mysteries and cruelties of the universe'. Astonishing, stunning and superb, the two of us walked tall for a bit: but I also felt I'd cornered myself, skewing the balance between work and life – I wasn't even making gingerbread. The whole lonely business was being observed with some concern by Mark and my parents. It would have been very nice to have a girlfriend during this time, but none would have put up with me for long: I was in any case learning some of Chekhov's evasive skills, turning Lika Mizinovas and Lydia Avilovas into sort-of-sisters before they swiftly decamped. You can imagine the next step.

With *Strider* still running, the National asked me to do a second play, Thomas Otway's Restoration tragedy (yes, there are some) *Venice Preserv'd*, and I was cagey – some said because it would be such a departure for me to do an English work. But I wanted to be free for Lyubimov's return to London with *The Possessed*: his wish to work with me again was a compliment, though a voice was also saying that some remarkable experiences are best not repeated. Then the National wanted to extend the run of *Strider*, and to strengthen their offer they made a suggestion. *Anton Chekhov* had been maturing, or perhaps rusting, for a year now; in my attenuated condition there had barely been room for the usual niceties of life, let alone Anton Pavlovich. However, word had got out; and they proposed that I take my show on a tour of schools and colleges on days when I was free from the other two productions, before bringing it into the main Cottesloe repertoire in the autumn – there could be space for thirty or forty performances over three months. I could see nothing wrong with this – in fact, it was obviously the best chance. The one commercial producer I had talked to about *Anton Chekhov* wanted permanent rights on it and most of the financial action. The NT offered sympathy and technical back-up, the Cottesloe was as perfect for this as it had been for *Strider*; and afterwards I could walk away with the rights intact. Meanwhile the schools tour – which would include some evening shows at Arts Centres round the country – was both commendable in itself and a great limbering-up: I could see Anton Pavlovich, exposed so variously, becoming as hardy as an old boot. Everyone's interests seemed to be served, except those of Lyubimov, who would make an attempt to sulk at me on the first night of *The Possessed*, royally swishing his scarf over his shoulder and turning his back until I made him laugh at his own tantrum.

After all the leisurely tinkering my bluff had been called, and I was racing towards a first performance of *Anton Chekhov* at Guildford Acting School on 14 May 1984. This meant four weeks' rehearsal, but what with breaking off for performances of *Strider* and *Venice Preserv'd* (some of them matinees) it really boiled down to about half that. My script was still all hunches and little method. I called up Irina Brown: luckily she wasn't working for the KGB, so could join my adventure, not as the director – that was me really – but as good company and Russian guide. In practice, I would be as anxious to please her, as being somehow related to Chekhov, as I would be any director; and apart from sparing me the withering prospect of being alone in a rehearsal room all day, she would ensure that things were authentic, having access to virtually every word Chekhov wrote, down to his last doodles. Alison Chitty, fresh from *Venice Preserv'd*, agreed to design – the workshop deadlines were ferocious, but I was unable to tell her yet whether I wanted an empty void into which Chekhov's ghost would walk, or the Cottesloe Theatre on an average day in 1984, or Yalta in 1903. I might need no props, or perhaps a nineteenth-century houseful.

As any Hamlet will tell you, getting started is the problem. How to introduce Chekhov? We began by proving that some things were never a good idea: hoisted upright after the years of theory, they collapsed under the weight of a surpassing archness. For I had sometimes wondered if he should wander into the theatre by chance, like the victim of a timeless *This Is Your Life*, to be confronted by a modern audience wanting to make much of him. Well, he would have turned and fled, as he did from Tolstoy in the bath-house. Or, in a small variation, what if the British Council had called the National to say that Chekhov was at large in London, and shouldn't he be captured for a question-and-answer session – after all, *Wild Honey*, Michael Frayn's version of *Platonov*, was about to open next door in the Lyttelton? The idea stood bare in all its silliness: this was a man acutely embarrassed by being dragged onto the stage on the first night of *The Cherry Orchard*. Or what if he arrived on a reluctant lecture tour (short of cash after another bad publishing deal) with an antique magic lantern, and dutifully offered the formal images of autobiography – slides of Taganrog, Melikhovo and Yalta – before digressing to enthuse about actresses and fishing and telling the stories I already had planned. It was better, in so far as it kept him in the building; in every other respect, worse. After a week, red herrings lay in piles around the room. How glad I was I had cancelled Edinburgh.

Reluctance is not a juicy theatrical value, and in fact I had already moved beyond such contrivances. But it was still going to be hard to find some energy behind Chekhov's reticence. What would set him going? He would need to feel in charge – essentially in his own world, but sometimes venturing out into the theatrical ether. I pictured some night late on in his life unknown to us, riddled with associations, regrets and remembered pleasures. Alison immediately designed a 'Chekhovian' set, as if for the end of *The Cherry Orchard* – suitcases, chairs under dust-sheets (specially good for touring, this, as dust-sheets can cover any low-grade thing), a desk and lamp, Persian rugs, all set on a wooden platform; and she then surrounded the whole unit with a moat of blackness across which Chekhov would sometimes peer at us. Bottles and glasses could be set in different areas of the stage so that he could visit each and talk to whomever he found there, compulsively reminiscing, the light gently shifting with him.

I was aiming at two halves of forty-five minutes each. I still wanted to introduce 'The Black Monk' close to the opening, but it was a hefty item which perhaps needed cross-hatching with something deprecatory. In 'A Dreary Story', written in some depression before Chekhov undertook his work on Sakhalin, the narrator describes the essential characteristic of his life with a self-mockery that Kovrin in 'The Black Monk' does not have:

> Every night I go to bed at midnight exactly and fall asleep immediately, then I wake at two o'clock, feeling as if I hadn't slept at all... I get out of bed and light my lamp... I walk from corner to corner of the room,

> looking at all the pictures on the wall...then, tired of that, I sit at my
> desk, without movement, without thought, without desire...

This sounds very like Chekhov to me, and if I add into it what he might easily have said – 'I step out into my garden' – and play the whole not with the anguished boredom of Professor Nicholas Stepanovich but with some of Chekhov's sweetness, it will be easier to move on to the strange story of the monk.

The thought that this apparition might soon return to earth then hangs in the air; and Chekhov sees that he must, after all, introduce himself. He does so mischievously, by dipping into 'A Dreary Story' again:

> My name is a popular name... I work hard, I have the stamina of a
> camel, and I do have talent...

As evidence of his fame, we'll turn to Chekhov's own biography:

> Josef Braz has just finished my portrait...he wants to present it to
> Moscow University...

Chekhov thought the University's medical school an important conditioning factor in the history of Russian pessimism, with the result that he never committed himself entirely to science. He once famously described medicine as his legal wife and literature as his mistress:

> When I get tired of the one I slip off and spend the night with the
> other. Not very respectable, but at least it's not boring...

Encouraged by the audience's appreciation of this, he begins a tongue-in-cheek CV. He is proud of having achieved six hundred short stories and a poem, but has to concede that he has dabbled in the theatre as well, and is perversely gratified that Tolstoy has such a low opinion of his plays. So far so good; but it all feels too bald, too written, in need of a good physical joke. If I briefly reveal the completed Braz portrait, propped against a chair – distastefully, raising its dustsheet with my stick – we can deal with the main question on everybody's mind:

> Do you think that looks like me?

Let's be clear: I'm Chekhov this evening, and better company than a starchy portrait that looks no more nor less like him than I do. In fact I'll drop the dustsheet back over it, as disgusted as Chekhov himself. Some counterpointing action would make all these introductions more natural. I recall that when Meyerhold was rehearsing *Three Sisters* and having difficulty with a line he felt over-blatant, Stanislavsky advised him to set about opening a bottle of wine during it – the small accompanying struggle immediately solved his problem. For us it could perhaps be the unexplained packing of suitcases, as if some disquieting journey were in hand.

With Chekhov, nothing was for ever and quite a lot for mischief: he said many contradictory things on the same subject, as most of us do, and he could be wayward. So he might speak like Sonya or Tusenbach about the necessity of work, but immediately celebrate the pleasures of idleness. Or of travel: if an open champagne bottle falls to his hand, he can become like Dr Dorn recalling his European tours. A journey always felt good to Chekhov as a means of avoiding other Russians, and when it failed he was irritated. He suddenly remembers an edgy encounter with a garrulous fellow-countryman in the Pension Russe in Nice:

> – Excuse me, perhaps I am unpleasant to you?
>
> – Why would that be? I replied.
>
> – Well, because of my profession. You see, excuse me, but I'm a spy...

This unusual Intelligence Officer proceeds to tell Chekhov his life story in one minute: he was a dunce at school, then his mother got a general to find him a job in the secret service. Now he tours the world, practising his dubious arts and (like Porfiry in *Crime and Punishment*) exercising 'gymnastics' if he gets into a corner. Candidly, he hopes to be a State Councillor one day. One thing, though: he would never lay hands on a famous writer such as Chekhov. The joke has a sharp edge. Does Chekhov sense the sacrificial part writers will play in an age of surveillance and midnight disappearances? As this thought occurs to us, he finishes the story abruptly and looks blankly out, unknowing, not altogether friendly. It's hard to tell what he is thinking: perhaps he's about to call the whole thing off. But the only point he's been making with his story is that he detests the Russian enclave in Nice:

> What fools...one ugly face after another, nothing but malice and gossip...

This surprising hostility is partly self-castigation. As he had little French, Chekhov reluctantly felt like one of the parochial group himself. Perhaps he saw its pettiness as the dark side of love of homeland, as a rooted inability to adapt. His own nostalgia, for his southern past in particular, now reminds him of his encounter with the Armenian girl in 'Beauties', the show's first sustained passage. However conversational he makes this memory sound, it should also have a finished feel, as if some literary method were at work.

A bitter segue follows: fiction is one thing, but Chekhov's real childhood was spent 'playing the hypocrite before God and man', in trousers so tight he was called the macaroni, beaten with a rope soaked in tar by a father who once reconsecrated a vat of oil in which a rat had died so that he could go on selling it. The memory of how he has 'squeezed the slave' out of himself brings on a fit of coughing – the evening's only display of illness, apart from a slight delicacy in getting up and sitting down. It brings the show to a halt. Feeling the audience's eyes as anxiously on him as Tikhonov's were that night in 1902, Chekhov swiftly climbs back into the saddle:

> Life is quite an unpleasant business, but it's not so very hard to make
> it wonderful. When your matches go off in your pocket, rejoice, and
> give thanks to heaven that your pocket's not a gunpowder magazine.
> If your relatives come to call, exclaim triumphantly, 'How very lucky
> it's not the police!'

He goes to freshen up at a washbasin, musing on how hard it is to live a good life without culture – which, by the way, has nothing to do with appearances. He remembers an inspiring old friend sicker than himself, the vagabond poet Liodor Palmin; the years drop away as he re-lives their evenings together:

> – Love lets you down…a woman will deceive you five times over
> before she's worn out a pair of shoes.
> – Anton Pavlovich, I think Shakespeare has already spoken adequately
> on this subject.

Palmin has a gargantuan wife who does little but bring him his beer at exactly five o'clock each day, and I can hear an echo – it is Andrei in *Three Sisters*, for whom, too, marriage is not a favoured subject:

> – A wife is a wife. A wife is a wife.

Chekhov then reports his literary progress to his friend – 'to think that such a genius would emerge from a privy.' He is off to Petersburg for the first time – and as he moves away, Palmin fades. In the capital, Chekhov tells us candidly, he became so drunk he mistook

> girls for bottles and bottles for girls…

He remembers putting on his new shoes with the pointed toes to visit Suvorin and flirting with his secretary, and Suvorin taking him for a boat trip, forcing him to talk so much about literature that he developed inflammation of the vocal cords. He only realised how tired he was when he went home to his lodgings and tried to read some Dostoyevsky, with the usual effect. Because of this fatigue, he now seems his own age again; and knocking the great Petersburger about provides a link into what I have already established –

Chekhov's observations about style and his invention of 'The Huntsman', which earn him an interval glass of tea.

Ninety per cent of this comes from his own mouth or pen, only a little embellished – actually it wasn't Suvorin in Petersburg but another editor, but never mind about that. Siberia and Sakhalin will occupy the first third of the second half and 'The Black Monk' end it – in between, I don't know. We open in nineteen days.

In 'House with a Mezzanine', Chekhov writes:

> For a moment I fell under the spell of something which was my own, something familiar, some landscape I'd seen in my childhood.

He could have been speaking of Isaak Levitan, and he should have one of his friend's paintings near him. Perhaps *The River Istra*, its translucent current running through a cornfield beneath a wide treeless horizon; or *The Oak and the Birch* or *The Village*. But really there is no contest with *Haystacks in the Moonlight*, the one dashed off that night in Yalta, in oil onto board, which Chekhov then put above his fireplace. I'm glad to get Levitan into the show, and while the painting is being forged by the NT's props artists, go further: the poster should be a still of myself as Chekhov superimposed on the tree-fingers and dank fen of *Autumn: Village Road*. Lovely.

Alec McCowen's one-man show about Rudyard Kipling opens at the Mermaid Theatre, and the reviews speak of an hermetically shy writer who hates biography and puts on his coat at the end to leave the theatre. I can't help feeling dismayed. However, it turns out to have quite a different method, guiding the audience chronologically through the life lived, whereas we aim to do it by free association. But the comparison is cautionary: however discreet our links, they must be compelling – an audience will get very uncertain if they sense no logic at all, so there must be some implicit pattern behind each digression. So far, the one moment where our garment could unravel (as you may have spotted) is around the washstand, the life of culture and Palmin, where the footwork is a little haphazard: perhaps I can take care of that in the playing.

Irina and I rehearse on Good Friday, in a deserted National Theatre. With a hint of paranoia Chekhov starts:

> There's not a single stain on my name.

Irina, from Soviet Leningrad, appreciates this: we reflect for a moment on surveillance, exoneration and rumour. The telephone in the rehearsal room suddenly rings, making us jump. 'It's Security here. Are you rehearsing in

Number Four? Just checking.' We finish the session with the writer being accosted while out walking in Paris: a young man approaches and asks him if he isn't Chekhov. Warily – is this a spy? – he agrees: the man is delighted, blushes to the roots of his hair, shakes him by the hand and runs off.

Then we break: I have a performance of *Venice Preserv'd* tonight. I step outside the building and look across the Thames: the sky is overcast and the river is dirty. No world soul here. For as long as I remember I have done nothing but spin my web; I feel significantly tired and a little sorry for myself, and even the lights of Somerset House seem as distant as a party I've not been invited to. It may also have something to do with the melancholy of Easter, which always affects me even though I am not pious. A middle-aged woman arrives out of nowhere and speaks to me very directly.

– Excuse me, aren't you Michael Pennington?

I acknowledge it.

– Oh, forgive me, but I do enjoy your work. Can I shake your hand?

She blushes and leaves as suddenly as she arrived, anxious not to intrude.

Ian McKellen comes in as a favour to watch a rehearsal. He is helpful and encouraging, but, since good-natured piracy is part of the trade, warns me cheerily that he will steal a technical trick I have found to alternate the characters in 'The Huntsman' for his one-man Shakespeare anthology, so that he can do duologues as well as single speeches. I've been wondering what Chekhov liked to eat, whether he should have a meal of sturgeon and oatmeal with us and how much he smoked: Mike Leigh would love me. I trawl antique markets for a period mousetrap of the type Chekhov used in Yalta, humanely trapping the mice and releasing them over his wall into a Tartar cemetery. I wonder whether he might not practise a little hornpipe to amuse himself, the sort of thing we all do alone. I also consider for a moment finishing the first half not with 'The Huntsman' but with the very early 'Romance With a Double Bass', in which a musician takes a swim in a river at the same time as a young fisherwoman. By a charming sequence of events she ends up naked in his instrument case, stepping out of it onto a concert platform, while he is left alone by the river with only his top hat and his double bass. Set in the lyrical open air, the story slightly debunks the impulse behind 'The Huntsman', and actually the idea is an aberration. One night I bump into Robert Stephens, who crosses the National Theatre bar as if he wanted to hit me, but instead lays a lathery kiss on my lips. He has long wanted to do a solo Chekhov and has planned to call it 'The Good Doctor' – but I have beaten him to it. He is generous to a fault. I think about how he might play the part, and for some reason how John Gielgud would – these encounters stiffen the sinew. In the third week I start to forget my own lines: I wonder if I should scrap the set altogether. As solitary as Chekhov, I talk all the time to my son and my parents, who continue to watch their anchorite with appreciative dismay.

Sunday evening, 13 May: the last of three dress rehearsals. Now I feel confident and secure, absorbed in my great invention. The first run, last Thursday, was for a couple of invited friends: with clothes and token lighting it really worked, having far more texture than such a run usually does. A second this afternoon was vocally tedious, as if the performance was stale before I had even started. It's all right – the arrival of fatigue means one is probably getting to the point. Before doing the third, I have rung my parents in the Lake District, where they always go on holiday at this time of year, to the same hotel, to the same room. I told my father how it was going, and about the very first performance at Guildford tomorrow. A new tone came into his voice, as of belief at last: 'You're really going to do this, then?' – he must have thought *Anton Chekhov* was a dream, or something to be called off at the last minute. He loves this sort of enterprise – professional self-determination, but without quite abandoning the institutions. They are travelling back tomorrow. I promise to talk to him after Guildford.

Monday 14 May, 8:15 am. I write in my diary that the day should be noted. Sunny pleasure battles with a sudden fear of memory loss during a hundred minutes alone. When Chekhov's passions are engaged, by some wrong for instance, I'm sure the show has quality: the times when he freewheels can be a little quaint. Still, I'm probably now as close to him as I could be – I no longer think of him as a bit like Astrov or Eric Clapton – and I'm inclined to think this is a proper piece of work, properly rehearsed, with excellent teamwork and an excellent wig. I don't know if it has all come together this fast because it was ripening naturally or because it had to. Either way, some guarded pride as I climb into a transit van at the NT, to messages of cheer from the building. Like Chekhov, I suddenly look forward to a summer 'rich with every kind of fruit'.

In Cheshire, my father also writes in his diary: the time and mileage at the service stop they've had lunch at on their return down the M6. Struggling with a cufflink in the improvised dressing-room at Guildford, I think affectionately that the men in his family battled with this kind of cuff, this kind of collar, most mornings of their lives. The telephone rings, which is irritating so soon before the show – perhaps it is for whoever normally uses this office. I think of not answering, but do.

'This is Rugby Coroner's Office… Mrs Pennington to speak to you.' Mrs Pennington? We were divorced in 1967 – we're friends, but not so much in touch that she would track me down here to wish me luck. Something is sinking through me. It's my mother of course. Her voice is soft and puzzled.

A few moments after making his diary entry, my father has died, of a massive heart attack, at the wheel of the car.

The room looks the same, but stiller, the collar studs on the desk, and I know Irina will be here in a minute to wish me luck. I have no idea what to do next, but I suppose I will have in a minute.

PART THREE

CRIMEAN RUBBISH

Darling, don't make sad faces. Angry, not sad. People who carry unhappiness around inside of them and are used to it just brood and whistle a lot. You must whistle!

    –Anton Chekhov to Olga Knipper, on playing Masha in *Three Sisters*

My parents are in for the matinee at the Theatre Royal Brighton – they form a large percentage of a tiny house that also includes the director Ken Russell. It is 18 November 1971. They came to Arthur Wing Pinero's *Trelawney of the Wells*, the other half of our repertoire, last night, and have stayed overnight not to miss *Three Sisters*. We have an early lunch – Russell is at his lobster at the table opposite. It takes me back to the many trips they took to Stratford, for and with me as a teenager, until I started going on my own, I'm sure to their relief; we would have lunch either at the Theatre Restaurant or the Mulberry Tree (now a shopping centre) before going to the matinee. I was always convinced I could spot one or other of the actors in the restaurant – a few years earlier in my life it would have been heroic cricketers, inexplicably passing our house – despite the fact that few of the Stratford company could have afforded to eat there, or would relish infant rubberneckers like me, or that by then they were probably getting ready for the show. Peter O'Toole broke all these rules, as he did many others, before *Troilus and Cressida* – he was in the Mulberry Tree all right, a bit close to the beginning of the performance, I primly thought, and enjoying himself more than one might expect of someone with such a serious afternoon in hand. But I also knew precociously (I could have won the $64,000 Question on Shakespeare in those days, had I entered, perhaps more confidently than I could now) that Thersites doesn't start till the fourth scene of the play.

Fifteen years later, with Chekhov in Brighton, I feel stranded for a moment between the world I grew up in and the one I've not so long ago entered. I look at my lawyer father, tensely, and then across the room at the farouche figure of Russell – not yet accepting that different planets can spin successfully alongside each other, I feel I must decide where I belong. Come the show, it is my parents' presence rather than his (as a potential employer) that makes me acutely self-conscious. There comes a day when performing in front of your ancestors stops being as excruciating as your first Nativity Play and becomes even a joyous business, a small celebration of what they have helped you turn into: but not yet. Come to that, for a long time I was fearful of playing in front of anyone at all I wanted to impress: far from the peacock showing his feathers, I would feel like a shameful fraud.

Perhaps it would have been easier had I come from a theatre family, rather than being an only child breaking away from everything expected of him. I was certainly aware of what my parents' loyalty was costing them. My father's anxiety had paradoxically turned him in towards the eye of the storm, and he had applied his skills as carpenter and electrician to building a world-beating model theatre (three foot by three foot by three foot, complete with four battens of lights and dimmers), inciting me forwards though he would have preferred me to turn aside; he later joined the Garrick Club, mostly for the pleasure of occasionally sitting next to good-natured senior actors who would duly compliment him on how well I was doing in the profession even if I wasn't. It was those evenings that his mood was lightest when he came home. My mother meanwhile would write to my granny that 'Mike's mania for the stage' was continuing, with the sure implication that this too would pass; later, adapting thoughtfully to the inevitable, she became the supreme archivist – I still have all her gathered press reviews, crumbling like papyrus – and would not be deflected from her view that it should have been me playing Falstaff at Stratford when I was twenty-one, or perhaps Lear. She once sent to me in South Korea a bad review of an actor she saw as a rival of mine, though really he was quite a close friend. Urged on like this, I had little to complain of, God knows; and all I could do in Brighton was be nervous.

I should have learned more sang-froid from working with Richard Cottrell, who had directed both *Three Sisters* and *Trelawney*. He had inspired me during the last three months of rehearsal and touring. At drama school you do an exercise, choosing what animal to be. Richard, both highly-strung and gentle, exuberant and fastidious, holds his head as proudly as some marvellous heron; and he has, or had, quite a striking stammer. Nevertheless, he set himself on our first day (an occasion even more gruelling for directors than actors) a surely daunting task. A formal semicircle of chairs confronted three trestle tables, with his own throne at their centre. The entire staff of his Cambridge Theatre Company attended – heads of departments, observers, secretaries, the lot. Richard started speaking about *Three Sisters* at ten-thirty and finished at one, without notes or any voluntary pauses. The implicit point was not missed: our company immediately began to work with the same full-heartedness, oblivious to any handicap, as its director and author. As if emulating the play's own community, a group of actors tends to develop a passionate sense of family in a Chekhov, and not only because of the odd reckless evening in Russian restaurants: with *Three Sisters* we were soon dreading our dispersal at the end of the job like the sisters fearing the departure of the military.

The only interruption to Richard's remarkable performance that day was when I slipped quietly away for fresh air. I was in a state of terrible nerves at the prospect of the read-through that would follow, and genuinely thought I was going to faint. I wasn't exactly a greenhorn, goodness knows, but this was different: I had not had a job for a while, and after seven years' work mainly as a kind of romantic juvenile, I was now to be Andrei Prozorov, the golden boy broken by his catastrophic marriage and the expectations of his sisters. This was a real character at last, and a graduation for me. Whatever looks I had been trading on were now helpful solely to establish a family resemblance with the strikingly blonde actresses playing my sisters: Virginia McKenna, Stephanie Bidmead and Patricia Brake. The rest of the cast were equally classy – Prunella Scales, Daniel Massey, Alan MacNaughtan, John Cater and, in the part of the Maid, Charlotte Cornwell. Cottrell had translated the play himself, and thirty years later it seems to me still one of the very best versions, inexplicably unpublished.

Overawed by the task, I determined not to go out in the evenings during rehearsals – for a routinely dissipated young actor, that was quite a resolution. When not reading, re-reading, learning the play, I had a list of Chekhov stories at hand, recommended by Cottrell as a way into the world behind the text, and many of them specific to the characters, not only my own: 'My Life', 'Ionych', 'The Duel', 'In the Ravine' (this, indirectly, for Natasha), 'The Order' (for Kulyghin), 'The Kiss' (for the garrison), 'Peasants'. Then there was Lermontov's *Hero of Our Time* for Solyony, Gorky's *My Childhood*, Tolstoy's *Childhood, Boyhood and Youth*; and we all had an invitation to imagine the sisters' dead father, General Prozorov, as being like Prince Nikolai Bolkonsky in *War and Peace* – but there are limits to how much you can read. Richard also recommended, from Turgenev's *Sketches from a Hunter's Album*, two stories: 'Singers' and 'Kasyan from the Beautiful Lands'. I failed at first to see why: 'Kasyan' is about an encounter with a sort of Holy Idiot and 'Singers' describes a musical competition; and though Turgenev's care for the peasant and his lyrical descriptions are marvellous they are undoubtedly long-winded, making you long for Chekhov's economy in 'The Huntsman'. Perhaps the point was a subtle one, to awaken us to things you can hardly begin a Chekhov without feeling, but which suffer a little in the discussion. Yakov, the champion in 'Singers', is said to produce a sound

> breathing with something, something of our birthright, and huge, as
> if the steppe were unrolling before us, unrolling without limit into
> the distance...

Listening to him, the storyteller remembers a seagull standing on the seashore, facing the crimson evening and spreading out its great wings to the sea; he recalls the sound again later when he hears a peasant boy calling to his brother over and over again, the voice echoing in the air, filled with the shades of night.

I felt as if, like this narrator, I was coming of age. I listened raptly to Richard talking in rehearsal about longings large and small – the distance to Moscow from the provincial town of Perm, even the loneliness of finishing a week's rehearsal to realise you have been so absorbed that you have forgotten to arrange a weekend. Subtly, he was directing us with these examples towards something central not only to *Three Sisters* but *Trelawney* as well, a link despite their obvious wide differences. The hope against hope of the Prozorovs translates in the more domestic world of the Pinero play into the embattled optimism of a group of actors facing historical change, while the theatre profession's dependence on good fellowship oddly corresponds to the Russians' clinging together for warmth seven hundred miles from Moscow. *Trelawney* is one of the genre of backstage plays that we love doing and the public more or less puts up with – not too sentimentally, it catches our edginess, vanity and helpless affection. It was entirely in its key that, at a particularly draughty matinee in Leeds, the sound of a single seat banging upwards during a silence caused Dan Massey to whisper to me, as if we could now go home, 'He's gone.' The press office, after a poor beginning crediting a photograph of Chekhov to his biographer David Magarshack, who was not yet born when it was taken, was making much of the fact that the two plays were written within three years of each other, but that is just the start of it. As for me, I was in a swoon, all the time: I was finally falling in love with my own profession.

Trelawney hardly required the same vows of abstinence and piety, but for the Chekhov I would come down and sit in the wings as the play started, and when not onstage or changing, that's where I'd stay, fully absorbed in my new-found world. I was thus very unlike a Petersburg actor of 1896, and, who knows, perhaps not that much like an Art Theatre one, though obviously the general approach would have to be called Stanislavskian. More probably I resembled a tyro Henry Irving, who used to wait for his cue for long minutes in the wings. It took Ellen Terry, an actress well ahead of her time, to see that he was giving the performance there rather than on the stage, and she taught him how to be nearly late, rushing down the stairs from his room. Losing its studied quality, his work improved greatly, it seems. My own devout behaviour caused a little stir at Brighton, one of the few remaining theatres to hire a Call Boy (an elderly gentleman named Harry) rather than a public address system to summon the actors for their cues. He had his timings, all written down in a little notebook, for knocking on each dressing-room door. Perturbed when, at 'Pennington 7:35', I would not be in there, he would come a little vexedly to tap on my shoulder ('Your call, sir') as I stood in the wings, bathed in the overspill of light, stage-struck and willing myself into Russia. He could not know that my life was beginning to make sense, and that I felt I wanted nothing more from the rest of it than to sink deeper and deeper into this world – into the passionately rag-tag life of a theatre company, and into the profound music of Chekhov.

I envy the rat that lives underneath the floorboards of your theatre.

By the time of *Three Sisters*, something was on the move in Chekhov – he had at last seen the Moscow Art Theatre's work and was reasonably satisfied. He was now writing specifically for actors he knew, visualising them as Molière and Shakespeare had done; and because of his deepening relationship with Olga Knipper, he was with them in the spit and the sawdust whether he liked it or not. There is no special reason why Tusenbach should be a Baltic German who keeps insisting that, despite his name, he is completely Russian, except that the actor Vsevelod Meyerhold was of German parentage and had taken the Orthodox Faith and Russian nationality a few years before. Conceivably knowing this, the audience might have chuckled at Tusenbach's anxiety to establish the point from the start; but in fact they never had the chance, as Meyerhold left the cast during rehearsals, annoyed that he had not been offered shares in the company. Meanwhile, long before the script was finished, Alexander Vishnevsky was being promised a role (Kulyghin) involving a frock coat and a medal on a ribbon round his neck, and Olga was being warned:

I've written you such a part: give me ten roubles, or I'll give it to another actress.

Though Chekhov was sensing a home for himself in their world, his suspicion of Stanislavsky was undimmed – this time he doubted, surprisingly, whether the director would be able to handle the four characters of the educated class that he (also from peasant stock) had written. His general attitude to the new play was the usual disingenuous scorn – 'just Crimean rubbish' – while his slyly mournful picture of the author at work veils a typical appeal for affection:

Well, I'm living in dismal Siberian Yalta, with my hair falling out, eating nothing but soup, and my Olga is in Moscow, going to balls in a plunging neckline…

With little more than Levitan's *Haystacks* for company, separated from his lover not only by the 700-mile train journey but 'by the germs in me and the love of art in you', Chekhov spent a long and laborious year in the composition.

Sometimes he would sit and think about the play all day but then pick up a newspaper. Or, he would teasingly write to Olga (waiting patiently in both her identities), the play would look sadly at him from his desk and he would look sadly back at it. Or one of the heroines would unaccountably 'go lame'. When Ibsen's *When We Dead Awaken* opened at the Moscow Art Theatre, the company sent Chekhov a group photograph inscribed with the message that they, the dead, would only awaken when he gave them his new play. When he did so, it was with the comment that the ending was like *Vanya*, but that was all right, because it was good to remind people of your other works.

Now Chekhov rushes to Moscow, to the theatre in which he said he would be happy to work as a janitor. He tells Olga he wants 'to talk and talk or even be silent' with her. He holes up in the Dresden Hotel, waiting to read the new play to the company, and Olga slips away from the theatre with chocolates, bread and honey and gossip, or to walk in the park with him. It is an honoured camp-follower's theatrical heaven, and perhaps almost as good as he had dreamed it would be. Then there is a setback. The reading leaves Chekhov excited but the actors confused: 'It's not a play, but a prospectus'; 'It's impossible to act' – and worst of all, 'I don't agree with the author in principle'. Perhaps unused to the need of actors to become windbags when they feel they have literary influence, the last enrages him most, and there is a good Chekhovian moment when Stanislavsky goes to the Dresden to find the author yelling: 'It's impossible. Listen! In principle!' So much for the joys of Moscow, Moscow, and the pleasure of sweeping theatre floors.

Much revision follows, at which moment, with instinctive timing, Vera Komisarzhevskaya asks for the play for Petersburg, only to be refused by the author because it is 'gloomier than gloom', even though he is simultaneously insisting to the Art Theatre that it is 'light-hearted, a comedy'. Suddenly he ups and deserts Olga and Moscow, leaving only two rewritten Acts behind. He had longed to be there; now he wants to be abroad. From Nice he sends a single line for the play, an apparent inconsequentiality which will be put to wonderful fugal use:

> Chebutykin: Balzac was married in Berdichev.
>
> *Irina hums.*
>
> I must write that down. (*Makes a note.*) Balzac was married in Berdichev. (*Reads his paper.*)
>
> Irina: (*Laying out her patience cards, absentmindedly.*) Balzac was married in Berdichev.

Then he completely rewrites the fourth Act.

Chekhov's demeanour is now that of the writer exiled from rehearsals, who nowadays would be bombarding the director with e-mails and faxes –

agitated, unable to let go, distrustful and enthused by turns. Fearful that the play's soldiers will be so caricatured they will offend the military in Moscow, he sends a friend, a Colonel, to check up on the company. This misfires a little, as all the man objects to is Vershinin having an affair with a married woman, which he professes to find improbable. Turning to Stanislavsky, Chekhov makes the point again, that these soldiers are to be played as the representatives of culture – 'simple, pleasant people, in old worn-out uniforms – no false military erectness, no shoulder-flexing and heel-clicking and so on'. He also insists that it would be a mistake to bring Tusenbach's dead body on at the end, as Stanislavsky dreams of doing.

From the Pension Russe he peppers Olga Knipper with queries, enlisting her help in areas which are not strictly her concern. Hearing that the Natasha (Stanislavsky's wife Maria) is busily putting out lights and looking for burglars under the furniture in Act Three, Chekhov perceptively demands that she go straight across the stage without looking to left or right, like Lady Macbeth with her candle. He unexpectedly insists that Knipper herself, playing Masha, should not look as she had as Yeliena in *Vanya*, but be younger and more lively – his sister lends a hand in this area by persuading the actress to drop a red wig that is making her head look too large. Knipper should also use her influence to stop the play's Olga, as reported, always taking her sister Irina by the arm – 'can't she get around on her own?' Knipper is briefly fired by Stanislavsky after a disagreement over how she should play Act Three; Chekhov's reaction is not recorded, but he is soon glad to hear that she has 'found the right walk' for Masha, and counsels that the character is fond of laughing and easily gets angry. I trust you, he says, you're a good actress.

The play opens on 31 January 1901, with Chekhov far away in Rome. It is rather disliked by the press, but loved by the public. The town chosen for the action, Perm, is seven hundred miles north-east of Moscow (the same distance, as the crow flies, as from Moscow to Chekhov's Yalta in the south), easy enough to reach now, but at that time with no direct railway and an infrequent connection to Petersburg; the nearest big town, Ekaterinburg, was twenty-four hours away. So the sisters might as well be in Siberia. But to the Moscow audience, Perm would soon feel so close at hand that people started talking not of going to see *Three Sisters* but of visiting the Prozorovs: the writer Leonid Andreyev would describe the play not as a story but a fact. Still, there are some surprises. Suvorin, coming out of the aesthetic closet and now rating Chekhov beneath Ostrovsky and Gogol, gives space in *New Times* to a skit by his resident critic Viktor Burenin, who denounces Chekhov as 'the minstrel of despair': his parody is called *Nine Sisters and No Husband*, and the whole of the first Act is a Stanislavskian stage direction. Trained cockroaches (though no crocodiles) also feature, and Burenin recommends (apparently forgetting that Masha is a married woman) that the sisters should all go and lose their virginities without delay. Suvorin's and Chekhov's friendship never recovered.

Chekhov did not see the production in its first season; but when it was revived in September he did something he had never done before – took over rehearsals. It was both a compliment and a reproach, perhaps. Now married to Olga (the actors thought the play should be re-titled *Two Sisters* as he'd stolen the third) and therefore finally to the Art Theatre, he worked continuously with Vasily Luzhsky, an actor he never very much liked, to improve his performance as Andrei. They went over every line and phrase (I wonder if I'd have welcomed that), and Chekhov suggested that he should be so excited in the last Act that he is almost ready to punch the audience. Turning to the existing production (I imagine Stanislavsky sitting in the stalls sulking), he cut the portrait of General Prozorov on the wall because he looked Japanese, and re-staged the third Act – he felt that Stanislavsky had made this into a 'hullabaloo', and insisted that the thing to be played was not blatant emotion but physical exhaustion. His views on such things as the actors imitating the cooing of doves were predictable enough. Stanislavsky's 'natural' sound effects, in the absence of recordings, must have been pretty crude, but they were ingeniously delivered: a mouse scratching behind the wainscoting was done by the cast running their hands over a bunch of goose-quill toothpicks. But Chekhov had the ear of a perfectionist, that of a radio producer before his time or perhaps of Harold Pinter: applying it to the Act Three fire-bell, he insists on a particularly jarring 'provincial' noise. He's right – no sooner has Irina poignantly cried 'Moscow... Moscow' at the end of Act Two than this very un-Muscovite bell is heard, and moments later Ferapont underlines the effect by harking back to the 1812 fire in Moscow. Also like Pinter, Chekhov was inclined to answer actors' over-intellectual queries by saying simple things such as Andrei should wear slippers, just as Trigorin made his own fishing rods. His reward was much better reviews this time and his own satisfaction.

So much trouble I had with this play. Imagine: three leading women, each a general's daughter, but each cut in her own cloth.

Just as the ache for Moscow has been in him as he wrote as well as in his Prozorovs, Chekhov's concern about the marriage he was contemplating with Olga flickers across the play, which deals very specifically with the malfunction that follows when a brother marries the wrong woman. Preoccupied with the subject, he even hints that Irina's and Tusenbach's incomplete but kindly union – or indeed Olga's humble certainty that she would marry anybody, even an old man, as long as he was good – might be a better foundation for life than the misplaced romanticism that destroys both Andrei and Masha. Meanwhile the extraordinary character of the cuckolded schoolteacher Kulyghin, with his endless capacity for putting up with things (an enormously deepened version of Telegin in *Vanya*), testifies to the dignity possible within a failed relationship.

Chekhov is also interested in what goes wrong within an orthodox family when a man loses authority. To the Prozorovs this happens first when the father dies and then when his son falters. The inadequacy of the three sisters to deal with life is less obvious while Andrei is still a bachelor and can still – just – be seen as the family's brilliant head and their father's male print. But as his grip is prised free by Natasha, their shortcomings, hopeless nostalgia and even pettiness are exposed – glaringly so whenever the realities of his new life stare them in the face. Andrei's fiancée's dress sense is a great and standing joke with them – she wears a yellow skirt and a red blouse! – and when the anxious outsider arrives for a family party at the end of the first Act, Olga, eldest sister and hostess, can't help herself:

> Oh, but you're wearing a green belt! That's not right, darling.

What value have breeding and education when they lead to such an unkind and discomforting remark?

Natasha's revenge on these exclusive girls is thorough and life-long: she takes over the house and emasculates their brother so comprehensively that Masha will compare him to the Kremlin Bell that still lies with a great chip out of it in Red Square. The real bell never got hoisted into position for a variety of technical reasons, but Masha extends her simile:

> Once upon a time thousands of people hauled up a huge bell – the labour and the money they spent! Then suddenly it falls and is smashed. For no particular reason. That's Andrei.

The cuckoo's triumph is such that the sisters soon betray their interests and butterfinger their responsibilities – though Olga does her best to help the victims of the fire in Act Three. While she does so, Anfisa, their old nanny, comes in for a rest, as some servants in old Russian households, almost members of the family, were accustomed to do. In one of the nastiest moments in Chekhov, Natasha flies at her:

> How dare you sit down in my presence! Go on, get up! Get out!
>
> *Anfisa goes out.*
>
> I can't grasp why you keep that old woman on in this house.

All Olga can manage in protest at this tyranny is that it makes her 'ill' when people are treated so. She is no more up to the fight than the exhausted Anfisa herself – you might wonder for a moment which of the two is the more useless. Masha is silent, and then, rather than engaging Natasha, takes a pillow and marches out of the room.

This very human moment is laced with politics. New despots can only establish themselves when the old guard lets them in, like the government preparing to throw open the gates in C P Cavafy's poem 'Waiting for the Barbarians'. In its opposed attitudes to life, *Three Sisters* anticipates the political changes of *The Cherry Orchard*, rehearsing big issues in a modest setting. It is not only that Tusenbach, prefiguring Trofimov both in his view of the future and in his love for the family's youngest daughter, speaks accurately about a great storm to come that will blow Russian life clean of boredom and laziness, or that Vershinin responds (when he wants the attention) about a glorious future when good-hearted men and women like the sisters will be the majority. Chekhov's way of dealing with change is to arouse his audience's sympathies at the same time as he sharpens its premonitions: the closer we grow to the Prozorovs, the tenser our intuition that they are being prepared for history's disposal and will soon be as displaced here in Perm as they would be in Moscow or Paris or Berlin.

Masha's plight is especially great because she is technically attached to this life, having grafted herself to the local schoolmaster, Kulyghin. For him (as he occasionally sees), Olga, orthodox and serious, would have been a more appropriate wife. Outwardly the most independent of the sisters, eccentrically dressed and with her unladylike tendency to whistle, Masha is actually the most snobbish. She certainly has the most potent memories of Moscow, if that means admiring such rituals as arriving home from the opera or the ball, dropping one's shawl on the floor and calling for the servants. Now she is inclined to complain about 'living in this climate' and having to endure 'all this talk as well' – even though it is the great and dubious speechifier Vershinin that she herself falls for. Meanwhile Natasha, insulted by the grand dispossessed, is oddly linked to Kulyghin: like him, she belongs here, and it is as if the background figures from *The Seagull* and *Vanya* were moving in to control the centres of action. Kulyghin regains Masha through the most determined toleration; while the equally tenacious Natasha, for all her affectations, ushers in a new world – more utilitarian, brutal, soviet if you like – in which everything must earn its place. Leisureliness will be criticised, and the pointlessness of deaf servants and resting nannies is obvious. She is the devil with, if not the best tunes, at least the comprehensible ones, and you must see her point, even if you wouldn't want to spend an evening with her. It is a miserable thing, of course, when she stops the carnival party at the end of

Act Two – a carnival, that rarest of things out here in the provinces: but then she does have a sick child. The attitude towards this problem of Second-Lieutenant Fedotik (a delightful character who gives everyone little presents and later dances when all his belongings are burned) is open and unprejudiced, and its fairmindedness contrasts strikingly with the grumbling bias of everyone else:

> What a shame. I was hoping to spend the evening here, but of course,
> if the baby's ill... I'll bring him some toys tomorrow...

When Natasha then arranges for Bobik to move into Irina's room, it is bad for Irina, but also certain that at that time, in that place, the child could easily die if not protected from the cold.

We listen to a quiet inner voice as well when contemplating Soliony, the play's other 'villain'. A mass of nineteenth-century Russian complexes quite hard for us to grasp, we should at least believe him when he confides in Tusenbach that he is perfectly all right when he is alone with somebody, and only becomes awkward and inclined to pose in company:

> Then I just talk rubbish. Still, I'm more honest than a lot of people. I
> can prove it.

He certainly has the gift of candour, surely speaking for everyone's darker side when he declares that he would gladly cook Natasha's baby and eat him; and whereas his commanding officer Vershinin is, by his own account, a man who can't choose books and so fails to read the right things, Soliony is literate enough to quote Lermontov and Pushkin and to write poetry himself. So he is not without dignity; and Natasha is an attentive if suffocating mother. Irina meanwhile longs to work, but lies in bed most mornings; she denies her childishness but squeals with pleasure when she is given crayons; and her longing for Moscow is both acute and very fanciful, since she is really too young to remember it. The yearning of all three sisters, felt by Chekhov as well, is discredited by the destructive Vershinin, a man prepared to use philosophical discourse as a means of seduction, rather as the love of nature was turned to that purpose by Astrov with Yeliena. He swiftly disposes of their dreams by declaring that he has been reading the biography of a French Minister who yearned for release from prison but afterwards failed to notice the birds in the sky. His point is good, but we will feel far less for him than for those who start the play by speaking of their return to Moscow – 'It's our home, you see' – and even name the month when they will leave, but who by Act Three have reached a tacit agreement to stop using the word and mention no more dates.

So Chekhov allows us to mock these characters without losing affection for them or respect for what they want. The ambiguities are reflected through the depths of the play's technique, which employs steep counterpoint even when it appears to be linear. Its opening, for example, seems bald, with all the necessary facts and helpful coincidences pitched in:

> Olga: It's just a year since Father died... The fifth of May, your Saint's Day, Irina... I thought I'd never survive it... Now a year's gone by and we think easily about it – you're in a white dress and you look radiant...

The clock strikes now as it did then. The sun is shining as it did eleven years ago, when General Prozorov got his brigade and the family left Moscow. On the other hand, last May the weather matched the sad event, and few people turned out for the funeral. For the last four years Olga has taught in this town to which they moved, and brother Andrei has got stout. But the exposition is never allowed to settle: as Irina discourages her sister from thinking too much of the past, our eye is caught by Tusenbach, Soliony and Chebutykin drifting in from outside, and while Olga longs for Moscow, a fragment of their conversation is heard:

> Chebutykin: Not at all, not at all.
>
> Tusenbach: Certainly, that's rubbish.

As Irina and Olga repeat their hopes of leaving, the men happen to laugh; when Olga says how much she would have loved the husband she doesn't have, Tusenbach is heard repeating to Soliony:

> You talk such nonsense, I'm tired of listening to you.

And the next stage of exposition is counterpointed by absurd talk of weight-lifting.

In a similar way, apparently random harmonies bloom with meaning. Chekhov is fully a man of the theatre now: apart from intervening in its practical life, he senses how much can be achieved by a single word or an isolated human figure. *Three Sisters* is dotted with moments of wonderful terseness. At the start, Masha's dawning interest in Vershinin is expressed by no more than the removal of her hat and a simple interjection, as funny and serious as in life:

> I'll stay to lunch.

In the next Act, her grand question about the meaning of life is answered by the suddenly laconic Tusenbach:

Look, it's snowing – what's the meaning of that?

Sometimes a simple call has to wait the length of the play for its response: at the start Olga says

I would have loved my husband

and near the end Andrei, torn between the loneliness of bachelorhood and the solitude of his marriage, replies

A wife is a wife.

Some of the bull's-eyes are virtually monosyllabic, like Chebutykin's repetitive last word *vsye ravno* – 'It's all the same.' It is also he who answers everyone's anxiety about the Baron's chances with Soliony –

Chebutykin: Joking aside, this is his third duel.

Masha: Whose?

Chebutykin: Soliony's.

Masha: What about the Baron?

– with, simply:

What about the Baron? (*Pause.*)

– *Shto u barona* it is, even more tersely, in Russian.

It is perhaps only by imagining them in the hands of his new colleagues that Chekhov could have made the diminuendoes of *Vanya* still more complex in *Three Sisters*. At the end of the second Act, Natasha stops the party. The group breaks up and everyone says a momentary goodbye, the visitors agreeing to meet in the street to decide what to do (the Russian celebration looking for somewhere to happen). The maid and the nurse clear the table and put out the lights, quietly singing. Andrei and Chebutykin (whom we have not watched together before) briefly discuss the dilemmas of marriage before leaving to gamble. Irina is obliged to turn away the carnival party and Soliony professes his love for her. Natasha bores Irina with talk of Bobik and gets a fateful invitation to go out driving with Protopopov, who will become her lover. Kulyghin, about to be cuckolded as effectively as Natasha's husband, passes through to check up on everybody, especially Masha – he is suspicious of Protopopov the transgressor, while his real enemy, Vershinin, is so desperate for company that he asks Kulyghin out – but Kulyghin is too cautious to do such a thing. Natasha leaves for her ride, and Irina, who has carried most of the burdens of the past few minutes, is left alone to dream of Moscow. The sense of steady musical decay while real life passes through at its own rhythms

– the quiet singing, the whistling, the putting on of coats, a troika with bells which reminds Irina of her dreams, the doorbell ringing, laughter, an accordion playing in the street – is so strong that Stanislavsky must have been astonished that Chekhov objected to his realisation of it. The fact is, the orchestration had already been done.

After the fire in Act Three, Chekhov goes further, injecting individual importunacies into the gradual return to normality. By confessing her love for Vershinin to her sisters, Masha starts a new movement just as everyone is ready for bed: within a few moments, with dawn breaking, he and she will be looking for a way to make love in the overcrowded house (his wife and children are in the drawing-room). With the same inappropriate energy, Andrei arrives to justify himself over the mortgaging of the property and Natasha's pocketing of the money; as he blusters he loses the women's attention, and finds himself breaking down in front of three blank screens. Into the middle of his anguish Kulyghin incongruously bursts, in pursuit of Masha. When he did this in Act Two she was harmlessly out in the street, but now, as he rushes helplessly about, the awful meaning of her absence bears down on him. The drunken doctor bangs on the floor. All these crises flare up and relapse while time ticks on, undisturbed. Irina reveals that the army is leaving and calmly decides to marry the Baron. She is the only one in the right pulse – it is just at such moments that big decisions can be quietly, clear-sightedly made.

All these technical developments greatly enlarge the characters' range and their persistence in the audience's imagination. They also make possible a final Act of astonishing power and grace. The routed sisters take up their burdens, stepping into a future of small efforts – perhaps becoming, like the ladies at Melikhovo, memorialists of a curious old life. Olga moves into town, to share a flat with Anfisa; Irina prepares to leave with Tusenbach, and when he is killed in the duel, she becomes the play's third lonely schoolteacher; Masha continues her blighted life, in love for the foreseeable future with an officer who not only will not consider staying with her but is worried that leavetaking might make him late. Like Lopahin in *The Cherry Orchard*, Natasha plans to cut down the trees, though for a less intelligent reason ('they look ugly in the evenings'), and is allowed the final revenge of criticising Irina's dress-sense as hers was mocked before. She and Andrei are left with their children (imagine Bobik and Sophie at ten, small-town Soviet cadets awaiting their turn) and her lover Protopopov, who may be the father of Sophie and who has bought Andrei off by making him secretary of the Town Council. As for Chebutykin, he will go away and perhaps come back in a year, but you feel he will be dead by then if he can manage it.

Odd new groupings are formed, as is Chekhov's way. It is Andrei and Masha, sunk in their own miseries, who are forced to react to the news that the Baron is liable to die in a duel. They don't want to get involved, of course, but it is interesting to watch the vestiges of courteous concern – just as Soliony, Vershinin and Tusenbach never quite yawned in each other's faces during their philosophising and as the whole company worried about Nina in *The Seagull*. This is the small change of basically decent people in the same hole – mildly, just helpfully, interdependent. Occasionally an intriguing clue is thrown up. Chebutykin has so far provoked little sympathy: his pain at allowing a patient to die was far more acute than Astrov's twinge in the same situation, but it was alcoholically inflated, and he was even more offhand than Dorn when asked by Andrei for professional help:

> Why ask me? Can't remember – I don't know.

Now we glimpse a reason for his darkness. His first words to Irina in Act One were to call her 'my little girl, my joy'; he now reacts with, for him, great passion to her plans to move to the brickworks and start teaching:

> My dear, wonderful girl…precious one…you've gone far on from me, I'll never catch you up. I've stayed behind, like a migrating bird that is old and can't fly away. Fly away, darling, fly away and God be with you.

A few moments later, Masha and Chebutykin, who normally have little to do with each other, peel off their camouflage as he miserably waits for the duel and she for Vershinin:

> Masha: You do nothing but sit.
>
> Chebutykin: Well?
>
> Masha: Nothing. (*She sits.*)
>
> > *Pause.*
>
> > Did you love my mother?
>
> Chebutykin: Yes, very much.
>
> Masha: And did she love you?
>
> Chebutykin: (*After a pause.*) I don't remember.
>
> Masha: Is my man here?

We may remember now that Chebutykin reminded Irina that he held her the day she was born, and that he loved her mother; that at the very moment in Act Three when she reiterated that she was going to Moscow he dropped and broke the clock; and we realise that, as with Dorn and Masha in *The Seagull*, there is a hint, just a hint, that he might be her father.

The accumulating effect of the Act, interwoven and self-questioning, is awesome, if that is not too big a word for something so profoundly moving.

Vershinin's almost wordless parting from Masha is no more heartbreaking than Kulyghin's attempts to amuse her with his confiscated beard and his determination that life shall go on. As the sisters comfort Masha they neither mention Vershinin's name nor refer to what has happened: this, together with his own silence, eliminates him from the play. As the soldiers leave, the shots from the duel are heard, and in the play's final moments, faith in the future, formerly a delusion or a courting device, becomes a jolting necessity. It was disingenuous for Chekhov to have said that this ending was the same as that of *Vanya*: the counterpoint is more daring, as Chebutykin mutters his grim little music-hall rhyme: 'Tara-ra-boom-de-ay, I'm sitting by the road today.' Everyone except Natasha, who has had her say, becomes touching in this Act, even the fatal Soliony with his scent. As for Kulyghin, his common humanity, his share in the Russian soul in fact, has been emphasised when he feared that the departure of Fedotik and Rodé, members of a regiment that he desperately wants to go away, would make him weep. The worst he will ever say about his adored, unfaithful Masha is that Irina has a slightly softer disposition – but that Masha has a nice disposition too. As you watch him standing with the sisters while they attend to her, his beard at the ready, you realise that if ever you dismissed him as ridiculous, you were in no position to mock.

On the way, Chekhov has also begun a new brief line in impermeable old retainers, who, like Marina in *Vanya*, offer a quiet comment from within. Ferapont is as easily overlooked as Firs in *The Cherry Orchard,* and like him releases into the action an element of nonsense and an odd liberation. Alone before his sisters' screens in Act Three, Andrei will be thrown off true by their invisible judgment on him; but he is quite naturally himself when he talks to Ferapont, who is as deaf as the Siberian wind. As if he were thinking aloud in an empty room, Andrei enthuses to the impartial old man how much he longs to be in Testov's or the Great Moscow Restaurant. It seems to be a futile speech, but there is always the possibility that it is not. In fact, Ferapont has grasped what is under discussion and claims surprisingly that there is a plan to stretch a rope right across the city, and that someone ate forty or fifty pancakes there and died. By the time the old man asks to leave, neither is more aware than the other:

> Ferapont: Should I go now?
>
> Andrei: Yes. Take care of yourself.
>
> *Ferapont goes.*
>
> Take care. (*Reading.*) Come back tomorrow and get these papers. Off you go… (*Pause.*) He's gone.
>
> *Doorbell.*
>
> What a business. (*Stretches and goes off unhurriedly.*)

Ferapont has also had a last word as conclusive and memorable as Chebutykin's – the family's yearnings are briefly put to shame by his stoicism, innocent of protest or humour:

> Andrei: Have you ever been to Moscow?
>
> Ferapont: No. It wasn't God's will.

Just as an ominous silence may lap around a word or a phrase, some things can't be spoken of at all; when, at the play's opening, Olga refers to her father's death, she is cut off by Irina:

> Why bring up these memories?

It is almost a point of honour that the sisters don't dwell on misery, but, paradoxical as ever, the play warns of the dangers of not acknowledging bereavement. A lost father continues to haunt his home – just as Serebryakov's first wife doesn't leave *Uncle Vanya*, and as the dead child whose image Ranyevskaya can see in the face of his tutor persists in *The Cherry Orchard*.

The wind howled in the chimney and Irina fainted clean away when the terrible moment arrived, either out of the blue or after the hushed weeks of a final illness. They buried their father in the driving rain with a military band and a salvo was fired over the grave though the attendance was small. Then the four of them came back to this house where they had lived with him for eleven years, and started again: General Prozorov's portrait continued to hang over proceedings, and they almost expected its eyes to move. And this was never some graceful country alternative to their Moscow home, but one that pitifully aped it, in layout and perspective. The view from an equivalent window was of no interest compared to the noise of the trams and horses' hoofs, the carriages rattling on the cobbled streets, the bells and the merchants' cries that used to greet them from the pleasant breadth of Basmannaya Street in Moscow each morning. Still, while he was there, there was some daily meaning. Now their home is a continual disappointment, and his loss insinuates itself into each corner of every room. Soldiers still come to visit of course, but the parlour is not nearly as full as it used to be, and the officers not as senior or as urbane; in fact the new lot are quite eccentric, arguing about the number of universities in Moscow or Caucasian recipes, and flying into rages that nobody has the power to control. The one they have always known is an elderly army doctor who rents a room from them and who is now so odd that he does dreadful things like presenting a samovar to a young girl on her Saint's Day, as he might to a married woman, and incomprehensibly breaking treasured ornaments. What help is there available to deal with him, apart from muted protests from Kulyghin and Tusenbach? The only officer who invites some comparison with the past is Lieutenant-Colonel Vershinin, who served in the same brigade as Prozorov before, like him, leaving Moscow in command of a battery; he used to visit the family when the children were small and for a time lived on the same street. It is as if the idea of the lost man, if not his authority, was somehow intact within Vershinin; he is, disastrously, fallen upon. Meanwhile, the women are losing the knack of talking about their father, as they have about their mother, who died earlier, and whose face Masha has almost forgotten. Mrs Prozorov is now only the owner of the ornament Chebutykin breaks and the possible object of his love. Silence surrounds her, and it is closing in on her husband as well.

And what would General Prozorov say to his daughters now, let alone his son? How would he deal with Soliony's excesses, and how much would he continue to humour Masha's dull husband? How would he help his youngest, whose disarray is becoming such that she feels as guilty for having snapped at a bereaved mother in the post office as if she had been involved in the death, and who in her intellectual decline can't remember the Italian for window or ceiling? Above all, how would he handle Natasha and his grandchildren, who might even be somewhere else now rather than spreading over every square inch of the rooms and garden? For his part, Andrei has said that since his father died he's shaken off a load, and so hopes to achieve something. In the event, not so, and even less his sisters: all they could report are continued careers at the local school, a post office job for a girl good enough to win a teaching diploma, an adulterous affair and a miserable marriage. There is nothing to give them pride in continuing, little to link them healthily to the cycle of life and death. Worst of all, the daily beauty in their lives, Andrei, is becoming someone they can no longer even look at. When they make a misjudgement it is as if somebody short of a limb has lost their balance: and when Olga reaches out at the end, part of the relief is that she feels she is standing up for herself at last. Until then, in their arrested state, beneath their sorrow and their refusal to 'talk about it', lurks the anger of the deserted. Losing a parent can liberate even the most loving children, if only into the further sorrow that they wish the parent could see what they are doing with their freedom; but their father's death has stopped these golden children in their tracks, paralysing them before their lives are half through.

RAISING THE DEAD

It's a cruel thing, isn't it, a disgusting punishment. People take you to the cemetery, make speeches, then they go home and have tea. Disgusting.

— Anton Chekhov

My mother sounded thoughtful, her soft Scots accent brushing the word 'motorway' as if she were learning a new language. She described what had happened – the steering wobbling, his head thrown back as he gasped for air, rattling in the throat she supposed. She never would be able to explain how she got the heavy car under control and onto the central reservation – which turns out to be the only stretch of the M6 for miles without a barrier she would have crashed into. Then, Mr Edwards the lorry driver – 'What's up, love?' – the ambulance, my father on the ground, the shot at resuscitation, her asking Mr Edwards was he gone, him cagey – 'We'll see, love.' This was just a sad and unexpected event in his working day, and now we will mention him often: he has become one of our company. Later she will say the Coroner at Rugby was very considerate, explaining why we couldn't have his clothes back, and the mad thought will occur to us that we might stay in touch with both these men, sending Christmas cards, I suppose. She who was always worried about losing her mind has studied everything carefully, backing away from the details only to see them more clearly.

Irina Brown's face, as she came into the dressing-room a moment later, twisted with shock. On my way out to the street I crossed the stage we had been about to play: after the bustle of rehearsal it was silent and abandoned, as if everyone had fled at the news. A surprising length of time had passed. It had obviously taken longer than I thought to change and pack, even though I wanted to get back to London to be in the house when my mother arrived in her taxi from Rugby. I couldn't get an outside line at Guildford to call her sister Jean, and the operator was quite rude, rather like Irina Prozorov being curt with the woman in the post office. Outside it was the same harsh morning, as if seen through jetlag, everything heightened and insulting. Irina watched me carefully in the cab back to London as I started to talk about him, as if I were a child who might stumble. He was kind, he was funny, the model theatre we built had Juliet balconies and a practical flying tower; he could talk about anything, and he did, Catholicism or cricket, art or the law. One day when I was ten he scared me into thinking he had lost a finger to his lawnmower. He thought Richard Burton and Liz Taylor were no better than the toms and cats that kept him awake prowling his garden.

This is not so much shock as dread. One thin thought flicks into the vacuum: how complicated it will be to change all plans.

Back at the National after only four hours, to change cabs, seeing faces who either know nothing and are breezy or have heard and whose anxiety makes me flinch. I get to my parents' home in North London just in time, ahead of my mother, to their house full of lemon geraniums (the smell now spoiled forever), brought by Jean, whom I managed to reach in the end. She is already inside when I arrive, I don't know how, and is having none of my trouble with vacuums – aghast and wailing, she's waiting for the moment when my mother will come and the whole thing start in earnest. We manage to let some light into the house, darkened by their two-week absence, throwing it open as if spring had come and re-connecting the water. Then the taxi arrives, my mother in the back, small and hot in the brown velvet suit she put on this morning to travel home, her picnic bits around her, looking blankly out of the window. The dread evaporates – this is just a big, plain fact. Inside the house, she is lucid and thoughtful, sitting in her usual chair, with Jean in the seat opposite where my father used to be: just once, words fail her and her hands flail briefly about her face.

It's inconceivable. He is so much in the room, moving gently around on his return from holiday, it must be our fault that we're failing to see him.

In the evening I get Mark out of school for a few days. I suppose this is an odd thing to do – his housemaster certainly thinks so: this was only a grandparent, after all. The fact is there aren't many of us available at home, just myself and Jean, who has a fragile husband to go back to; it is both that Mark is needed and that in some way he shouldn't miss this. The years starting now will turn him into the tenderest of men, tolerant of the bizarre and unreasonable, until his fervent sense of a family's history will illuminate his own children. At the moment he is seventeen, and looks thoughtfully at the floor as I sit and tell him what's happened – he is as unknowable as any teenager, but he smiles at me and packs his bag, as if to say we do still smile.

Clouds scud across the sky like thoughts adrift. I cook an inexplicable chocolate pudding for the three of us and we drink a bottle of my father's white burgundy to prove that everything continues. There are moments of lightness, even joy: for two days I cater ridiculously, cooking for ten. We're simultaneously disposing of him and keeping him here – I close his wardrobe quickly so that the live smell wafting out of his clothes doesn't escape, then go and choose his coffin. The clothes I'm not wearing myself, that is, trying to be him: he was far more barrel-chested and generous in the girth than I am (this year especially) so I'm not quite sure what I look like.

May 16. Is it too soon to work again? My mother is going about like a mouse, quiet and grateful: she rests after lunch, as she's taken to doing in recent years anyway, sitting calmly on the bed, her hands folded in her lap, looking quietly across at the window. In between the dreary litany of phone calls – with the dread of having no more to make – the bookings with the National have been sorted, and I honour my date at Goldsmiths College, trying *Anton Chekhov* out on its first audience. I feel a little breathless, as if something threatening was at my shoulder. I've the idea that the whole script might have been wiped from my memory, or that some line from it will rear up and bring things to a halt:

> Why do we never try to stand again when once we've fallen? If we lose one thing why don't we search for another? I want our lives to be holy, sublime and solemn as the vault of heaven. Let us live! The sun only rises once a day, so take hold of what's left of your life and save it...

For the first time in two days, I feel alone with my father, as if he is a little way above and ahead of me, in an imaginary dress circle. It's not so much that he would be enjoying the performance, these wonderful things being spoken, but that he quite obviously is. He surely wants me to think carefully about what I'm doing this evening. When in doubt, Chekhov should be humorous. It's clear that the Siberian section that opens the second Act needs to be brisker, more matter of fact – he has been travelling for days and can still feel carriage-wheels rattling beneath him.

The next date is Christ's Hospital Horsham: a gathering of sixth-formers cower in their characteristic blue Tudor gowns and yellow socks while I try to make common cause. Chekhov's story about the Armenian girl – the main chance in the first half to assess how we're going – now moves forward arrhythmically, less a lyrical reminiscence than an excited writer falling on clusters of language. This seems a strange thing to be doing this afternoon; but I came across an interview with Bob Dylan before the show, and his point of view is simple enough, like Käthe Kollwitz's father's: if you've something you do well, you have to keep doing it, nothing else matters, even when you think it should.

May 20. My father's birthday: we eat a topside of beef with a bottle of Beaune, such as he might have chosen. He wasn't a wine bore, but he loved his small cellar. Feeling bad after years of teasing him, I'm working my way through it in bibulous homage. The next day is the funeral. An advertising balloon appears over Maida Vale – it seems to have 'Shell' written on it. My father was latterly that company's legal advisor, and I confusedly think this is something they've run up for him on this sad day: but in fact it's an advert for

Snell, the estate agents. I remember that during a brief spell as a Parliamentary lawyer before the war, he worked on A P Herbert's bill to prohibit advertising from aeroplanes and balloons. At the service a couple of his Shell colleagues, boardroom men both, weep openly – 'Oh, Vivian...' It's less than a week.

Mark goes back to school, but it's clear to us both what's happened. We've moved into the house. He's spent much of his life here in any case – creeping downstairs in the evenings to eavesdrop from my old vantage-point – and now he can stake out a teenage room you will hesitate to enter; more than ever, he'll need his kingdom. The days spread out a little. At the third performance, at Banbury Arts Centre, Yegor in 'The Huntsman' seems to me too bullying and Pelageya too pitiful, whereas he should be as lost as she is, trapped in his male expectation of himself. Obviously. Then Guildford, where the news came ten days ago. The dressing-room and stage look dull, insignificant. A full house, their enthusiasm perhaps mixed up with sympathy.

The last play my father saw was *Venice Preserv'd* a month ago. He didn't need to hold my mother's hand in that one, I'm glad to say: free from those alarming Russians, the boy was heroic and well-dressed, slugging it out with McKellen and Lapotaire. Much more like it. Now that the show comes back into the Lyttelton after a two week break, I have to meet colleagues I haven't seen since he was alive, and I'm nervous. I wish it wasn't so hard for them, but I'm relieved that they're trying, and quite surprised at who are the most embarrassed. On top of which, it's Ian McKellen's birthday, so we're celebrating at the same time.

I collect the ashes from Levertons. They're presented by a somewhat theatrical undertaker with a scrupulously shaped beard, stepping forward as if to offer Richard II his orb and sceptre. But a moment before, I've caught a glimpse of him through a flapping plastic curtain that would have looked well on a shower – he seemed to be pulling the goods out of a filing-cabinet. I tuck the unmistakable box under my arm like an awkward piece of shopping. This is all fine and even humorous, but I slightly misjudge the run across Haverstock Hill and have to do a dash and swerve – the casket jumps briefly out of my hand and I catch it nonchalantly.

Irina and I go into a rehearsal room again, to review where we've got to. The show's first half now seems tight but the second slightly flabby, though neither of us can spot why that is. It should be the other way round, since the first Act is rather episodic while the second has boiled down to three broadly coherent movements. The first of these is Siberia and Sakhalin – doubters in the interval will see that there is a serious intent in all this after all. Chekhov is delighted with the people he meets on the road, learning that the wives are too strong to be beaten by their husbands and that Siberians don't belch in front of you or look for insects in their hair. Early one morning his carriage crashes into another hurtling in the opposite direction; stranded, he takes refuge with a Siberian family, resting in a room decorated with sweet wrappers and vodka labels: someone's painted a tree on the door growing out of a vase, together with some red flowers and birds that look more like fish. The husband is careful to wipe the teaspoon on his behind before offering tea, while the wife bakes bread in front of a window, so that she seems to be kneading sunlight into the dough. From the sleeping platform Chekhov is accosted by Grandpa, who argues with him about how little a human being needs to be happy, while an idiot boy makes a mooing sound in the corner of the room. The 'mooo' becomes the foghorn on the ferry as Chekhov crosses the straits to Sakhalin.

His experience on the island is represented by exemplary cases: a man who's killed his wife with a hammer and now lives in a tidy little room – with her portrait above his bed; a convict who stands in silence for hours looking at the roof of a neighbouring house – 'What is he thinking about?'; the sadistic flogging of a not necessarily guilty prisoner. It's best to handle the latter as Chekhov did, by getting out of the way. A light is left on a single chair in the middle of the stage: the executioner quietly offers the victim a glass of water (which he bites in his agony), the indifferent doctor counts out the ninety lashes like a church warden, and a medical assistant enjoys watching the punishment. Chekhov stands in dark profile to one side, as oblique as the details he notices.

For the second section he returns home to Russia – but not in the way he actually did, with a long party on the high seas interrupted by a few stabs of fatalism. I'm more interested in the odd dullness, which I certainly remember, of being suddenly back in the same dusty room after a life-changing journey across Siberia. Jump-cut into this by a lighting cue, Chekhov yanks off his great satchel and makes a final comment, with the utmost simplicity I can muster:

> God's world is good. Only one thing in it is bad. Ourselves.

Now that he's back – and I've moved him a couple of years forward, to Melikhovo – he's ready to talk to anyone, about the gooseberries he plans to grow, his apples the size of three kopeck pieces, his divine cabbage, the cherries that he's nervous to pick because he used to be beaten for it as a boy:

> The soil hereabouts is so good that if you were to plant a shaft in it,
> in a year's time a cart would grow out of it.

About fishing too, with special reference to Isaak Levitan's unusual summons – 'Are you there, crocodiles?' – the smell of hay, anything. But the burst of exuberance falters: Sakhalin has taken the bounce out of him. He's replaying his earlier bonhomie in the relative minor and seems significantly older, because of the extra energy such cheerfulness requires. In truth it seems that every pleasant thing – the moon, the quiet wood, the sharp points of his garden fence – are 'waiting for me to start dying'.

His reminiscences now fill up with vexation, then anxiety, then anger. He has too many visitors, all bringing presents, but none of them has the sense to give him new fishing-rods:

> Sometimes they bring me antique embroidery…look here, what am I to do with such things? Do they think I'm an archaeologist or something? What a shame.

To escape he heads for Moscow, but is astounded by the literary establishment, men who pointedly complain about

> mediocre writers who lose the ability to look straight at life and go running off to Siberia and Sakhalin…

Rather than hang about in the salons, he flies out of there 'like a bomb', home to his peasants. He describes a little of the country doctor's life – this includes the Astrov section with the maps – and then attacks the culture of official neglect that allows socialist agitation not just to flourish but to corrupt itself:

> Russia is an enormous plain across which wander mischievous men, convincing our people that their crass prejudices are the truth, as if some beautiful future could justify deceiving them now.

But then he apologises:

> Oh dear. I've fired off a leading article from a radical newspaper at you.

These graceful retreats are a little disappointing. But the plain fact is Chekhov is not a liberal, a conservative, an impartialist, a transitionalist or a monk. There's too little time left for all that:

> My holy of holies is the human body – health, intelligence, talent, love and the most absolute freedom imaginable – freedom from violence and lying, whatever form they may take. That's the programme I would follow if I were a great artist…

Finally he returns to 'The Black Monk', and we see that this is the end of his life. Kovrin's last encounter with the apparition, his consumptive attack and his death, are told in the first person, with the name of Kovrin's wife changed to Olga. Chekhov finishes by drinking another glass of champagne before speaking his recorded last words and shrinking into himself:

It's a very long time since I last drank champagne.

We need to lose some of this material – reluctantly, for in itself it all works well enough. The right version should emerge on the road if I try different permutations by the night. It is also important to concentrate on Chekhov's intellectual exactitude, perhaps matching it with a certain physical daintiness. As if they were watching a brain surgeon catching butterflies, what already excites audiences is his sudden, exact recall, and his readiness to modify rapture with precision. They get the feeling that he is at the top of his form tonight, just for them, giving his best. By now the text feels a little too familiar and easy. It must be more jagged or Chekhov will escape us, and I actually imagine him doing so – looking in at the back of the auditorium for a moment in his dark coat, he soon turns and slips out again.

Why is he so helpful to me? Why does he sometimes feel like my father speaking and then like me speaking to my father?

At a programme meeting for the National I boast that our first preview there will be on 2 July, the anniversary of Chekhov's demise in 1904 – so eighty years to the day, he may die the death again. It's a good joke, but Irina knows I'm cheating, as that's the Russian calendar. In the rest of Europe it was the 15th. I've developed the quaint habit of matching my diary to eighty years ago, starting with our 4 June, when Olga Knipper bought the tickets for their last train journey to Berlin and Badenweiler. My game is a countdown to the moment of Chekhov's death, a progress away from my father's, and an acknowledgment of my deadline. The comparing of dates is the sort of thing newspapers do all the time, while a daily calculation can be poignant. When my father left on a year's Fellowship for Harvard during their courtship, my mother carefully marked down the rising number of days going by and the falling number ahead – down to zero, whereafter there is silence, except that certain dates have interesting circles drawn round them.

On my birthday Chekhov, with great unreasonableness, writes to demand an agreed 4,500 roubles from Maxim Gorky for the right to publish *The Cherry Orchard* in his magazine *Knowledge*. Gorky's offer to do this was imprudent, a fairly clear breach of Chekhov's contract with his main publisher Marx, with whom Gorky had often battled on his behalf: apart from the scoop, he probably wanted to help. Marx stopped him doing it, but Gorky now sent Chekhov the 4,500 all the same. I celebrate the occasion with a rarity: laryngitis, from accumulated strain no doubt, and do *Strider* that night on a whisper, which in fact is possible. Twenty-six days to the NT opening.

The next day I entrain for Norwich while Mark and my mother make a secret birthday cake. The Premises Arts Centre is diffuse and unnerving, with a big pillar in the middle of the audience: many of them are close to me but there is a splashy echo in the acoustic for those at the back. Excuses, excuses:

actually it was a stinker, mannered and cute after a rather assured rehearsal. When it goes this badly I feel keenly the lack of an author or director to share the blame, or at least to drink with. Look, I rail at myself in a way I wouldn't if they were there, it's not enough to feel fond of Chekhov if you've nothing to say about him; he's a champion performer when he's minded to be, and what do you think you are? Screw it. In Wolverhampton I realise I'm losing the character by taking my props too much for granted: Chekhov should always handle his books appreciatively.

Home from there past midnight, I sit in my parents' kitchen with the window rattling – how many years has it not been fixed?

> What a superb night it is. I can see the little wizened tree under the window. It's bright and peaceful – not a cloud in the sky, everything quiet, not a leaf stirring…

He was very brilliant, trapped in his talent really, though he wore it as lightly as he could. I certainly couldn't measure up to him, and the effort to turn my life into a fitting contrast caused us grief at first, since eminent men, however kind, are inclined to see the world in the terms in which they have conquered it. Almost by definition, the theatre, half art and half trade, makes fun of the intellectual life: I was the grit in his oyster all right, but the question I posed was worth his answering.

When it became clear that I was going to throw myself out of paradise, his colleagues were soon surprised by his passionate and informed views on the theatre. He never accepted the hackneyed comparison between his advocating profession and mine, but in another way he understood very well what had happened to me, how one thing provokes its opposite. It was his own story. By the time I knew him, he seemed the entire English gentleman, except for a tendency to grow his hair to a point almost farouche, so that you thought he could be some kind of artist after all. In fact he was neither an artist nor English, but merchant-class Welsh, a coal agent's son. Not that he'd fought his own way out of the valleys like a Nye Bevan; he'd been pushed hard at every step by his ambitious Baptist mother, to whom he always seemed, by some quirk, to be less than grateful. As, like the young Chekhov, he dispatched his homing pigeons from his barn, he may have felt too many decisions had been taken for him. Perhaps it all involved too much bullying by his mother of his father, a mild and clerkly man of no intellectual pretension.

In fact I grew up hearing my father talk with a surprising theatricality. He remembered with sensual recall the Dickensian fog out of which the distant sound of George V's funeral hearse rattling down Kingsway towards the Aldwych had reached him. It was the most melancholy thing he had ever heard, and the smell of hay in the Suffolk barn where he slept when he was first posted in the War was the sweetest he ever smelled. Every girlfriend I ever had fell for him, and any who were too late to know him wished they hadn't been – he glittered with sexual appreciation, though he was profoundly faithful. He was generous, intolerant, inordinately gifted, a sort of left-wing Tory who was nobody's man, and I have dedicated many pieces of work to him, such as the disappointed soldier father in David Edgar's *Destiny* and the brilliant lawyer turned independent politician in Harley Granville Barker's *Waste.*

Fifth week. A batch of London schools dates – the real test of nerve, perhaps, among the bells and crashing doors. At Fulham Cross Girls', there's only an anglepoise lamp to make up by – best to do one side of the face, then move the lamp round for the other side. The young audience in the woodworking studio starts out asleep but I'm not having that, and the show is detailed and defiant. Now the boys: at City and East London College daylight pours through the windows at eleven in the morning and I turn to see a dozen heads of rasta hair, graffiti on the walls, woolly caps above young London faces to whom Chekhov will mean nothing. They get the best too, in the fighting spirit that pulls you through a tough matinee.

I learn my lessons. The trick is to buttonhole these kids, really look them in the eye – asking them one by one whether the classroom wall is worth a short story, whether they're interested in Astrov's maps, if they realise that we did in Australia what the Russians did on Sakhalin. It doesn't matter if they don't know who Chekhov was, as long as they meet an interesting man who's interested enough to treat them properly. The young streetwise faces remind me that he must never seem English Establishment: I realise that in a show which is all to do with easing gently in and out of a man's thoughts, I've developed a slightly hearty, even military manner, hammering first syllables with a most un-Chekhovian brusqueness. God knows why. At Thomas Tallis School in Blackheath, they seem very young. Anxious not to bore them, I rush the transitions a bit, become shallow, and so bore them, I suppose. At St Mary's College Twickenham I learn something else important: we need scissors in the desk draw, since the coarse string holding Astrov's portfolio of maps is capable of jamming into a tight knot as it's untied. At St Christopher's Letchworth I reach for the little paper cone during the coughing fit and knock out a contact lens: it lands bluely on the desk. I keep talking and pop it in the drawer as if it were some tiny thing of Chekhov's.

Eighty years back Anton Pavlovich goes for his last carriage ride in Moscow before leaving for Germany – where he will querulously write to Masha that he's not seen a single handsome German woman and he will be back in Yalta soon. I am becoming concerned about the boy Chekhov meets on Sakhalin, irritating him by not being able to provide his father's name for the census –

lacking a real character, he's just an all-purpose scamp. The catch is, his mother has killed the man and is here with the boy and her lover. On the train to the Plough Theatre Torrington I read Chekhov's short story 'Murder', as a sort of refresher. A young American sitting opposite asks me what I'm reading. I'd have to say Chekhov's 'Murder', and as I have an NT leaflet explain that too. We're still an hour from Torrington. So I mumble, feeling bad to be unfriendly, and he is offended. I was working, but perhaps he was in need. What would Chekhov have done?

Not a bad show if I didn't know how much better it can be.

Sixth week. Chekhov visits Berlin Zoo. In Northampton, I try some spare bits and pieces while there's time, as if still looking at materials for a suit that's nearly finished:

> In 1891 I made a European tour, during which I drank some excellent white wine and ate oysters. In 1892 I attended a birthday party with V A Tikhonov, who danced on top of a taxi, which gave nothing but general pleasure.

A Shell man, who presumably draws a fee for doing this, arrives to counsel my mother, who stares at him through her one working eye as if he had come from Mars. She has had her hair done for the first time as a widow. She is both resolute and much older, weak, smaller and undeceived. If my father had gone away for six weeks and walked through the door now, he would seem more a stranger. I feel his weight through the air and his voice as a booming whisper in each room. My mother now sleeps in the mornings as well as afternoons, and strains for hours to remember what he told her to do with any Busy Lizzies left over after their planting in pots. Her concentration is tremendous, as if she were at a seance, and she moves deeper and deeper into the past, her new home.

The last lap of dates, and the show has developed a pleasant, conversational feel – it's like an unbroken string weaving and snaking back on itself. I remember to let things happen. It is the accident of catching the medicine bag in his eyeline that gives Chekhov his idea of talking about cholera – he hasn't prepared a speech on the subject. And he coughs not exactly because he has had a painful memory from childhood, but because he stands up while he is still upset by it. Waiting to begin, I doodle a map of the Straits approaching Sakhalin, since if I can no longer see them clearly the audience won't. It turns out more like what I saw when I arrived at Nakhodka in 1975 – sparse brushland, derricks, sheds and warehouses, a cast-iron hammer and sickle; whereas Chekhov saw harbour lights, forest fires and mountains, dark figures stock-still on the dockside, those reefs like black monks. In Wigan, he is nowhere to be seen, except for a couple of moments when he puts his head round the door – to see me playing an old man instead of a prematurely sick one. I still can't decide where to put a cut into the second half.

Chekhov arrives in Badenweiler and is asked to leave his hotel because of his coughing. He is irritated by his regime, bored with 'stupid cocoa and porridge'. He writes to his mother that his health is returning not by the dram but the hundredweight, and he'll be completely well in a week. A setback at Hornchurch for me. On reflection, it's simple – the stage is rather high above the audience, and I can't see them too well. Chekhov would hate to be elevated like this, but next week at the Cottesloe, the seating rising away from him, it will be a meeting of equals.

The boy on Sakhalin is better now, but almost too late I realise that the old peasant Chekhov meets in the Siberian cottage has been neglected as well – he's just a cliché, some silly old countryman in the middle of nowhere, whereas he should be foxy, alert to being patronised by a Moscow visitor. He doesn't understand at all about the planned Trans-Siberian railway:

> It'll work by steam, I understand that. But if it has to go through the village isn't it going to knock over the houses and crush the people?

However he is sharp enough to reject Chekhov's easy assumption that human beings only need the bare necessities:

> Grandpa: A Siberian's a good man…but his life is wasting, like a mosquito, shall we say, or a fly…
>
> Chekhov: (*Now a bit tired of the conversation.*) Well, I suppose he works and eats and clothes himself. What more does a man want?
>
> Grandpa: Your honour. A human being is not a horse.

It's a rare moment – Chekhov caught out in a little condescension.

July 5. Practise the cherries – they might jump out of my hand on a Press Night, or I might swallow a stone. I still can't decide on the cut. After all these weeks. I'll see how things go and make one, or not, when the moment comes. Suddenly there's no time to think.

As the lights go down in the Cottesloe, Alison Chitty looks around at the usual suspects – the press, the NT people, the first night lot. Next to her a man has been reading in his programme my quote from Ivan Bunin's *Memoir of Chekhov*:

> It is a wintry day in the Crimea: grey, cold, with clouds settling on the river. It is quiet in Chekhov's house: only the slow ticking of an alarm clock can be heard… Chekhov sits at his desk…then he leans back and looks off into the distance; he stays like this for an hour, perhaps an hour and a half.

Alison knows that for the last twenty minutes I've been hidden in a deep chair at the back of her set, invisible because black on black. Also that I won't leave the area for Bunin's hour and a half, longer than any of them, as Chekhov will stay on through the interval, continuing to pack, surveying the comings and goings. This is not just a matter of passing the time for those who don't want a drink, but signals a little anxiety: the hour is moving on, to Siberia and towards dawn and death beyond it. The clock begins to tick, and there's a hush. Alison thinks one thing only: Why is he putting himself through this?

It's going well, though. I slow down a bit, probably with fatigue, in the second half, around Astrov's maps. To compensate, I edit on the hoof, leaving out the story about two well-dressed ladies who come to discuss the Graeco-Turkish War with Chekhov, only to be manoeuvred into a discussion about candied fruits. I also decide, just as the cue arrives, to keep in another, about a country woman who falls from a cart and with her last breath begs her husband to get the oats threshed as it's been such a good harvest. A furiously buzzing fly bothers me, as it does a section of the audience – it seems to like the smell of beard fixative. I get to the line:

It's so fiendishly dull, the very flies drop dead

and it stops. Yes indeed. The last ten minutes take the most concentration, like coming in to land:

A light breeze blew in from my window, sending my papers to the floor…

The Cottesloe is more or less a sealed room; there's been no recent movement from me, or, I'm glad to say, from the audience. But now a paper on the desk flutters to the ground. I belong to a superstitious trade, forever hoping that Godot might turn up: now I suddenly feel approved of, and not only by the public.

I last saw my father standing in his doorway, waving me off as brightly as always, before turning back inside for my mother's blessing and another gin and tonic. Nowadays my recurring dream is that, let alone visiting, I've forgotten to ring them up for a year or two: guiltily I rush for a telephone and even find the money before realising that they're gone and waking up.

He had been the only Law Double First of his university year (he could equally well have done it, with a bit of notice, in Mathematics or History), but the odd thing was that the great scholar never seemed to read a book – the shelves groaned with them while he and my mother read the newspapers. And they didn't half talk. They'd met in their third undergraduate year – in fact she was a Cambridge girl, one of two gentle daughters of Glasgow parents come south. Suddenly her diary notes, in among the 'Lunch Charleses' and the 'Coffee Toms' (and even a 'Breakfast Jim'), a 'Lunch Pennington Trinity', but a month afterwards the more mollient 'Lunch Vivian'. After the May Ball, discretion falls from empty pages for the rest of her year, while his letters to her achieve a quite surpassing daftness. In fact they're assembling a repertoire of endearments, nicknames and plain silly talk that accompanied the rest of their lives, causing me great fear on their visits to me at school. Time has shown, I am told, that without achieving his intellectual heights, I've inherited his combination of serious intent and intimate foolishness.

They were so taken up with each other that as they got older it was said, with varying degrees of bitterness, that they might not even open the door to you. My father certainly became uninterested in strangers, but to his own he was simply wonderful. As Chekhov learned about Tolstoy from his daughters' attitude, I get something about him from the fact that his sister-in-law's children were completely devoted to him for his generous interest, not to mention his skill with a cocktail. I never loved him more than when he took his courage in both hands and came to see me in an extremely rackety lunchtime show at the Kings Head pub in Islington (rackety venue too) in a cast drawn from the wilder edges of the profession, standing in his Garrick Club tie, a slightly high colour in his cheeks, the corners of his mouth dragging with tension, doing his best, which was certainly good enough.

Now the summer opens out; his favourite magnolia blooms and begins to drop, and my mother's small circle of friends gathers tightly around. A hand in his glove for over fifty years, she is already reversing the idea he loyally held to, that it would be a disaster if he died first. He once sat weeping at the kitchen table when he was convinced he had throat cancer, and what would happen to her. But then he did so a second time because he thought she was becoming so absentminded as to be ill in some way, though I suspect she was only taking a break from listening to him. His general position on mortal matters was, no doubt out of fear, bluntly aphoristic: if he kept me out of the hands of lawyers, I must promise to keep him out of the hands of 'the medics'. Well, he couldn't quite do the first, and he didn't need my help to achieve the second – the result of his nonchalance was this stroke of lightning on the motorway. For all his love, he left her too soon, to drum her fingers characteristically on the arm of her favourite chair, wondering why someone else's husband couldn't have been taken, and me to deal with a little hypochondria in the cardiac region. The truth is they should have gone together, in some moment devastating for me: they were so interested in each other, above all interested. After a lifelong conversation of such quality, a dull silence was filling the house: I decided that from now on, if it was at all possible, she would go wherever I did.

INCOMPREHENSIBLE DARING ARDOUR

> And so goodnight, friends, who understand about one's mother.
>
> – George Bernard Shaw

In their eagerness to see him on his return from Sakhalin, Chekhov's mother Evgenia and his prudent brother Misha took the Odessa train south from Moscow as far as Tula so that they could meet him, turn round and travel his last hundred miles or so home with him. Evgenia always had a little trouble with what her gifted son was up to: Chekhov once complained to a friend that she thought he wrote poetry, and, except for the one time at Yalta when the Art Theatre visited, she never cared to see his plays. Before he left for Siberia she had counselled him to take care, never to travel by horse after dark and to beware of boats – arming him for the journey with coffee and a coffee stove, which three weeks later, approaching Tomsk, he finally discovered how to use. As if he was going on a jaunt, she also asked him to bring back a fur collar in the local fashion.

What her welcoming party found at Tula was unexpectedly raffish, and the reunion may not have been exactly as a mother would have hoped. Chekhov was accompanied by two travelling companions from the East – Irakli, a Buryat monk who looked like a Red Indian, fresh from missionary work among the Sakhalin Gilyaks, and a certain Midshipman Glinka, the son of a Petersburg baroness, who had conspired with Chekhov to buy three mongooses in Colombo. The animals were now sitting up at the table with the three travellers in the station restaurant, surrounded by a curious crowd. Chekhov had christened one of them Ruffian ('he's something between a rat and a crocodile'), and, obviously feeling that such a pet was for life, continued to be unaccountably fond of it, claiming that it cried when left alone. He also kept a second, but this was eventually identified as a civet, and fell from grace by systematically biting his visitors' toes and his mother's nose. In the end Ruffian was presented to Moscow Zoo, his place at the hearth taken by the dachsunds Quinine and Bromide – much to the relief of Chekhov's father, who had denounced the animal as little better than a heathen.

Although he testified dutifully to her unbounded love for her children and theirs for her, Chekhov loses some of his precision when it comes to Evgenia; our view of her, as hers of Anton, is a little shadowy. Like her assertive husband, she came from a family of peasants turned merchants (her father, like Pavel, was bankrupted), and her adaptation to the Chekhovian world was incomplete: she was so superstitious that she once refused a pair of false teeth that her son Alexander had bought for her because he had done it on the thirteenth of the month. Little as she may have understood a success built on such a different view of life, Anton's career presumably atoned for much. Living only for her family, terrified of being thought to complain and always complaining, she spent her life under his eye, from his youthful arrival in Moscow till his death. No-one is one thing of course: religiose and prejudiced as she was, Evgenia's insights could be deadly. When she perceptively declared:

> Anton never sees anything through

she was echoing other friends who felt that Chekhov couldn't stay still anywhere for more than a moment – even if she couldn't understand that his restlessness and panic were connected with the black monk he kept expecting to meet. There does seem to be something intermittent about his tenderness towards her, even a coldness – at any rate a discretion from a man who has been candid with us about most things. Perhaps he forever associated her with the shambles of his father's bankruptcy and his premature adulthood; and though it was hardly Evgenia's fault that his tuberculosis came through her side of the family, perhaps she occasionally looked to him like the black monk as well.

Meanwhile history has not been kind to Pavel Chekhov: there he is, fixed, the burdensome despot, overbearing and self-deluded. What looks out from the pictures is certainly a face of dangerous stupidity. Anton's childhood, crippled, as he was to say, by tyranny and lies, sounds comparable only to the misery of that of Pavel himself, who as a young man had inscribed on his signet ring, 'To the lonely man, the desert is everywhere.' His self-respect abandoned in Taganrog with his debts, Pavel sways like some awkward giant through the Moscow years, idiotically issuing timetables for the family's churchgoing and domestic duties – 'Crying after punishment is forbidden' announces the 'Father of the Family', though he is by now one of its dependents. Once in Melikhovo, he takes on a slightly touching air, and his punctiliousness as a diarist, down to the itemisation of meals, happens to provide much of our knowledge of the Chekhovs' day-to-day life. Even his Bible-thumping accents gradually soften with age and country life, except at the odd moments when he is convinced he's seen Beelzebub in the night. A man without a job, looking for something to do as the dispossessed male will, he changes the house's wallpaper, reorders the rooms, supervises his much-loved clocks and consecrates anything he can lay his hands on – all the while locked into an uncomprehending relationship with the peasants around the estate, who can smell the remnants of his old-fashioned tyranny and hate him for it. This always bewilders him – what has gone wrong with the world that people won't do what they're told? He has always loved Anton in his way and understood him hardly at all, even feeling ashamed of his theatre connections. Alexander's and Kolya's dissipation, to which his sternness had contributed so much (they wet their beds almost till adulthood), makes him wretched; and he is really closest to the teacher son, Ivan. Pavel the bully turned loser, declining from self-made grocer to warehouse clerk to a foolish retirement on a pension probably paid by Anton's publisher, his last twelve years a fatuous and clumsy effort to retrench: there he goes.

A couple of months before the Moscow Art Theatre premiere of *The Seagull,* Pavel died after a bungled hernia operation, wretchedly, on a surgeon's improvised table. Chekhov, a better doctor no doubt than the one who had operated, was looking for a house in the south at the time. He received the news late, that's true; it would have taken him three days to return, also true; but the fact sits there staring at you: he didn't come back for the funeral in Moscow, which was paid for by Masha, preferring to continue his search for a new home. His last word on the event, rendered impersonal by its euphony, was that the main cog in Melikhovo's machine had slipped.

Evgenia used to refer to Pavel as 'the Authority', and Chekhov asserted that she didn't mind his death too much. She certainly expressed the view that he would have been surer of entering the Kingdom of Heaven if he had died more slowly – and therefore more painfully. This milder form of his father's religious stupidity enraged Chekhov, no doubt. With untypical vagueness, he advised her 'to do your duty…you have to be ready for anything', and soon wrote to her, in a tone infinitely open to interpretation:

> However badly your dogs and your samovar behave, winter will always be followed by spring, just as youth is followed by age, and unhappiness is always followed by happiness – and vice versa.

Evgenia survived him by fifteen years, as she did three other of her children and her husband.

As for my own mother Euphemia, Effie for short, she watched spring succeed three more winters from a deep chair by her window in St John's Wood, drumming away, a reel of memories always turning. Just as my father had been struck as he drew an ordinary breath, there were times when some recollection would impale her in the middle of a room, in the middle of a day. Then I would find her stroking and smelling a plastic mug they'd used for their picnic on their last holiday, or writing notes on a yellow pad beside her bed – things to ask him, things that had interested her. Sometimes I would be brought short too, unsure what to do for the best. I was an only child, there was hardly anyone for Mark and I to talk to, and if I made an error, like rearranging his bookcase too soon after his death, I would be dumbstruck by my inability to right the grief it caused. On that day I felt like Lopahin, letting the sound of the axes in the cherry orchard be heard before the family has left.

The Red Sea is dismal. I stared at Mount Sinai and was moved.

A year went by: I noted the anniversary but didn't remind my mother of it. *Anton Chekhov* had completed a nap hand for me, even making me a little 'hot'. *The Sunday Times* ran a piece headlined 'If This is Venice, I Can't Be a Horse or Chekhov' on my twists and turns in the NT repertoire – 'Michael Pennington seems tired…his face is colourless, he passes a hand repeatedly across his forehead and his speech is slow' – not a bad description considering I'd done the interview over the phone. My show had opened to something between a blaze of glory and a sort of deep acceptance, as if it was inherently right that there should be such a thing at last, that it should be mine, and that it would probably be there for keeps, a bit like a person's Hamlet.

I was quite unable to stop working. I conceived the idea of adapting Maupassant's *Pierre et Jean* for a radio serialisation, had it accepted, and started timing out the episodes. At least it wasn't Chekhov, I told myself, forgetting that Maupassant was one of his favourites. Meryl Streep then cast an eye over me as her next leading man, before – at length – dropping me, over a most discomforting lunch at that discreet table round the corner at the Caprice. On the same day the BBC offered to do a television documentary on me for the arts programme *Omnibus*, all about my Russian 'obsession', my Trans-Siberian wanderings, my 'thing' about Chekhov: sometimes our profession feels like the Big Dipper.

Pennington's Chekhov was well-intentioned but made my toes curl. By happy chance Lucien Stryk was in London, and so it was agreed that we would re-enact our original meeting on the Yokohama-Nakhodka boat, going to and fro on a cross-channel ferry sweetened by a good lunch in Boulogne, which we managed despite the fact that, in homage to Chekhov's transit difficulties, I'd forgotten my passport. We then went to Peterborough to join the Nene Valley Railway, which is what you must do for any filming involving old locomotives: punctuated by close-ups of hissing steam and turning wheels, we jabbed our fingers at each other in reanimated conversation. Finally, back in London, I repaired to the Athenaeum, where amid billowing lace curtains I looked seriously out of the window, drank tea ('in the Moscow manner – nine glasses straight off'), and generally tried to explain 'my life with Chekhov'.

Lucien spoke with humour and elegance, much better than I did, while a gloomy piano plonked away, and Humphrey Burton, fronting the programme, adopted hushed tones while referring to me mostly by my surname. It was excruciating, fortunately going out late at night unobserved by my more rumbustious friends, and I blame myself for not being able to control the phoney lyricism of the thing. Perhaps I shouldn't complain, since those were the days when television might still respond to an arts idea like this: nowadays I'd have to beg for a mention. My mother regarded all the gauzey drapes, soft focus and brooding voice-over as good publicity. I'm not at all sure what my father would have thought.

The 1985 Jerusalem Festival was *Anton Chekhov*'s first overseas date, and we made a strange little package of four. Mark got a break and stayed home, but my mother came with Fionnuala, a friend whom she trusted to take care of her, and I had Irina Brown once again to help me – her aunt Leda lived at the centre of a small Russian enclave in Rehovot, just south of Tel Aviv. Leda, also widowed, would make a good shot at bonding commiseratively with my mother, but Effie would have none of it: no, she was one of the Chekhov team, and she was going to go sightseeing, to the Wailing Wall, the Dome of the Rock and the El'Aqsa Mosque and everything; and while I was rehearsing she'd sit by the pool.

Her diary entries had always been of a quite Chekhovian terseness. In 1936, as the local press trumpeted 'A Cambridge Romance', she notes: '4th Sept: Hair 9.45, Teeth 12:15. 5th Sept: Get Married'. The year of my conception is the one diary missing in sixty years, as if in an excess of discretion, but the next year I find: '7th June: Michael arrived 6:15. 9th June: Indigestion. 10th June: Feel better.' However the widow is now positively expansive, curiosity and apprehension arcing together:

> Interesting & entertaining – Israelis very thorough re our motives for the journey... Lovely reception for us all. Fionnuala brought apricots and a peach – delicious – & sat with me for a while, which was nice. Mike visited the theatre which he liked very much.

Well, I *quite* like the Khan Theatre: incomplete props, the dressing-room a thoroughfare, flashlights throughout rehearsals, the impossibility of silence. But the encounters are rich enough, as they can be at Festivals – on my way out of a radio interview I meet Dizzy Gillespie going in. My lighting designer Yankele is a man who lost a leg when he was a deep-sea diver, welding pipes: it happened just before the Six Day War, so he couldn't fight, and he watched his closest friends go out, and every one of them died, 'only God knows why'. Only God knows why he is divorcing his third wife either, he says: his bachelor flat is like a bohemian Parisian apartment of a generation ago, with someone unremarked sleeping on a shelf. Yankele is highly skilled but short of equipment, lacking the means to do business with Strand Electric for the newest lamps – rampant inflation is making the shekel a hard currency to take seriously. He certainly has no computers, which will make the show's final lighting cue – a very slow cross-fade as the black monk returns – specially difficult. It involves bringing one circuit imperceptibly down over a minute and a half, while another lifts for fifty seconds within that time: it will be like stomach-rubbing and head-patting in two different tempos. Irina watches spellbound while Yankele, one hand on each fader, delicately executes the cue without ever taking his eyes from the stage so that he can monitor the effect. I'm not altogether surprised – as he shinned one-legged up ladders to focus, he expressed what he was after in a manner his English equivalents tend not to: 'A dawn coming, not a welcome one, but a kind of awakening to death.'

A long ride on the day off to Masada, where a thousand Zealots defied their Roman conquerors by killing each other. Our host is Avital, an affable lawyer who compares Arabs to the animals at the side of the road. It is less a conversation than a promotion. To him the use of the word Palestinian in PLO is a joke – pure mythmaking, there is no such concept. Some things are not pejorative, just facts: one is that there is no question of trusting an Arab. Hearing a demurring silence, he explains patiently that Islam requires that they be scrupulously honest with each other but are entitled to pull any trick on an infidel, so if an Arab cheats a Jew he is immediately baled out by the firm. In his polarising scorn he ignores the proverbial corollary that he has the same prerogative to cheat his persecutor if he can.

Herman Melville said that it's hard to breathe the air over Jerusalem, so saturated is it with prayers and dreams. As we drive home through a gorge Avital lightly points out that it is impossible for two sides to share the land when these cliffs positively demand to be graced by snipers: he also wants to take us along the Hebron Road, presumably to see how bulldozers have curtailed Arab life in the West Bank. As we wind up hairpin bends past burnt-out tanks towards the city, it seems stony and ramshackle, the buildings dusty outcrops in a dull grey forest. I hear panic in Avi's insistence that the Arabs will only negotiate when it suits them, and it's nothing to do with wanting peace. To understand him, you perhaps have to come to this narrow strip of promised land perched between the sea and the critical mass of Islam: I think he feels as if he's permanently at the front of the terraces at an overattended football match – and it's a home fixture. Blocking out his logic, I recall the kibbutznik Jacob we met working in a new centre that helps young Arabs and

Jews forget the past, and remember that the Haifa Theatre is preparing a production of *Waiting for Godot* half in Arabic and half in Hebrew. Do we realise, says Avital, his volume rising again, that Arabs don't even have a 'p' sound in their language, and have to say 'Bolice' and 'Beyot' – whereas the Jews are linguists and communicators who respect a contract?

He turns triumphantly to me. Is all this what we're finding? He bets we expected to find a lot of idiots running around in the desert. No, I say (wondering briefly why any Arab would want to pronounce the word *peyot*, which is the side-lock of the Orthodox Jew), it is as I thought it would be – a skilful and sophisticated commercial culture in a tourist paradise. And circumstances have prevented us from getting much of the Arab point of view. The advocate in Avital seems to like this, but I think he is disappointed that he hasn't shocked us.

> Have you noticed when something is wrong within us we always search for reasons outside? We say the Jesuits are to blame, or the freemasons, we say the Jews are behind it.

Alexei Suvorin was given to anti-Semitic outbursts, but Chekhov remained his friend until *Three Sisters*, travelling with him and corresponding several times a week. He disliked Suvorin's prejudices, but a certain jocular pre-Holocaust anti-Semitism was part of his own repertoire. Potapenko's punishment for abandoning Lika was to be called 'a yid and a swine'; asking a Jew for a loan was as hopeless as defending oneself from gossip; critics were 'Jews who don't understand Russian'; and he teased Olga Knipper for looking like a Jewish dentist. In fact, as his biographer Donald Rayfield has said, Chekhov exemplified the type of southern Russian who liked Jews somewhat as they liked women: they were only just Russians, and never geniuses, but their rights had to be defended. He accordingly championed Jewish schoolfriends and had two detectable Jewish romances; Levitan was 'a Jew who's worth five Russians'; and the innkeeper Moses and his wife in 'The Steppe' affectionately re-create the couple who nursed him when he caught pneumonia in a Cossack village as a boy. Closing his case at the end of his life, he also offered his great fellow-writer Shalom Aleichem carte blanche to use anything he'd written as a fund-raising piece for the victims of the infamous Kishenev pogrom.

In other words Chekhov's record was not bad for the times – times blemished by such day-to-day outrages as police purges, the exclusion of Jews from the legal profession and the fact that they had to convert to marry Orthodox Russians – as Ivanov's wife has done, only to be cut off both from her family and her husband's affections. Overall he looks not unlike Dickens, who created Fagin and was then shamed into eliminating his Jewishness in a later edition. When focused, the Russian shows a prophetic touch:

> There's been a great fuss about Captain Dreyfus – it's a messy kettle of fish, fuelled by anti-Semitism, a thing which reeks of the slaughterhouse...

This notorious business may have been what flushed Chekhov out rather as the Sakhalin experience had. Sitting in the Pension Russe in Nice in 1898, reading Emile Zola's passionate defence of the Jewish Dreyfus – wrongly imprisoned for espionage instead of the gentile Esterhazy – he was spurred to furious admiration. He was specially appalled at the propaganda claim that Zola was being paid for his favours:

> When the French start talking about a Jewish syndicate behind him they feel a worm chewing away inside them and they need a bogeyman...

I've planned to insert a longish section about the Dreyfus Affair for the Jerusalem performance of *Anton Chekhov*, before the President of Israel: I've had to drop some favourite bits to make space, but it feels right. The show, and I suppose the insertion, is enjoyed – nobody comments much about the latter, and when I hopefully mention it at the party, everyone shrugs in a cosmopolitan way – very much as French friends will do later when I play Henry V in Paris and ask them about Shakespeare's treatment of the enemy. That indifferent cheerfulness: civilians don't care that much what the theatre says. In any case, I'm not pleased with myself tonight, realising that on this first overseas date I have fallen into a trap – uncertain of my points of reference, I busily Explained the Exotic Figure of Chekhov rather than letting him speak for himself. How stupid, but Jack Garfein, co-founder of the West Coast Actors Studio, has come round and invited me to bring the show to the States. In bed I think sourly of a recent row I've had with the National Theatre over £25 worth of salary, and go to sleep thinking both about President Herzog and the man who directed Ben Gazzara and married Carroll Baker – both of them entertained tonight by my own invention.

Between this summer and the next, like a parsimonious cook boiling every part of the pig, I tried to get a film version written and financed. I could see how to do it: Chekhov eye to eye with the camera as with the audience, the locations called up by what he says, his painterly words realising the field of rye, the streets of Petersburg, Siberia. Eventually, as if it were the house on the hill in *Psycho* without the frights, the camera would leave him in his home, creeping away as the lights blazed. The effort may have been a bit half-hearted, and the response of producers certainly was, though counterweighed with many professions of respect. The stage show was then briefly discussed for New York, but on condition I gave it a snappier title and told more theatrical anecdotes; and I did a heavily abridged radio version for the BBC World Service, that undersung station with its audience of tens of millions.

I also continued to indulge Chekhov's passion for travel. These were the days when the British Council could still promote overseas tours, before Margaret Thatcher tightened her grip on it – not that she was against cultural imperialism, but she wouldn't want to help anyone to enjoy what she didn't. *Anton Chekhov* stood at the ready, weighing in at seventy-two pounds in a trunk, but, if the clients could provide that bit more equipment at their end, forty-two in two suitcases. Lighting plots were dispatched weekly, and my wig stood on its block in the bedroom as if I were a Victorian actor-manager waiting for the call. Sometimes the dates would have intrigued Chekhov – Sydney, Brazil, Madrid, Valencia: others, like Istanbul and Ankara, he might have specially appreciated, since he peered across the Black Sea towards them for large parts of his life. Between the more exotic destinations I instinctively alighted on some English dates and ignored others: also – and we all do this sort of thing sometimes, for some less than perfect reason – I accepted and then cancelled a few, with the result that there was a serious falling-out with my booker and I was threatened with legal action by Hemel Hempstead. Many Sundays I found myself in some English town, spinning away. At Tatton Park in Cheshire, I resolved to enter through the audience, which involved hiding behind the not specially stout front-of-house manager until the customers were all in, then taking a fifty-yard walk to the platform. I did it, and then dried stone dead on the first line. The audience stamped at the end, perhaps against the cold, perhaps not; the short-sighted Chairman of Cheshire County Council especially liked Chekhov's red tie (actually a handkerchief) – he didn't know Chekhov was Labour. I played a disused grain mill at Wells Next the Sea, sponsored by Holiday Homes. At the Cheltenham Festival, Chekhov appeared inconveniently on an unlit lecture platform but I was rewarded by a long discussion afterwards with Michael Foot. Less cheery was Bognor Regis, where instead of my oil lamp and pedestal desk I found only a wilting aspidistra and a lectern, so that I concur with King George V. Arriving at such dates was like driving into some rolling metaphysical fog – where's the theatre, nowhere for a cup of tea, a gloomy Sunday with the age of miracles definitely passed – but by the evening I seemed to have been there for weeks and would be reproved by the eagerness of the audience. However, at the theatre at Hereford, where my father went to school, everyone had gone home for the weekend. Trying to open a closed theatre for an evening with a Russian writer with a car full of props is a fair recipe for mania: I played, but to too few people and an apology from the local press. However, you never know who'll be in: astonishingly, Roger Rees turned up from New York, raised a glass to the play's restrained showmanship, and we drank to our mutual RSC past.

The animal still hadn't been cooked quite enough: I hankered after a fuller radio treatment. One way would simply be to adapt the stage show; but I was frustrated at how much material I'd had to leave out even of that, especially from Chekhov's journey to Sakhalin – not so much once he got there, but from his encounters on the Siberian road, the moments in fact when I had crossed his path in 1975. There are small narratives of surpassing tenderness here as well as scathing observation, and some insights into the man that intrigued me greatly: the more you look at it, the more mind-boggling the journey was, and I wasn't sure the stage show quite did justice to it. If I could assemble a whole programme from this material, Jane Morgan, a great radio director, promised to set up *Chekhov in Siberia* for me, at ninety minutes on Radio Three.

> Why is Michael Pennington being invited at this particular time? After all, wasn't he already here for the Jerusalem Festival?
>
> – The *Ma'ariv* newspaper, Tel Aviv, November 1985

It's as if I were trespassing. David Hare, researching his *Via Dolorosa* twelve years later, was often met with infuriated bewilderment: 'But what are you *doing* here?' – as if there are places where good intentions and curiosity are dangerous. Back in the Holy Land, I'm again just doing the job I've been asked to do; though since last week was Belfast, I also feel like some linen-suited correspondent hopping from one trouble spot to another. Flying into Ulster, I woke from a doze sure that the pilot had just said something about 'exceptional bravery'. Had it been Dublin, my hand-luggage – Russian teaglass, small paper cones, a sound tape, a sealed cardboard wig-box and surgical spirit in a plastic bottle – might have provoked some cheery banter about Micheál MacLiammóir; but here the box was opened and Chekhov's hair briefly caressed by two beefy hands: the officer flushed as if caught out in a small indecency, and eagerly re-sealed it. My day in the Province turned out quite loyalist, more like twenty-four hours in Shaftesbury Avenue – mostly spent with Jonathan Miller, there to lecture, inveighing against the National Theatre and inviting me to join his new company (I haven't heard from him yet); and Kenneth Branagh, who passed in a crowd in those days. He was back in his home town to enjoy the gossip – not least the fact that in the Arts Theatre's week I was in a programming sequence that went Bertice Reading/ the Vicious Boys/*Anton Chekhov*.

And now Tel Aviv, to play the Cameri Theatre. My mother has gone to stay with friends and Mark is here to stage manage – so far he seems very silent. By way of welcome, Zemach, our producer, who looks like a lecherous hoodlum, arrives for breakfast, depressed at having had to cancel one performance already, at Kfar Saba ('Village of the Grandfathers'), for lack of interest, he announces bluntly. Now we have four performances only and two days off, which is anathema to him. He boasts resentfully that he has just toured Geraldine McEwan's Jane Austen show and Ian McKellen's Shakespeare (did he use that trick I showed him?), both to 'fantastic success'. A fantastic success too was Timothy West in *The Homecoming*. Courteously supporting his new protegé, the Cameri's Uri Ofer demurs a bit at this. Rather wishing Jonathan Miller were here, I detach, as one must, and, thinking of my mother's garden, see from the high window Tel Aviv's arteries of pizzerias, piscinas and snack bars snaking down to the beach:

> We sat staring at the table. The wick of the candle was crusted with soot. The rain beat on the windows and I was thinking again of home. In Russia it's May now, and the forests are green, and the lilac and acacia are in bloom. But it seems to me that there too the wick of the candle is crusted with soot...

The Cameri stage is enormous: I'm in among the silver birches of *Wild Honey*, Michael Frayn's adaptation of *Platonov* – which is odd, since it was this play, with the same sort of set, next door at the Lyttelton last year. Stacked in a remote corner, the furniture they've found for me looks good, but there's no-one around to set up. We have two hours only to get the show ready, having been let in an hour late; but by the sustaining logic of our profession, Brian ('Basher') Harris, a fine lighting designer whom I've known since 1964 at the RSC, is here doing *Wild Honey*: with the collusive air of a compatriot earning an export dollar, he takes care of my liaison, which essentially means shouting at anyone who shouts.

What am I doing here? Part of every hour, as if in a wave of flu, I feel undefended and unbefriended: I might as well be looking at crashed carriages on the Siberian highway. The only validation apart from Basher is the courteous attention of Saul Hyman from the British Council, who at least knows how to talk to a visitor, and is suggesting companionably that I work up a show about Byron and Shelley for him next summer. He is a seagull fluttering in the airless rooms of his organisation, and I wonder how long he will last.

> The best cure for melancholia is work. You have to sit at your desk and
> force yourself at all costs to concentrate on a single idea...

It's not just that I want to use all my research, but I'm nostalgic for a certain
kind of company. At some sort of three-way junction, I sit in Israel, thinking
of Chekhov far from home in Siberia, and also of myself aping his journey in
1975. For some hundred days, Chekhov saw golden tones in the dawn sky and
heard the heathcocks calling, watched flames eating up the grass and birch
trees covered with hoar-frost like powdered sugar; while a week staring through
an icy train window at rolling blue shadows left me with a fondness for the
suspense of daybreak: streetlights giving way to sunrise, empty factories lit
from within like Halloween pumpkins, half-asleep suburbs. Chekhov
complained that six thousand miles from home he felt overcome by apathy;
but it was more likely the neutrality of a cleared mind, on which every image
was leaving an equal mark but none made the blood run like a familiar face
or a good joke or an idea for a story. Feeling blank and uneasy now on these
car rides, in these empty theatres and hotel rooms, I guess that this is the
right place to prepare my pig's last boiling, on Radio Three.

Diffidently introducing himself as usual, Chekhov will take a new tack:
disgusted at a life of 'idleness and fornication', he has equipped himself with
a sheepskin coat, a knife to cut sausage with and keep the tigers at bay, and a
small flask of cognac to be opened on the shores of the Pacific. This is good
radio – you can follow him on the map (as Pavel anxiously did on a wall
chart at home) by train to Yaroslavl, on the Volga riverboat to Perm and
onwards by overnight train across the Urals to Ekaterinburg and into Siberia
proper. A year later the first tracks of the Trans-Siberian would be laid, but
then the railway stopped at Tyumen; thereafter Chekhov negotiated the rutted
mud roads, the fleas, cold and wetness in a springless carriage, bouncing
along on an improvised straw floor over his luggage, which must have efficiently
passed on the energy of the wheels beneath him.

The diversity of his correspondence en route is interesting: he writes a
batch of articles for Suvorin's *New Times*, keeps a diary, but also sends letters
to his family, different ones to individual members. So the same events are
variously described, as if he were practising for some definitive version,
metaphors mushrooming speculatively. At first, unsure of whether he is up to
it all, he falls back on Chekhovian mannerism. His soul is like jelly, he says,
neither cheerful nor bored; the Volga riverboat whistles with a sound halfway
between an ass's bray and a celestial harp; the occupation of the local people
seems to be the manufacture of clouds, and so many of them warn him about
Kozulka ahead that he dreams that it is a bird with a long beak and green

eyes. Here and there he finds his stride, as if falling into step with some unnerving stranger: the Volga barges pulled by their tugs suggest

> a stylish young intellectual being pursued by his fat wife, his mother, his sister-in-law and his grandmother – they have him by the coat-tails.

At Ekaterinburg, still straining a little for his similes, he notes a river the colour of coffee grounds: the terrifying people have big bones, huge fists and little eyes, and he expects the waiters to murder him. At the end of the railway line, he crosses the Tom River (inhabited only by toads and the souls of murderers, he mutters), in the company of a ferryman who groans like a pigeon. He is happy to be back on land:

> It's good to be a coward; it takes so little to cheer you up again.

Beneath the warmth of the household which shelters Chekhov after his carriage-crash, an incident already covered in the show, lies a darker story which isn't. A cradle hangs between the bed and the stove with a baby crying in it. This is little Sasha, whose mother has left him with Chekhov's hosts and gone back to her husband in Sretensk, promising to return in a week. The childless foster-parents love looking after Sasha, becoming closer and closer to him as two months go by and there's no sign of the woman's return. They don't know if he is theirs now: they don't know the mother's name or where to write to her. The wife gives the baby a piece of bread tied in a rag to suck as she tells Chekhov this story, breaking off as her face reddens and she begins to cry. The husband looks at Chekhov shiftily. He feels the same but can't allow himself to show it. How will this story finish? Nobody knows: Chekhov has moved on.

The traveller continues in his 'wicker basket' to Tomsk, where he is taken up by the chief of police, who threatens to read him a play he's written but instead gives him a nugget of gold and accompanies him to the brothels. Relieved to be gone, Chekhov moves forward in a new carriage, 'looking down on God's earth like a baby', past ice-covered lakes, a bitter wind pricking his cheeks. He always loved the sound of the bittern, and now he imagines its strange bass tone as speech, puncturing his solitude:

> 'Don't be afraid. I come from the River Psyol: Levitan sent me.'

For all their vivid beauty, the days pass by as in a lingering illness; he becomes sick of the stars in the sky and the silence as of the grave. In these shifts, sudden but completely coherent, lies much of the character I've come to love – this level-headed man who will suddenly abandon all proportion, who hugs misery as tightly as its alleviation, an ironic stoic who so dreads the happiness of a full-time wife that he welcomes endless lonely spectres. On he goes towards Krasnoyarsk and Irkutsk, according to his complex and confidential nature:

> My socks blow their noses. The inside of my felt boots feel like a water closet. All that keeps me going is some incomprehensible daring ardour...

A great reception at the Cameri – over a thousand people, the biggest house the show has ever played. It's set me alight: in fact, I don't quite know who was at the wheel, though thinking about this fresh Siberian material has certainly brought me close to my subject again. Now that he's seen this, Zemach has warmed up – he's going to make some money after all. I sit on the balcony of the hotel like Chekhov in Nice, watching the foreign city go by, swishing my cocktail of curiosity and homesickness. Chekhov was struck by his exhausted chambermaid at the Pension Russe who nevertheless 'smiled, smiled like a stage duchess'; with me it's the waitress in the breakfast room, closely followed by the large daughter of some British Council type at last night's reception. Chekhov's occasional ideal was 'to be completely idle and love a fat girl'; he'd have approved of them both.

I left him just near Krasnoyarsk. The rivers in Siberia travel south–north, so he had to keep crossing them. His timing was bad: the ice had just thawed and many were impassable – nevertheless it was the coldest spring Siberians could remember. How he wished he'd brought something soft to rest his head on instead of this wooden trunk: but he is now so used to the jolting that if ever he finds himself on a smooth dry stretch of road he becomes bored and depressed. All the time he pays more than he needs to, does what he didn't mean to, doesn't say what he should have done and expects what doesn't happen. There's nothing to eat on the road but bread and garlic. He notices that if you call out, Siberians call it 'roaring', so that the bear, the sparrows and the mice all roar. His occasional travelling companions are coarse: he decides you should always go solo, alone in a carriage with your thoughts. The brothels (except for one – Japanese-themed – in Blagoveshchensk) are more than usually depressing.

> Heaven only knows where the Siberian plain ends... Wild ducks take wing from my carriage wheels and fly lazily off into the birch trees: never before have I seen such a multitude of ducks...

Now he watches thirty convicts in a procession, their irons clattering. How insignificant their crimes seem suddenly, and how small their sufferings compared with the forest, in which each man's death is like the death of a gnat. He meets a group of migrating peasants. One with a blond beard has

> an irony in him, but directed inwards as if playing over his own soul.
> It couldn't be worse, he says, smiling with his upper lip only.

But it will be worse, says his brother Misha, a frail man travelling with two violins wrapped in cloth, one under each arm. Misha is useless for anything but fiddle-playing, but like one of Turgenev's singers, he is a master at that, fiddling in the taverns, in the fields and at weddings. The two men have abandoned their home and they're off to Siberia, hoping for a better life – but Misha is frail and will surely die of the cold. His fiddles will be sold to a convict for twenty kopecks, children will tear off their strings and break the bridges, and water will pour into them.

> Oh, go back, Uncle Misha…

Chekhov calls, as they recede behind him.

When Alec McCowen toured his solo show *The Gospel According to St Mark*, he would wander round the theatre all afternoon, just looking for someone to talk to. But I have my son, warming to his task now and able to set up alone even here, attending to details well beyond the call of duty. At the Weizmann Institute at Rehovot he organises every slight fold of our dustsheets as if painting a canvas, observing how the light touches them, bothering me for confirmation only rarely. He has been thoroughly befriended by Gadi, the local stage manager, and can now operate a dimmer board as well. It's lovely: I stretch out in the auditorium, counting my blessings. Gadi has a polio leg: like Yankele, he shows a mix of finesse and bloody muscle all the more for his handicap. However, there are no extending ladders here: you aim the lights by lowering their flying bars to the floor, guessing at an angle and then hoisting them back up till the height is more or less right for what you've guessed. As usual, we transform nothing into something in nothing flat. Rather to my surprise, five hundred people here want to see what Chekhov might have been like: we gather around a small flame, as at Lyubimov's *tagan* in a cold room. The show works well. In general, an audience can enjoy two opposite things: secure if they sense the actor is confidently in charge of what he is doing, they will come to the edge of their seats if he can trick them into thinking he isn't. Their encounter with Chekhov, with its possibilities for embarrassment or stalling, suits the latter well: there is more danger than reassurance tonight, as if the whole thing could break down. For some no doubt other reason, when Chekhov realises near the end that 'every hour is precious' there is quite a loud rueful laugh.

A trip to the Sea of Galilee and Zefat, near the Lebanese border, the Golan Heights to the east. Snipers often have a go at the road through these green trees. The mountains are like crumpled brown wrapping-paper. The sun sets a deep mauve, glowering over the country's agonies, yellow, white and red in it too. I hope I can describe it well to my mother, this effect of blazing oil colours gradually bleaching out. I hear a familiar voice:

> Sometimes, you know, clouds huddle in disorder on the horizon, and the sun behind them colours the sky with every imaginable shade: crimson, orange, gold, violet, pink... The sunset glistens on a church cross or the windows of a manor house – it's reflected in the rivers and it quivers on the trees. Far away, a flock of wild ducks flies homewards...

That's how it's done.

Arriving in Haifa mid-afternoon, we're firmly refused entry to the theatre by an aggressive girl at the stage door, who knows nothing of us and isn't about to hear us out. Rehearsals will finish on stage at six, she snaps, and then we'll see. But we've been promised we can set up at four-thirty, as we need to. Impossible. Well then, can we make a phone call? No, the lines are very busy in the service of the theatre. As Saul Hyman and she slug it out, having at least the satisfaction of a little creative abuse, I remember Chekhov in the fields between nowhere and nowhere, listening to the drivers cursing each other, eclipsed, his heartbeat tiny:

> There I stood before dawn in the open fields, looking at the flames eating up the grass and my smashed bags and the horses in a black mass on the ground, and I felt as if I was in another world and that soon I'd be trampled to bits. You can't imagine how desolate it was.

Once the rush of blood has receded, it's easy to see what's happened. The Cameri, who are responsible for the whole tour, have booked us in for the night but forgotten to follow up. Once we're in, the company manager is routinely rude, but he lets us drink coffee for an hour and a half and secures a dressing-room of some sort with a shattered bulb in the single socket by the mirror – no Basher here. Here it comes again, the soloist's great *cafard*: no-one knew we were coming, just like Hereford. I'm very nervous. When Saul writes a letter of complaint to the theatre management later, he is at pains to point out that the girl at the door was wearing leather trousers.

Our flight home to London has been delayed. *Chekhov in Siberia* has to be ready for the BBC when I get back, and during the long wait I again drift between Tel Aviv and Siberia then and now. The highlight of Chekhov's journey was in the middle, as it was for me, and that should be the centre of the new show as well: Irkutsk, perched on the shores of Lake Baikal, best and most beautiful of all Siberian towns.

Lake Baikal, by far the world's biggest freshwater resource, is a world to itself. There is a breed of sturgeon in its depths that can live up to three hundred years, but also the *golomyanka* fish, no more than a backbone surrounded by fat – if brought to the surface it bursts in the sunlight and melts away. As befits his massive reservoir, it is said that Father Baikal had three hundred sons and one wayward daughter, constantly trying to flee into the arms of her lover the Yenisei. Her father pursued her with a hail of stones, one of which became the Shaman's Rock, which the bear-worshipping tribes used for human sacrifice, somewhat like Rome's Tarpeian Rock. This daughter grew up to be the crystal-clear Angara, queen of all Siberian rivers, where a small coin could be seen thirty feet below; by the time I arrived she was maintaining such a hydroelectric rush that she could only ever freeze from the waterbed upwards. As I crossed the Yenisei river, it too was jammed with dams. When Chekhov stood on its banks in 1890 he saw it, in contrast to the pellucid Angara, as a fierce and mighty warrior unaware of its own strength. Like Vershinin thinking of a better future, he dreamed that one day such energy might be transformed into a great audacity for the Russian people, rather than into the exquisitely-dressed pessimism engendered by the Volga. To him, at the beginning of summer, the approach to Irkutsk was like going from prose into sheer poetry. He felt indescribably contented, and even his haemorrhoids 'modestly withdrew'.

I was there later in the year, towards the time when you can buy milk in the market in solid blocks, but I concur. In 1975, untouched by the ills of post-perestroika Russia, you could still sense Irkutsk's old, liberal spirit. This, for instance, is where the Decembrists ended up in 1825, that cell of liberal officers who, 'between the claret and the champagne', had attempted to force a Constitution on Tsar Nicholas I. Specifically, they wanted Constantine, the Tsar's brother, to be allowed to succeed, even though his intention to divorce his wife disqualified him. But the cry 'Constantine and Constitution' that rang out in Senate Square that day was misunderstood by most people, who thought *constitutsya* was the name of Constantine's wife. All the rebels really provoked was the beginning of censorship and a retaliatory police force, but the common cause briefly linked the people and the highborn. The Decembrists were feted and garlanded in all the villages on their way to Siberia, partly perhaps because of the quixotic element in their coup d'état. So quixotic, in fact, that its leader, Prince Trubetskoy, failed to turn up on the day, but was banished anyway. Like many others, he was followed here by his wife: in the churchyard of the Znamensky Monastery by the Angara I saw her grave, which, by an odd union of ideas, stands close to that of the fur trader Grigori Shelekhov, who established Russia's first colony in Alaska.

These aristocrats were better colonisers than revolutionaries – Pushkin, who invented the claret and champagne tag, obviously repented and dedicated a poem to them:

> Have faith;
> The wakeful sky foretells a day of wonder
> Russia arising from her ancient sleep.

Though he didn't say, Chekhov knew the fate of these men well enough – from a time when his grandfather was preparing to buy his freedom – and of their achievements as the schoolteachers and agricultural scientists of the new Siberia. He must have wondered how their story compared with the colonisation of Sakhalin, looming ahead of him, where the same hopes were invested in murderers.

Resting for a moment, the long-distance traveller feels master of all he surveys while feebly longing for home. Chekhov went to the bath-house, and the colour of the suds coming off him made him think he was a horse being scrubbed down; he strolled past a theatre, a museum, a park with a band playing. His interest surging, he wired his family in Moscow, asking them to put money together to send him a telegram with even their smallest news. He specially wanted to know if his mother's leg was all right and whether Misha had fallen in love yet. He urged them to say a Mass for Nikolai and not to forget his father's birthday (some chance, I should say). He thought of women at home who had never much interested him when he was there, even Lika Mizinova, whom he normally nicknamed 'Jamais': the King of the Medes worried that she might be inclining her ear to the notorious Levitan. Considering the conquests he might make in Irkutsk, he complained that Siberian women were 'chamberpots', hard to the touch and

> so fish-cold you'd have to be a walrus or a seal to make love to them.

All this from a quiet hotel where he stayed for a week, 're-learning what sleep means', that happened to include my future birthday.

By 1975 this hotel was a grocery where, without knowing its significance, I bought vodka before going to the circus. It was the anniversary of the 1917 Revolution. For once the shop was packed with a surplus: cognac and vodka, just those two items, just the one brand of course, rows and rows of it, for the holiday. The streets were surprisingly empty, as the tradition was to visit your relations on such a day before hitting the town in the evening. Still startled by solid ground, I felt I was having a private view of this monumental, makeshift city, of its *izbas*, spires, its shaded parks and Polish church; as if I'd abandoned holy orders, I strode through the streets imagining I could penetrate all secrets. I thought of a girlfriend in England who no longer saw herself as such – I knew that, but still needed her as a destination, for lyrical reasons only. I conjured up Mark, then nine, and wondered what was happening at that moment – was he sitting or running, was there a football at his feet? The circus in the evening was packed, even if the band had to start the applause for the ballet acts. A bear once laid a cable through swamp in the taiga, it's said, during the building of the Irkutsk–Bratsk highway; now, his descendants stare back from the centre of the circus ring, mocked and humiliated, surrounded by a parliament of doves, bears, hippos and monkeys.

Back on the train heading for Moscow, I again watch the endless taiga, and hear Chekhov's voice wondering what mysteries it holds. Only the migrant birds know its limits and what lies beyond it; men on sleighs drawn by reindeer enter it, but who knows where they come from? And as for destroying it, you might as well try to burn down the sea:

> A path winds stealthily through the trees and vanishes. Where to?
> Another secret? A village nobody knows of, not even the police?

I want to step into it and walk, perhaps in the summer, when the birches are covered with leaves – to cross the Bratsk dam, drive across Baikal in winter, breathing the clean sharp brilliant air. Instead I sweep through – somewhat in the manner of the Tsarevich Nicholas, who by coincidence was comfortably touring Siberia at much the same time as Chekhov, surrounded by an idiotic suite of Guards officers. Hailed as a 'genius of peace and mercy', he seems to have noted little except the weather, the distances and the company at table. I hear Chekhov's ringing voice again:

> Have you noticed how well-fed people have this habit of lecturing the hungry? Those that seem more stupid and filthy than them they call the people. But we are all the people, and the best we are doing is the people's work. The real dregs of our society can be found in the Pullman cars.

He moves on in the other direction, into the Russian Far East, and recedes into the distance, his voice fading to ominous silence. Everything he has said has implied its opposite:

> Allah kerim, what bread I've eaten, what tea I've drunk, what thoughts I've thought... Thank God I've had the strength to make this journey.

> I've lived through so much, it's all so new and interesting to me, not
> as a writer but as a human being. Wonderful! I'm in the fresh air all
> the time, I've seen the sun rise and set every day...

But I also know that he spent much of the time in a dream of going home to
Taganrog and starting a library there. The simplest longings wouldn't let
him be:

> I fell asleep for a time and dreamed of my own bed in my own room:
> I dreamed I was sitting at my own table and telling my friends how I
> was nearly killed by a carriage on the Siberian highway.

You that way; we this way. Looking westwards, I beam at Lucien as we ease
away from Angarsk station. He is writing to his wife in Chicago, and I am on
my way to Mark. I miss my creaking floorboard at home, the split wallpaper,
the uneven stair; but I also feel the beginning of nostalgia for a place that
isn't mine, Siberia, where I have no business. I start on a song for him, such
as I did in those days:

> Six thousand miles is not too far
> To hurry home to you
> By crystal light beneath one star
> It seems
> I haul across the world
> These dreams...

but then, for fear of embarrassment, write him a postcard instead, about a
dubious food purchase at a railway stall:

> At Chita we eata biscuit and risk it...

And now he grins back at me, my nineteen-year-old stage manager, climbing
onto our El Al flight home, another tour toured. He has been wondering
what I was thinking.

A FOUR-ACT VAUDEVILLE

Three years from the first idea to the end, and mostly as monotonous
as a cobweb. How hard it was for me to write this play, and it had
nothing to do with laziness.

— Anton Chekhov on *The Cherry Orchard*

In its strict meaning, nostalgia has to do with place rather than time –
somewhere you need to get back to rather than a season when you were
happier. Chekhov saw through it in his Siberian cottage – much as he longed
to be home, he imagined that there too the wick of the candle was crusted
with soot. However, thirteen years on, struggling to complete *The Cherry
Orchard* in Yalta, a longing as sharp as that of the three sisters overcomes
him. In his eagerness to get to Moscow one last time, he declares to Olga that
he'll be so happy he will even live apart from her if that's best – all he asks is
somewhere to sit in the theatre (always the playwright's problem) and a large
lavatory. In fact, she can take a lover if she wants.

The hour is late. Despite Olga's special diets, Chekhov is being reduced
to nothing by an illness he still plays down for fear of all the sympathetic
faces around him. He has the strength to write a few brief lines a day, that's
all, however hard the Art Theatre press him for the 'four-act vaudeville' he's
promised them. He writes to his wife of fatigue and unproductiveness – but
very much as if he were an old man and it was only to be expected. In the no
doubt incomplete body of his letters, the rare moments when he acknowledges
poor health stand out shockingly. All of us may turn away from the dire facts
of our flesh, to be sure, but Chekhov's temperament had always driven him
into a particularly secret retreat. Good health – the birthright only conspicuous
by its fatiguing absence; when was the last moment, he must have wondered,
that he had lived on equal terms with the world? Why had he not treasured it
more? Now his voice is flat and his breath short: his digestion is wrecked, he
has emphysema and one lung has gone, so his vision of his new play is like
a dream of wellbeing:

> It's a faint glimmering in my brain, like dawn breaking. There will be
> cherry trees in bloom. A branch of cherry blossom coming into the
> house through a window. The orchard a sea of white, girls in white
> dresses...

In fact the view is so hallucinatory that Ranyevskaya will think she sees her dead mother leaning over like a bending tree, and Trofimov will glimpse the faces of the oppressed in the trunks.

Playing for time, Chekhov tells the Art Theatre he has lost his touch – but that the new work will feature a billiards enthusiast with only one arm and a loud voice, so that Vishnevsky should please research some billiards terms. He suggests to Olga that the playing of Ranyevskaya will involve her in no more than inventing a smile and a way of dressing. Meanwhile, old memories jitter round his subject. He recalls the sound of a cable breaking in a mine that he once heard as a boy and which he turned into a breaking string for an 1887 story, 'Fortune'; and that his family's Taganrog home was bought by a friend promising to save it for them who then kept it for himself. He remembers his hospitable friends the Kiselevs, with whom he used to stay in the country nearly twenty years before: especially Alexei, the owner of the estate, 'an elderly, good-hearted infant', who tried to ward off bankruptcy by begging a rich aunt to save them – and, while she's at it, to buy them all sweets – before taking a lowly job in a bank. For Trofimov, he calls up cadences he's used before, like the denunciations of those who own human souls in 'The Bride', a story in which a consumptive idealist wins an Anya-like figure with his thrilling opinions but disappoints her in his own person.

Soon it becomes clear that these fragments are failing to make a play fast enough for the Art Theatre to open their new auditorium with it. They are moving from the Hermitage Gardens to premises on Kamegersky Lane – once used by Fyodor Korsh and now redesigned by Franz Schechtel – where they will be financed by a textile millionaire. This man, Savva Morozov, has become in effect chairman of the company's board; pleasingly, he has made the actors' quarters a priority, as Stanislavsky always wanted, as well as installing a revolving stage, a new lighting system and furnishings that include the famous seagull on the curtain. But as Chekhov can't meet a deadline any more, the company realise they'll have to do *The Lower Depths* instead – a good thing for Gorky and for them, and good too in that it allows *The Cherry Orchard* to become, piece by piece, what we know.

There seems to be something unfeeling about the theatre's pressure on Chekhov to deliver – though his virtuosity in keeping his illness secret can't be discounted in this – and Olga's position on both sides of the fence must have been particularly hard. All Stanislavsky would ever say about his author's health was that he 'sometimes felt ill', but he had eyes in his head, and some knowledge too. There was an occasion around this time when the director had boasted about his skill with the hypodermic needle, so that Chekhov asked him to administer his arsenic injection. Chekhov lay down on a bunk, facing the wall, and Stanislavsky tried to inject what his biographer tactfully describes as his back. At first Stanislavsky was so overcome and nervous that he was unable to penetrate the great man's skin, and after several botched attempts did it like a piece of business in a play – by laying the needle sidelong and expelling the fluid along Chekhov's back. Chekhov smiled sweetly and thanked him, but there was no further talk of assistance.

When he received *The Cherry Orchard* Nemirovich-Danchenko incomprehensibly leaked its plot to the press, where it was inaccurately reproduced. Chekhov published a denunciation, and there was a bitter to-ing and fro-ing such as the papers love. Stanislavsky and Nemirovich were quarrelling too, and Chekhov threw his hat into the ring – if Nemirovich left the Art Theatre, he would too. Stanislavsky and Chekhov continued to bicker. Having been given jocular licence by the yearning husband, Olga took to going to parties with Nemirovich and coming home at four – gossip began to surround them. The author insisted on attending all rehearsals, ill or not. Angry at the intrusion, Stanislavsky went so far as to declare that the visitor was blighting the play's blossoms just as they were coming through. As the sound plot characteristically developed, Chekhov snapped at him:

> Haymaking takes place between the twentieth and twenty-fifth of June; at that time I think the corncrake no longer cries, and the frogs are silent too. If you can show a train without any noise, in absolute silence, that's good.

He went on to say that the last Act should run for twelve minutes, not forty – which is very fast, too fast in fact, since twenty is what he specifically refers to in the script, and stage time seems on this occasion intended to be real. Anything Chekhov said about *The Cherry Orchard* should be taken cautiously – he was ill and dyspeptic, and didn't expect to be quoted in a hundred years. As for his last word on his old adversary and patron, it depends very much on the now inaudible tone of voice: 'Stanislavsky has ruined my play. But bless him.'

It's funny, definitely funny…there's an old woman and a silly girl.

With the portfolio closing, we can see that he has always been writing the same story, about the same people. Just as Eugene Atget was photographing the familiar alleys, street corners and commonplace faces of Paris, it's as if Chekhov has looked all his life at a single landscape by Levitan, compulsively re-peopling it. He returns to that country estate, and the sound admittedly so poetic to him, to the same stewards, sponging neighbours, selfish divas, second-rate writers, embarrassing relatives, ne'er-do-wells with guitars, family retainers of both sexes, guilty doctors and hopeful girls. They talk reminiscently about Moscow and other European capitals, but it's unclear how much they really know about them: their nostalgia often sounds like cheap sentiment. They struggle on in duplicating pairs – Ranyevskaya and Gaev, Sonya and Vanya; they philosophise together – Vershinin and Tusenbach, Lopahin and Trofimov; they fail to say the life-changing things on their minds – Lopahin with Varya, Sonya with Astrov; sometimes they barely understand each other – Anya with Trofimov, Yeliena with Astrov. Anya and Irina worry about their grasp of foreign languages. They even use the same phrases: 'I haven't any money,' cry Arkadina and Ranyevskaya; 'I really don't want to leave,' hints Trigorin to Nina and Lopahin to Ranyevskaya. Spinning on their music-box, their action is increasingly jammed by daunting new men – merchants, beggars, revolutionaries and cynical, far-sighted survivors. Apart from *The Seagull*, there is, since *Ivanov*, only one exterior Act per play, and those of *The Cherry Orchard* and *The Seagull* end with calls from beyond while an onstage soloist dreams of the future. Three of these plays devote their final Acts to extended departures. By the time of *The Cherry Orchard*, however, there is no doctor, and though Yepihodov carries a gun in his pocket in case he needs to kill himself, it doesn't appear.

For all this, the play, with its improbable props and its heightened realism, marks a final move forward. Its orchard is preternaturally huge (and the writer Ivan Bunin thundered that there were no orchards exclusively for cherries in all Russia), while the odd fact is that the action starts with day breaking at 2:00 am – which would be all right if we were further north (it's May) but this is close to the dreaded Kharkov. Perhaps the cherry blossom, blazing in Chekhov's mind, is creating its own false dawn. Vsevelod Meyerhold, now far estranged artistically from the Moscow Art Theatre, viewed the third Act – when the anarchy of her party flows round Ranyevskaya as she waits for news of the sale – as flat-out expressionism, 'the nightmare's vortex, the dance of the puppet show'. Certainly, to lay the ground for such a climax with magic tricks and ventriloquism, with waltzes and poetry readings, and above all with Charlotta's unexplained prestidigitation of Anya and Varya, is extremely bold. The decisive moment is also attended by the local postmaster and stationmaster, amidst the burlesque of Simeonov-Pishchik and of Yepihodov, who, 'reduced to a state of mind', makes nonsense of language. Yasha laughs openly while Ranyevskaya frets; the news of the sale makes Anya excited at first and she dances. But the Act's best jokes, such as Varya clouting Lopahin with Firs's walking-stick on his crucial entrance, as her subconscious would require, and the presence of real billiards (Yepihodov breaking a cue) to distract Gaev from giving the news, are old-fashioned Chekhov. In some ways, the play is very simple, with no aimless philosophising and little sense of meandering time – even at the most discursive moments in Act Two there are pressing negotiations behind the talk. For all his experimental instincts, Chekhov was ending with a plain story, told with the acquired simplicity of genius.

In the human wave spilling on at the opening – relieved, exhausted, delighted – it's quite easy to miss some of the facts. One might assume that the brother and sister, Gaev and Ranyevskaya, have arrived from abroad together, since we don't see them greet; but in fact they have done that at the railway station. Gaev is a resident here, while Ranyevskaya is ostentatiously back from Paris. However, the one who's been away longest is Yasha. It seems likely that Ranyevskaya met him in France and hired him there: he is described as her footman, and trusted to give her her pills, whatever they are for. She has been away because six years ago a double tragedy befell her. First her lawyer husband died of a surfeit of champagne; then, in debt, she fell in love with someone else, a dependent personality like her husband, and had an affair, whereupon, in a somewhat Ibsenesque manner, her little boy Grisha drowned. She fled, followed by the lover. Recently Anya, her daughter, seventeen, has joined her in Paris, chaperoned by her governess Charlotta. Anya was shocked by her mother's way of life, conducted way beyond her means, but now that she's back delightedly remembers going up in a balloon. In each of them, nostalgia, running in both directions, has triggered reversible emotions.

Of Gaev's staff we meet Dunyasha, Firs and Varya. There are satellites: Yepihodov, who lives nearby and works for the family as a clerk, so no wonder they're in a mess, and Simeonov-Pishchik, a Micawber-like figure who is always borrowing money. It will be quite difficult to stop these two, delightful at first, from becoming comic turns in the theatre, items from a Chekhov one-act play, but part of their purpose is to discredit the story's solemnity. At least an English audience doesn't know that Pishchik means 'the man who squeaks' and Yepihodov, roughly, 'promenader'. In fact it is Yepihodov who squeaks, because of his new pair of boots, and he starts his part like a vaudeville Vanya, dropping a bouquet of flowers and crashing into a table; but Pishchik achieves a certain glory by surviving an overdose of Ranyevskaya's pills as effortlessly as he recently did a bucket of pickled cucumbers. Even his prediction that something will turn up proves true when English businessmen find 'white clay' (gold, we suppose) on his land, and he leases it to them for twenty-four years. Unaware that the orchard has been sold, he then comes joyously round to the big house, scrupulously paying off his debts; hearing the news he bursts into tears and leaves in disarray, having offered the family a few roubles and compared himself to an old horse.

First on of the residents is Dunyasha, an unsentimental picture of a stupid working girl who thinks she has the sensibility of a lady – even though she is warned by her fellow-peasant Lopahin to keep her place, and what's more to wait upon him. She is followed by Firs, who enters like a herald, muttering inaudibly in old-fashioned livery and hat, and is in fact near to tears that his mistress is back. His name has a sort of phoney classicism, like a black slave being called Virgil. He is also perfect for Chekhov's purposes, an enriched development of Marina, Ferapont and Anfisa. Because of his age and deafness, he can take to an extreme the author's liking for the non-sequitur, or demi-sequitur:

> Ranyevskaya: I'm so glad you're alive still.
>
> Firs: The day before yesterday.

– although at other times he hears remarkably well:

> Ranyevskaya: You've aged a lot, Firs.
>
> Firs: What is it?
>
> Lopahin: She's saying you've aged a lot.
>
> Firs: Well, I've lived a long time.

Varya is Ranyevskaya's nun-like adopted daughter, probably peasant-born, and like all slightly bossy châtelaines in Chekhov, she cannot but remind us of Masha Chekhova. Chekhov's descriptions of her over the long period of composition are mystifying indeed: first she is to be 'a simpleton…a fool'; later 'crude, stupid and kind hearted'; eventually 'a crybaby'. However, the author was not above building up one part and decrying another when persuading his actors of their casting, and he specially didn't want Knipper, to whom he was writing here, playing Varya. In fact, Varya is an awkward personality, but extremely sympathetic: loved by almost everyone, she irritates them all by turns, and you worry about her in the future as you do for Masha in *The Seagull*, Sonya in *Uncle Vanya*, and Olga in *Three Sisters*. Lopahin's failure to change her life by marriage much disappoints us; and by a wonderful stroke – terrible for her – she finds herself saying goodbye to him by pulling an umbrella out of a bundle in such a way that he thinks, quite wrongly, that she is going to hit him.

When Varya talks quietly to Anya in the first scene about how difficult it has been to keep things going at home – even the tramps dossing in the servants' quarters criticise her housekeeping – Anya falls asleep. Inadvertently, she is introducing a motif in the play: everyone is inclined to drop off at the wrong moment. Lopahin started the action by kicking himself for taking a nap just when he meant to go and meet Ranyevskaya at the station. In a short while, Simeonov-Pishchik will have a few winks in the middle of touching Ranyevskaya for a loan, and will even sleep in mid-sentence during the Act Three party, before losing his money and then finding it again. Chekhov's characters have always found great energy for pursuing their interests and ignoring those of others; but even that seems to be flagging now, as if they are going through wearisome motions.

In point of fact, though, when she falls asleep Anya is not uncaring, just young and very tired. Chekhov insisted that this character was always gay and lively like a child, with tears in her eyes only once. To him the part was 'not very important' – though he presumably didn't say that to Lilina, Stanislavsky's wife, who was preparing to play the seventeen-year-old at nearly forty. He also vigorously denied that Anya was related to Nina and Irina, just as he did that Sonya and Varya were close cousins, but that would be authorial pride. In fact, Anya turns out to be a heroine, embodying Trofimov's hope for the future without the cant, growing up at speed, always practical enough to ask the right questions.

However, she does have some of the intolerance of youth: she utterly ignores the devotion of Dunyasha, who wants to tell her about her marriage proposals, particularly that of Yepihodov. Dunyasha is in fact about to fall for the phoney rhetoric of Yasha, who doesn't really remember her after such an absence, only declaring that she has grown from a child to 'a tasty little thing' and acting accordingly. Now he's back he won't even meet his own mother, who has been waiting in the servants' quarters since the day before. He insults all the local people, including Gaev; he calls Firs an old bore and suggests he drops dead. His form of nostalgia – the Russian love affair with France, also parodied through Natasha in *Three Sisters* – is quite perverted: in fact, he would be a natural partner for her, and together with Serebryakov in *Vanya*, has to be one of the most unpleasant men Chekhov invented.

Off to the side, Charlotta enters the play with a fine non-sequitur – 'my dog even eats nuts'; nevertheless, this is a bleak picture of absolute loneliness. It is the first of a remarkable series of entrances – pretending the sexually timid Lopahin has designs on her, playing a card trick or ventriloquising a baby with a bundle of clothes. What is always emphasised is her rootlessness and sorrow, even as she leads the dance: after all, she comes from a fairground family, though she doesn't remember her parents and has no idea how old she is. She seems to be part of a Chekhov story rather than a play, and in fact she comes from his life. In the summer of 1902, the Stanislavskys invited the Chekhovs to use their house at Lyubimovka, north of Moscow, while they were away. It had been a troubled few months – Olga had had what may have been an ectopic pregnancy and nearly died, and was still ill. There is some question whether the baby would have been Chekhov's rather than Nemirovich-

Danchenko's, and it may be significant that Chekhov walked out on her at Lyubimovka, provoking the angriest exchange of letters they ever had. (This very much depends on the daring of individual biographers, working with straw and remembering the mysterious paternities in some of the plays.) Everyone knew Chekhov was ill and supposed to be working, so they left him in peace and even the local church muffled the sound of its bells – however all he had achieved by August was to notice that there was a maid called Dunyasha working in the house. Then he had some luck – one day, as he took a walk, an English governess, dressed as a man but with pig-tails, leapt out at him and insisted on being piggy-backed, raising his hat for him to passers-by: this was Lily Glassby, who was looking after his neighbours' children. She was no conjuror, but she kept Chekhov entertained from time to time as he worked, with ice cream and little flirtatious notes.

> You shouldn't go to plays. You should look at yourself a little more often.
>
> – Ranyevskaya to Lopahin

Within this diverse group there are unexpected intimacies, generally involving Lopahin. In her longing to regain grace, to 'lift the millstone...after the storms and cold of winter', Ranyevskaya turns to the past, when her mother was alive and she occupied the nursery, waking each morning to the sight of her cherry orchard. As she does so, Lopahin is preparing for its sale. But he has also worshipped her since she looked after him when he'd been beaten by his father as a fifteen year old – taking him into the great house, calling him 'little peasant', washing his face and putting him to rights, with a promise that he'd be all right by his wedding day. This fatal seductiveness is replayed in the action, even while he destroys her life: when she woos him into proposing to Varya, all she achieves is to deepen his infatuation with her. As a result, Varya's heart is broken and the estate remains unsaved.

Another link is between Lopahin and Trofimov the student, who gives him a word of advice:

> Do stop waving your arms about – cure yourself of the habit, it's stupid.

This is a little unfair: Lopahin, aware of the problem, has admitted that he just doesn't know what to do about it:

> Look, they flop around as if they belonged to someone else.

Unlike everyone else in the play, his loss of co-ordination has to do with frustration at not working: he can't bear not to have many projects on the go. The remorseless student points out that his great plan for summer cottages is just another way of waving his arms about – before, astonishingly, admitting:

> I like you. Your fingers are sensitive, like an artist, and you have a fine
> soul too.

So much for Lopahin the boor, often encumbered in English productions with a thumping northern accent while the rest speak received pronunciation – an insult both to the north and to the character. Lopahin's father was a peasant and so was Chekhov's grandfather, but that makes neither of them coarse. Likewise beaten by a shopkeeper father, but without a Ranyevskaya to tend him afterwards, Chekhov had a lifelong preference for delicacy and good manners: Lopahin's inclinations that way coexist with a tough vision of his entrepreneurial part in Russia's future. Like Trofimov, he believes he understands the country's destination, and he describes how two of society's traditional modules – gentry and peasants – are being joined by a third estate, the summerfolk, with whom he can do business. He would agree with Trofimov that Russia is full of wonderful places: he genuinely loves his fields of poppies, though he can't keep from boasting about how much he has made from them – 40,000 roubles already, much better than cherries. The aesthetics and the agronomics have about equal weight.

As the play's axis, he receives the most detailed individual description Chekhov ever provided. He was really anxious about Lopahin, particularly as directed by Stanislavsky – though in fact Stanislavsky was close to the character, being a rich man of peasant origins. This should be a gentle person, Chekhov insists, dignified, intelligent – after all, Varya loves him. He must wear a white waistcoat, brown boots, walk with long strides, meditate. He should throw his head back and comb his beard absent-mindedly – but always from the throat towards the chin. Notice that he calls the servants by the familiar *ty*, while they address him by the formal *vy*. He should be a cross between a merchant and a professor of medicine at Moscow University. He mustn't shout, because rich men don't need to. None of this, obviously, has anything to do at all with English class stereotypes.

Trofimov, on the other hand, calls everyone else *vy* but Lopahin *ty*. This is the character who makes better sense of Vershinin's and Tusenbach's muddled talk about the future: in Trofimov's mouth the ideas blossom so that you feel Chekhov's very breath. But such sense is he inclined to talk that his aspirations also had to be made ridiculous. The reasons were expedient. Chekhov had taken great interest in the Petersburg student uprisings of 1899 and 1902, which were brutally suppressed, and he was well aware that too heroic a treatment of a student *narodnik* would now be censored. And indeed it was: Trofimov's playing text was milder than the one we now have, which is based on Chekhov's original: lines about his expulsion from university and unfed workers sleeping thirty to a room were softened at the Art Theatre. These were the first political cuts Chekhov had had to make, and they left the part resting on a hinge. As Lopahin can be boor and idealist, Trofimov ends up as visionary and clown, which indeed suits Chekhov's preference for ambiguity: he electrifies the company with a wonderful speech about the need for hard work and less conversation, but he sleeps in the bath-house and is capable of declaring fatuously to Anya that they are above love and of losing his galoshes. Nevertheless, like Gorky, he has put on his bark shoes and traipsed all over Russia – he tells her inspirationally that the whole country 'is our orchard'. At moments too, he shows genuine wisdom, as when he points out to Ranyevskaya that the path she wants to go back down to the past is now overgrown.

> What a strange creature a Russian is. As in a sieve, nothing remains in him. What we have to do is work, work, and the rest can go to the devil.

Beneath these subtleties of character lies an inexorable historical pattern. One consequence of the great reforms of Alexander II was that landowners like Gaev and Ranyevskaya were now unable to depend on serf labour, just as the serfs could no longer rely on them for protection. Land in southern Russia was worth something, but the ill-trained gentry were failing as farmers, and the peasants were at a loss. Old Firs, brilliantly chosen by Chekhov to be a critic from the ranks of the liberated, is so reactionary that he calls Emancipation 'the disaster' and harks back:

> Everyone used to be happy, but they didn't know what about. The peasants belonged to the masters and the masters to the peasants. Now it's all higgledy-piggledy, it makes no sense.

We don't know what proportion of the estate the orchard represents, but the railway line that has brought Ranyevskaya home has certainly given her a commercial opportunity. Lopahin claims that a minimum rental for holiday homes of ten roubles an acre on the combined orchard and land by the river would bring in an income of 25,000 roubles a year: therefore, he is talking about a holding of up to 2,500 acres, so big that some critics have taken it as a vast symbol. As for the cherries, now that such work has to be paid for, who will harvest them? In any case, the trees are exhausted: they only crop every second year, and nobody seems to want the fruit – not like forty years back, when as Firs says, with the vivid recall of an old man's memory just before it clouds over:

> ...it made good jam...the cherries were sent to Moscow and Kharkov by the cart-load, they were soft and juicy and tasty. They had the knack of it in those days.
>
> Ranyevskaya: And now?
>
> Firs: Forgotten. No-one remembers it.

Both Ranyevskaya and her brother know that the game is up. After an initial objection – the fact that their beautiful orchard is by so much the most interesting local feature that it's mentioned in an encyclopaedia – neither seriously queries that it has to be sold: they may evade the 'vulgar' question, but they are focused on it in their own way. The nub is that there is an outstanding bank loan and the family have not been or felt able to pay it back. Ranyevskaya's approach is to secure a marriage between Lopahin and Varya, but, as noted, the plan misfires because of Lopahin's preoccupation with Ranyevskaya herself. During the action, the bank, with insulting helpfulness, offers Gaev a job for 6,000 roubles a year – twenty times what a factory worker might have got then, but paltry compared to the scale of his problems. Gaev meanwhile, like Chekhov's friend Kiselev, thinks he can raise the money through his relatives: there is a disapproving aunt in Yaroslavl, a Countess, who might still be touched for 10,000–15,000 roubles, though it seems by Lopahin's account that they need ten times as much as that. Gaev also prattles on about a general who might lend them something – with interest, of course. In the end the distrustful aunt gives them 15,000 roubles to buy the estate in her name – a pitiful bid, and not enough even to pay the interest they owe: Lopahin has to part with 90,000 to cover the debts and secure the property.

Beyond this, the siblings counter the fearsome practicalities with little more than hopeless nostalgia. They have a repertoire of displacement activity such as Gaev's 'air' billiards and excessive talking, which both Anya and Varya try to stop: 'You're off again, Uncle.' As you would expect, their foolishness is earthed by flashes of insight: Ranyevskaya ticking Trofimov off for his lack of generosity, and Gaev seeing clearly that if too many cures are suggested for an illness, the illness must be beyond help. But earlier, his aim lost, he has made a great speech to the bookcase, which he loves as uselessly as his cherry orchard:

> Dear book-case, I salute your devotion for a hundred years to the ideals of goodness and justice... (*He weeps.*) You have called us to a faith in a better future, a future of work and social conscience...

He cries not because he's a sentimental duffer with no sense of scale, though no doubt he is either funny or embarrassing if you're related to him. The fact is, Gaev has done his best as a man of the Eighties – that is, the type of landowner who belatedly tried, in a period of adjustment, 'to know your peasant'. This sincere desire aimed to reverse a disillusionment which, as it happens, is the central matter of *Ivanov*, at the other end of Chekhov's career. Succeeding in 1881, Alexander III viewed liberals like Gaev with such suspicion that they received few seats on the local councils (the kind that Protopopov and Andrei – who couldn't have managed it without his sinister sponsor – serve on in *Three Sisters*), and certainly no favours. By 1903 such a man's melancholy and sense of alienation, deepened by the succession of Alexander's girlish son Nicholas II, would be considerable. Chekhov complicates matters further by making Gaev, by training and reflex, an incorrigible snob – a man who keeps commenting on Lopahin's cheap scent, who feels his greatest sin has been to waste his substance on fruit drops, and who is so out of date and babyish that Firs normally dresses and undresses him.

In this political stasis, the relationship between Lopahin and Trofimov, two men whose eyes are trained on an uncertain future, becomes particularly sharp. In Act Two, they meet for a routine but idiosyncratic bark at each other. Trofimov is still under thirty, but Lopahin insists he will be a student at fifty, and immediately asks in return for Trofimov's opinion of him, which is given with stylish offhandedness:

> Oh, that's simple… Just as nature needs wild beasts destroying everything they meet, so it needs you, I suppose…

Trofimov turns to the company, stilling their appreciation of this by denouncing the intelligentsia for their illiteracy, their empty philosophising, their failure to do better by Russia:

> Where are all these crèches we've heard about? Where are the libraries?

– whereupon Lopahin, spotting the element of rhetoric, points out that for all this preaching about hard work, it is he, Lopahin, who gets up at five in the morning and labours through into the night. Then, in his brief hours of rest, he often lies awake, reflecting on human nature and how few honest people there are:

> God – you've given us the great forests, the land, huge horizons – we should be like giants.

Gaev then exemplifies Trofimov's criticisms by making a nonsensical speech about the sunset, whereupon a famous and unexplained sound is heard, interpreted by Lopahin as a cable in a mine, and by Gaev (perhaps choosing an animal he resembles himself) as a heron, and by Trofimov as an ominous owl. This is followed by the arrival of a tramp, a Gorky-like figure who intones a disturbing poem of the oppressed, angering Lopahin and frightening Varya – but about whom, significantly, Trofimov makes no comment.

When the two men meet again in Act Four, they are once again accompanied by evidence of change: Lopahin's arms are waving, an axe is slicing into the cherry trees, and their courses are set. In the contorted Russia of the future they could find themselves on opposite sides of a table in an unfurnished room under a single bulb. However, mollified by parting, the tone is this time more placatory:

> Trofimov: Man is marching towards the highest truth, and I'm at the front of that march.
>
> Lopahim: Will you get there?
>
> Trofimov: Yes. Or I'll show others the way.
>
> Lopahim: Well, dear fellow, the two of us may look down our noses at each other, but life goes on anyway. When I work…I know why I'm alive, but there are lots of people in Russia, you know, who don't know why they're living.

Then they leave the play together. Lopahin, the lonely victor – like Chekhov, a barefoot boy who came to own Melikhovo and Yalta – will go to Kharkov for the winter, while Trofimov goes 'to town' with the party before peeling off for the insurgent political life of Moscow. A particularity of *The Cherry Orchard* is that the whole process of the company assembling and scattering – trying to look forward to meeting again, while knowing how unlikely that is – is visible: the last Act begins, as the first did, with Lopahin standing in the nursery and Yasha's mother vainly waiting offstage for him, this time to say goodbye. Ranyevskaya, after a last greedy attempt to imprint the knots in the wood of her nursery walls onto her memory, is going, with Yasha in tow, by express back to Paris. There she will manage, though perhaps not for long, on the unused roubles sent by the Countess. Gaev and Anya will be left behind, he to work at the bank, she to study and pass her exams, believing in a future when she will be reunited with her mother and they will read together and build a new world. Varya, disappointed by Lopahin's failure of nerve, is going to work as a housekeeper in Yashnevo, fifty miles away, leaving Yepihodov nominally in charge of the estate in preparation for its re-building as holiday accommodation.

Meanwhile someone has been left behind to die. An audience always gasps when, after a great silence, Firs wanders on, as alone as when he preceded the company at the start of the play. The reaction is partly at the audacity of the writing, partly at our collusion in the terrible event. It's not even that he has been particularly lovable, though we always wanted him to be; the fact that he's forgotten is a last word on the cruelty of people who half-care. Ranyevskaya loves her country and her nursery and her table all in the same breath, but has forgotten about an old man, while her brother hasn't registered his decline at all as long as his own boots were ready.

The moment has been generated carefully. The first hint came just after Anya complained that workmen were already cutting down the orchard before Ranyevskaya had gone. Everyone could agree how tactless this was, and Lopahin rushed off to stop them. In the slipstream of that, Anya turned to Yasha:

> Anya: Has Firs been taken to the hospital yet?
>
> Yasha: I told them to see to it this morning. They must have done, I suppose.
>
> Anya: (To Yepihodov.) Please find out if Firs has been taken to hospital.
>
> Yasha: (Offended.) I told Yegor to do it. Why are you going on about it?
>
> Yepihodov: Old Firs, I see, is past repair. Time he was gathered to his fathers. I envy him, actually. (Places a suitcase on a hat box and squashes it.) Oh, that had to happen, I knew it would.

So far the women are doing better than the men; but Chekhov has distracted everybody with the awfulness of the trees being chopped down too soon, and then by the latest of Yepihodov's twenty-two misfortunes. Meanwhile, Yasha is the perfect vessel for anything to do with not bothering, the last person you should trust with a message that doesn't interest him. Varya and Anya try again, until the subject is exhausted by repetition:

> Varya: Has Firs been taken to hospital?
>
> Anya: Yes.
>
> Varya: Then why didn't they take the letter for the doctor?
>
> Anya: We'll send it after him.

Even for them, the problem is now too elusive among their other concerns.

Watching these derelictions, we realise we haven't done so well either: for us, too, the question was not quite interesting enough. In fact, if we imagine the play written from one end to the other, we are being denounced in virtually the last words Chekhov wrote. As his and Ranyevskaya's houses darken, we may remember that he once told Gorky that all he ever wanted to say to his audience was:

> Look at yourselves, how stupidly you live.

Meanwhile, the imagination reels: an old man entombed in a locked house with not half the physical strength to call, to climb, to rattle. Even if he could break a window he'd still have to open the shutters, locked fast against a Russian winter. We wait for him to realise what he faces, but he edges his mind onto the fact and off again:

> They've forgotten me. Never mind, I'll sit here for a while. They're so silly.

Perhaps Yepihodov will pass by on his rounds in a few weeks, or perhaps builders starting the work, and then Lopahin himself will come back in a few months: the first thing any of them will notice is the smell.

> The only thing I fear about death is the kind of oration someone may make over my grave.

According to Olga and Stanislavsky, Chekhov next planned a play in which a scientist would go to the North Pole after an unhappy love affair; in the last Act this hero would stand on the deck in the silent Arctic night, the northern lights would gleam and he would see the shadow of the woman he loved floating past. It sounds more like a story than a play, but the change of style is not so surprising – there are signs of repetition in *The Cherry Orchard*, and it's hard to imagine Chekhov working that seam any further. It's also good that, leaving that sort of thing to others, he finally stood by his earlier statement:

> Why should I write about a man who gets into a submarine and goes to the North Pole to secure a reconciliation with the world, while at the same moment his beloved hurls herself with a shriek from the belfry? No. You should write about simple things: Pyotr Semionich married Maria Ivanovna. That's all.

As Chekhov approached death, Olga Knipper was arranging the dismissal from the Moscow Art Theatre of her rival (and Gorky's mistress) Maria Andreyeva, who had been accusing Olga of sleeping with Nemirovich. Her husband's last six months turned out to be a sad mess, one way and another. The impact of *The Cherry Orchard* was much muted by the declaration of the Russo-Japanese War a week after the premiere, immediately followed by the sinking of the Russian fleet. As for the first night, the Art Theatre threw a jubilee for Chekhov to mark the date, which was also his birthday, perhaps fearing that the occasion needed cranking up a little: it was suspected by the police of being an 'unauthorised gathering', and it was certainly unworthy. How could they have put Chekhov through an event that, quite apart from his frailty, combined everything that embarrassed him most – a man who had boycotted the jamboree of Tolstoy's seventieth birthday because the great man's life felt like some unending celebration anyway? They brought him onstage between Acts Three and Four (he had been hiding till then) – the audience was shocked to see him coughing and coughing. Someone shouted, 'Get him a chair,' but there wasn't one to be had. Meanwhile everybody who felt they should speak did so, at length, somewhat in the manner of Gaev to the bookcase. As a last transaction between Chekhov and his theatre, this cruelly inappropriate event emphasises incompatibility as well as clumsy love, and it certainly raises the question of whose benefit a benefit is for.

The company took *The Cherry Orchard* to Petersburg, where it had much better luck than in Moscow. Back in Yalta, Chekhov tidied the play up for publication and started two more stories, but they never stood a chance. In the teeth of Masha's objections, Olga took Chekhov away to Germany for the last stage of his life. In the midst of a heatwave he sat on his balcony at the Sommer Hotel in Badenweiler, a spa town near Basel in the Black Forest, studying ship's timetables for imaginary journeys, or lay in bed, making up a last story for Olga's amusement – in this, a group of American and English gourmets wait for their dinner in a hotel dining-room, unaware that the cook has gone home. Then he lost coherence and started babbling about a sailor, his brother Nikolai, the Japanese; Olga dispatched two students for a doctor, and would always remember their running feet on the gravel of the hotel drive. Once arrived, the doctor straight away called for a bottle of champagne. Chekhov looked him in the eye and said it for him – *'Ich sterbe'* – drank the champagne, turned on his side and immediately, quietly died. As Olga sat beside him, the champagne cork, jammed back in the bottle, flew out again with a pop and a huge moth got in through the window and started beating its wings against the lamp.

With Chekhov gone there were changes, and further decline. He had once made a prediction about Tolstoy's death, an event he might have expected to experience:

> Many people are ashamed to do evil simply because Tolstoy is alive. As long as he is, it is easy and agreeable to be a writer, but without him we would be like a flock without a shepherd. I dread it.

He could have been speaking of his own. Within three weeks of the loss, Suvorin, presumably in political panic, was trying to recover his personal letters to Chekhov, dismissing his friend as 'never great – just a poet of the middle classes'. He then began publishing petty denunciations by rival writers in *New Times*, to which Chekhov had given so much. Just under a year after *The Cherry Orchard*'s premiere the Petersburg military killed two hundred protesters on Bloody Sunday, and nine months after that, following a summer of strikes, Tsar Nicholas published a manifesto guaranteeing civil liberties, a constitution and a cabinet government. That he did so was largely due to the Lopahin in his life, Count Witte – a former railway clerk – who finally convinced him that the world had changed for good. While trying to avoid this move, Nicholas invited his uncle to become dictator of Russia: in a somewhat Chekhovian moment, the Grand Duke responded by mutely pulling out a gun and pointing it at his own head.

Chekhov's party began to scatter. Alexander hit the bottle again; Masha, rich from his inheritance (Olga, with a career, had renounced all claims), took up responsibility for the archives, for Evgenia and for the Yalta house, with the help of brother Misha; Ivan continued to teach. Soon after the death, Stanislavsky staged *Ivanov* at last, with Olga as the tragic Anna Petrovna. It was a poignant occasion – and though few people would have known it, Olga was going home at night to continue her correspondence with her husband:

> I speak to you out loud, but my voice gets lost in the room... I can feel you everywhere, in the air, in the grass, in the murmuring wind – it's as if you were walking with me, light and transparent, leaving no mark on the ground...

In the absence of new plays, however, Stanislavsky was wearying of Chekhov – death had released him from any obligations to his major inspiration. Meanwhile in Petersburg, Vera Komisarzhevskaya's thrilling voice, ringing out as Sonya that autumn, sounded to her audience like a clarion call not only for Uncle Vanya but for the Russian people.

Naturally enough, everyone began to trim. The Moscow Art Theatre had the foresight during the following years to withdraw *Vanya* from their repertoire as stale, at odds with the time, and to institute special workers' performances of the other plays. Stanislavsky, though he sincerely understood the change, hated working for proletarians, and would break off to reprimand them for cracking nuts during the performance. On 26 October 1917, the day after the Revolution began, the company was playing *The Cherry Orchard*: the play's valediction to the old world drew a huge ovation, no doubt made up of contrary emotions. In due course the Art Theatre was recognised as a People's Theatre, and by 1918 they were presenting *Vanya* again, at the Polytechnic Museum. A new audience was presumably ready to share Vanya's views of Professor Serebryakov; they certainly still wept at Sonya and her uncle, and Alexander Vishnevsky was sent a present of game from a fan because he seemed to have suffered so much in his part – no small thing, as this was in the middle of a famine. The company began travelling, across Western Europe to London and the US, beginning to notch up thousands of Chekhov performances – only a minute percentage of which, by the way, were of *The Seagull*. In 1923, Stanislavsky declared plaintively from the loneliness of a foreign tour that, after all they'd all been through, who cared about an officer like Vershinin going and his mistress staying? You can see his point. In 1928 he is caught shaking his fist at Varya during a curtain call. The far-sighted Nemirovich-Danchenko meanwhile went to Hollywood in 1925 as an adviser to Paramount, then to Italy and Germany, before returning to what was now Stalin's official theatre, where in 1940 he put on a major revival of *Three Sisters* neatly adjusted for optimism, in which Chebutykin wasn't allowed to puncture the upbeat end by intoning his hideous little song. In increasingly sclerotic company, Olga Knipper was still playing Ranyevskaya in 1943, at the right age at last, her privilege having reversed the tradition that Russian actresses started by being too old for their parts.

Onto Chekhov's blameless page the Soviets had by now worked long and hard to sign their names. It was awkward that the plays (somewhat like Shakespeare's) contained no outstanding peasant or worker: so Trotsky denounced them, while the People's Commissar for Enlightenment, Anatoly Lunacharsky, declared *Three Sisters* to be 'dangerous and decadent', and took the view that Masha should have followed Vershinin, thereby sacrificing herself for a great cause. However, both he and Lenin, like Stalin ahead, could see the advantage of middle-class culture in the new disposition – the more attractive the Whites, the more righteous the ideas that overthrew them – and both had a way of dropping in for performances (Lenin particularly appreciated *Vanya*). Producers of revivals of *The Seagull* found that Nina could be justified as an archetypal heroine standing for humanity's belief in useful art. Well, sort of, though her starting-point –

> If I had your talent, ordinary people would have to pull my chariot through the streets…

– sounds distinctly pre-Marxist to me. However, the seagull stuffed and poised for flight could certainly be reimagined to be somewhat like the famous statue *Worker and Collective Farm Girl* – which in the latest reorganisation of Moscow now hovers over the entrance to a shopping mall.

While these deadly adjustments were on foot, Chekhov had been smuggled out of Russia, and the greater the distance, the bigger the welcome. Having derided the idea of having his work translated, especially into English (on the basis that a man like Lopahin would be incomprehensible to non-Russians) he would have been most surprised. In 1905 Bernard Shaw was asking the writer and actor Laurence Irving if he had heard of some fellow called Tschekoff, a Russian novelist who'd written 'The Black Monk' – on acquaintance with the plays a little later, he declared, rather like Gorky, that he wanted to tear up all his own and start again. Shaw championed Chekhov as he did Ibsen, though he was closer at heart to the Norwegian, and many of us find that his 'Chekhovian' play, *Heartbreak House*, suffers dreadfully by comparison with *The Cherry Orchard*. Still, he got the amateur Stage Society to put on the latter for the first time in 1911. It was a flop in a way that eerily recapitulates the first Petersburg *Seagull* – hurriedly thrown together, misunderstood by actors and public alike, it provoked so many walk-outs that Firs was almost as alone in the theatre at the end as he was in Ranyevskaya's house. It is, once again, hard to account for the high sense of insult in the reaction.

However, when *The Cherry Orchard* had its first full-scale airing in London in 1925, there were cries of 'Author!'. John Gielgud was playing Trofimov, in a little beard and round glasses – he declared later that it was the first time he had really felt he might be able to act. The great half-Slav (who was even alive for a few months when Chekhov was) went on to do all the major plays except *Vanya* at least once – *Ivanov* most of all. At times he has seemed to have as direct a hotline to Chekhov as to Shakespeare: and the Russian's unassailable position here owes much to Gielgud's efforts as advocate as well as actor. Partly as a result, the English have come to feel they own Chekhov with the same possessiveness that sometimes allows them to forget that Oscar Wilde was an Irishman. This, by the way, rather amuses Russians, to whom Chekhov may now mean less than he does to us.

Virginia Woolf saw that *Cherry Orchard*: she felt as if she was a piano being played for the first time, all over the keyboard with the lid left open – consciously or not, she was parodying Chekhov's remark that his piano in Yalta and he were two of a kind, uselessly waiting for someone to play them. J B Priestley was there too: to him, Chekhov was the model of a new sort of man badly needed and never found again – the mould had been broken before 'our blind mad century' was five years old. A 1926 *Three Sisters* directed by Theodore Komisarjevsky (half-brother to Chekhov's original Nina) perpetrated something Chekhov hated – all reference to Tusenbach's plainness was cut so that John Gielgud could reluctantly play up to his romantic image; but it was still good enough to inspire Rodney Ackland to become a playwright – he went home on the No 9 bus after the performance 'in a state of exultation'. It wasn't even the great ending that had done this for him so much as Masha dancing on her own in Act Two, quietly singing, 'The Baron is drunk, the Baron is drunk.' In a lighter way, the effect on him must have been like Masha dancing alone in the last Act of *The Seagull* in the original Art Theatre production: it was said that her damaged life had never been so evident as in those wordless moments of automatic waltz steps. Chekhov's effect on the literary community invariably results in such bulletins of tender capitulation. The Art Theatre arrived in New York in 1923 and were a sensation, though curiously enough they didn't affect local practice, which remained stuck with Broadway values: in 1930 George Jean Nathan was urging Lillian Gish, preparing to play Yeliena, to get out of the show since Sonya would wipe the floor with her at the end. Some of this slow reaction was because early American Chekhov translations were very poor; but in 1935, the young Tennessee Williams recovered from a nervous breakdown by working through the stories, then the letters, then the plays: thereafter he always kept a picture of Chekhov on his desk.

By this time Maxim Gorky, the author's friend and hysterical champion, had become the highest paid author in Russia and Minister for Literature. He was effectively imprisoned in a great Art Nouveau house in Moscow as Stalin's informer from the world of letters: a specially printed copy of *Pravda*, prepared for him alone, was delivered each day, so that he should suspect nothing of the purging of his fellow-writers. All that is another story, a terrible end to the life of a great figure; but back in 1904 he had bidden farewell to Chekhov in the same tones with which he'd greeted him six years before, feeling like 'screaming, crying, yelling with indignation and anger' at the casual insults of the funeral. This event was famously in the manner of the dead man, and if ever the old cliché 'he would have loved it' had weight it is surely here. The body was brought back from Germany because both Suvorin and Chekhov's brothers insisted that he be buried in Russia: all sorts of permissions had to be secured to attach a refrigerated car to a passenger train travelling across the border. Thus Chekhov arrived in Petersburg and then went forward to Moscow, to be greeted by old girl friends and a Government minister; but that gentleman was there to pay his respects to a dead General from the Russo-Japanese front. The military refrain continued as Chekhov's body, which had arrived in a van marked 'fresh oysters', was borne to its resting place accompanied by a military band: the mourners had been surprised by the odd transport but were now grateful for the honour, until they saw that the music was intended for the General. Chekhov's procession now headed for the Novodevichy Cemetery, led by a constable on a white horse, while (according to Gorky) the mourners discussed the virtues of their dogs and their dachas. Gradually it swelled to four thousand and in the centre of town public transport came to a halt. The cortège stopped for a short service outside the Art Theatre – Masha, Misha and Evgenia arrived late at this point and the police nearly excluded them from the procession. At the cemetery the event turned into a riot: flowers were trampled, trees climbed and the rubberneckers shouted. Gorky complained that Anton was being buried next to a Cossack widow. Chaliapin broke down in tears.

The great singer would be buried there himself in 1938, close to Kropotkin the anarchist and Molotov the Stalinist. Over in different sections are Andrei

Gromyko and Svetlana Stalin, with Ostrovsky uncomfortably nearby – Innokenti Smoktunovsky lies in a little actors' corner on the (expandable) edge of the cemetery. Chekhov (with his father) lay on his own in a row until Nemirovich-Danchenko slipped into a place to his right, to be masked from him shortly afterwards by Ivan Moskvin, their original Yepihodov. When I first saw Anton Pavlovich's unassuming headstone in 1975, it made me think of the spinning-top in *Three Sisters*. I've been there twice since, and it's always seemed to be a bright, crisp day, silent except for early birdsong. A few steps away from him is the great actress Maria Yermolova, whom he venerated as a beautiful wildflower in a world of carnations, even though she had rejected *Platonov*. He is now safely in the midst of a small community: Bulgakov, Levitan too, I'm glad to say, and there's Gogol over there. With the latter too, fate mimicked a writer's tastes: when he was moved from an earlier resting-place in 1931, the police went onto high alert, as if he was going to rise up – and indeed when the coffin was opened there were scratch marks on the inside and Gogol's body lying on its hip, giving rise to the idea that he might have been buried alive. Beneath a simple white headstone with a little black roof in the *Modern* style, meanwhile, lies Chekhov, his name seemingly hand-written on the rough plaster; the flowers are always fresh on his grave. Again the quietude, the mute acknowledgment, the odd sense of intimacy: it seems that there are many great figures in here and one friend. And I hadn't noticed it before – until another actor interposed his body in 1943, Chekhov's and Stanislavsky's tombstones would have stood back to back, as if they were sustaining their differences beyond the grave.

CONCLUSION: MOSCOW AND LONDON

Every hour is precious. Keep well, and cheerful, and don't suffer from indigestion and bad temper.

– Anton Chekhov

February 1998

Basmannaya Street, where the sisters and Vershinin used to live, has had its name restored after all those years as Karl Marx Street. Muir and Merrilees, the Scots-owned department store that Chekhov loved – he named two of his puppies after it – was nationalised after the Revolution as TsUM, and has kept that name, but it hardly matters: through the Soviet period Muscovites clung to the original. On the fabulous Moscow metro, there have always been stations named after Dostoyevsky, Pushkin, Gogol, Mayakovsky – now there is Chekhovskaya as well. The Slavyansky Bazaar burned down only a few years ago. Meanwhile at the Moscow Art Theatre's birthday celebrations recently Yuri Lyubimov achieved a rare feat of prestidigitation: when he stood to pay tribute to 'the two most important men in Russian theatre' who had famously dined at the Bazaar, the accompanying slides of Stanislavsky and Nemirovich-Danchenko got stalled, and two pictures of Lyubimov himself came up.

Their company is still where Morozov installed it in its Art Nouveau palace, but there has been a split since 1987 – half of it, under its long-standing director Oleg Yefremov, is known as the Chekhov Art Theatre and works here, while Tatyana Doronina's breakaway team, the Gorky, is based round the corner on Tverskoy Boulevard. Yefremov has abandoned the Moscow Art Theatre equation between long service and casting privileges, so that he can now put on a *Seagull* in which the Nina is under forty. Philip Morris sponsorship or not, the organisation stubbornly continues on its idealistic way: a twenty-play repertoire across its two auditoria dominated by Ostrovsky, Dostoyevsky, Gogol and Chekhov, with Richard Nelson's and Alexander Gellman's *Misha's Party* (1993) as contemporary as it gets. (Ray Cooney's *Out of Order*, rechristened as *Number 13*, will open in 2001, its London hotel setting for some reason realised in tartan patterns, which will extend to the seagull on the Art Theatre curtain.)

Their 1991 *Platonov* plays once a month in the studio – the night I was there, there were perhaps a hundred people in, but there is no thought of taking it off. Watching its four and a half hours, sustained by actors so good that you can smell their breath when they're drinking, I can see the power of the later, actor-led Stanislavsky Method in a Chekhov – in that respect the two men were half a step out of time with each other. The adjustments that the Art Theatre, like all Russian institutions, has had to make in order to survive in such style are remarkable, of course. The 1917 Revolution separated Chekhov from his audience as effectively as the Puritans cut us off from the vitality of Shakespeare's theatre – we can imagine the immediacy, but it is brutally difficult to get it back; now, in fact, it may be as hard for Russian directors to catch the tense balance of the original plays as for us to sense them from another culture. For every under-attended winner like this *Platonov* there is a more popular, wayward cousin: a 1966 *Seagull* directed by Anatoly Efros with a strikingly vicious Nina, her lake replaced by a scaffold for Konstantin the artist to die on, or the 1980 production of the same play by Yefremov himself which ended with Nina recapitulating her speech from Konstantin's play from the ruined stage. Asked by an English visitor what Chekhov would have thought of such a thing, Yefremov shrugged and said, 'Chekhov is dead.'

The best tickets in town at the moment are the Youth Theatre's version of Bulgakov's *Heart of a Dog* and Oksana Mysina's magnificent implication of her audience in the story of Katerina Ivanovna from *Crime and Punishment* – implication because the audience is locked in a room with her as she confides in them one by one, like the women with small children in the metro begging with cardboard signs round their necks. Such shows are as much extrapolations on known texts as Yefremov's and Efros's Chekhovs or Lyubimov's Dostoyevskys; meditations on the classics clog the vacuum into which new writing might have rushed since 1990. This lack of creative nerve is typical of what is called freedom; but while Russia waits for its new agonies to find a voice there is at least a sincerity in its theatre not always typical of the West – the assumption of first-class acting in a company style puts to shame our creeping find-a-star-and-build-him-a-luxury-vehicle paralysis. Here, drama is definitely not just a means to pass the time: an English professional worn down by casual humiliations should take a bracing trip to Moscow, where artists are celebrated as they always were. Certainly, for a week, doors have swung open for me at the drop of a Raskolnikov.

> Our psychology is a dog's psychology: when we're beaten we whine
> and run to our kennels, and when we're stroked we lie on our backs
> with our paws in the air. How little justice there is in us, and how
> limited our patriotism...

This week's gala performance at the Taganka in memory of Vladimir Vysotsky, actor, singer and poet, is a postponement of one of the shows the Soviets cancelled before Lyubimov came to London for *Crime and Punishment.* The director has been reinstated at the Taganka, technically free but within a power-sharing structure that severely limits his spontaneity. The Vysotsky evening is attended by Boris Yemtsov, Yeltsin's Deputy Prime Minister. In it, a young actor brilliantly impersonates first Brezhnev ('who is this Vysotsky?'), then Gorbachev ('Vysotsky started the ball rolling, I followed it up'), and finally Yeltsin himself, promising that in future the hero's birthday will be celebrated by payment of Russian workers' overdue wages. This light reference to a topical scandal brings the house down, and Yemtsov and his pals are seen to roll in the aisles. The Taganka, whose walls used to hum with provocation, has become a harmless freeway for political cabaret which weighs in like *Spitting Image.*

It would have been Vysotsky's sixtieth birthday, and I wonder what he would have made of this evening, both necrophiliac and opportunist. 'The keeper of the nation's spirit, of our pain and all our joys' typically used to work not in concert (he was hardly permitted to) but in private apartments and the street, as the spirit took him, and people would simply gather, squat down and listen: the best image in Lyubimov's show is of twenty-five actors crouched attentively on the floor while a block of theatre seating covered with a vast white sheet swings gently from side to side above them. The trade in bootleg Vysotsky albums (many sounding as if he were singing down a distant telephone line) is healthy still – they include snatches of conversation and general *pensées* as well as the raw-voiced songs; but little candle-lit shrines on street corners are less common, since his audience is becoming less fervent with age. He died at forty-two from heart disease aggravated by chronic drinking, but with no diminution of his energies up to the end, leaving Marina Vlady, the French movie star, a widow; he lies not in Novodevichy but in the Vagankovskoye Cemetery, and buses leave the Taganka at regular intervals to visit the grave.

Glad-handed by Yemtsov and his cronies at the after-show party, Lyubimov is slapping backs he would at one time have preferred to stab. It is like a sponsors' reception. As the speeches boom forth, Alexander Trofimov, his original Raskolnikov, stands to one side, desperately ill at ease, but not for that reason. He makes a real effort at politeness on meeting me. I gather that the part was his moment of triumph preceding the actor's fearful decline – humbler and humbler casting, and the ethic of Lyubimov's ensemble allows for little protest. Other symptoms are painfully evident: his hands shake and his blood pressure looks wrong. A ditch runs either side of our road, first to last: I think immediately of Christopher Guinee in our production, who would give a wonderfully full-blooded performance as Marmeladov before slipping out to the pub for the second half. Of course he shouldn't have, but then who's to say? I realise I've barely seen Christopher since, professionally or otherwise; if I did but know it, he has just three more years.

The premiere of Lyubimov's version of *The Brothers Karamazov* at the Bolshoi Theatre in Petersburg later in the week is an emotional event, largely because the invitation to stage it here came from Giorgi Tovstonogov, the theatre's boss (and first director of *Strider*), just before he died, and because the new show more or less coincides with another birthday, Lyubimov's own. I go for the day and spend rather too much time walking about Petersburg in the cold, looking at the statue of a great nose dedicated to Gogol on Vosnesensky Passage, or sitting in the stalls watching Yuri's rehearsals all over again. It's melancholy: St Petersburg (which on the Russian tongue sounds disconcertingly like St Peter Brook) was, even in my memory, the showcase city; but now Moscow – the bleak, 'real' Russia – is the glamourpuss, while the old capital sinks into decay, violence and despair. In the absence of an infrastructure, so much these days depends on personalities. Moscow's Mayor Luzhkov – known as the Walrus, because of his preference for bathing through holes in midwinter ice – is a showman and entrepreneur who has encouraged investment, whereas Petersburg's Anatoly Sobchak was found guilty of corruption this year. It seems all of a piece that sitting in the Bolshoi stalls I am approached by a stubbly young man who gives me his producer's card – perhaps this is the Petersburg equivalent of the Bush or the Royal Court, I reflect, seeing the tragic and comic masks printed in its corner. However his soubriquet is 'producer of erotic shows' – I look back at the masks, which now look not so much tragic and comic as Before and After. He wants to make me an offer: I advise him to contact my London agent, a dignified and well-mannered woman, and imagine the rest.

Then I join Lyubimov at a Press Conference, where he insists that his was never political theatre like Brecht's but purely classical – this astute stance allows him to feel he is hovering above events, albeit in a rather leaky cradle. He is somewhat sneered at nowadays, as if he was as out of date as the system he repudiated, but in another way he represents continuity. *The Brothers Karamazov* is certainly unrepentant: the musical stings, unpredictable lighting and his actors' off-the-cuff theatricality sometimes compete and often crystallise into brilliant single images, first cousins to the moving door and flailing spotlights of *Crime and Punishment*. The only real difference is that Yuri is now virtually on the stage himself, sitting in state at the front like an orchestral conductor but without the concealment of a pit. It is clear that even after his losses at the Taganka, which rankle deeply, his energy is colossal. News reporters with video recorders charge down the aisle during the performance; there is a groaning buffet upstairs afterwards, with many speeches and bouquets, while cadres from various Petersburg theatres sing new lyrics to old pop melodies along the lines of: 'Oh, how good, Yuri Petrovich, how talented you are, you are here with us, Yuri Petrovich from Taganka...'

Once again, the only people not listening are his actors, in a corner getting drunk, fast. At a certain point someone calls out for a chair for Yuri, who is after all eighty, and I'm reminded of the premiere of *The Cherry Orchard*, though I can't say that Yuri demonstrates Chekhov's modesty under pressure. I leave soon after. We cling to each other in what is probably a real goodbye this time, even though he's been suggesting we work on *Timon of Athens* and *King Lear* together: for the latter he will have me play both Lear and the Fool. When I query the practicality of this the old Yuri flashes out: I shouldn't bother my head about it, he'll decide how it's to be done. Meanwhile I have lost my journalist companion, Marina, a statuesque woman in a tweed twin set and pearls who I know earns only ten dollars for a half-page article. I last saw her downing four glasses of champagne as if they were an investment. Where is she? I finally spot her up at the end of the table, scooping apples, bananas and oranges into her handbag in the old Soviet manner.

For all but the experts, visiting Russia from time to time is like adding touches to an unfinishable picture: another layer of romantic colour gets painted over, some detail of exaggerated importance returns to its true place. These days the sound of the Russian language is almost a surprise: but behind the fake fur and the buzz of the mobiles, the Austrian cake-shops and the cappuccino bars, beyond the empty cashpoints and the restaurants making an awkward transition from boorish *traktir*s to millennium watering-holes, the old Russian question stays unanswered: how in the world do people survive? Always, like Marina, they will shrug, 'Oh, we get by.' In a world somewhat resembling Chicago in the 1920s with its bent cops, gangster politicians and tax collectors who prefer cash payments, this is a mystery so deep as to be sinister. Nevertheless, most people, from the multimillionaires to your neighbours, proclaim and very likely feel an intense love of homeland, and those who travel complain that when they return the country has changed again. By the autumn of this year the average wage will have plummeted from $150 a month to $60, while Russians' overheads continue to include the extended families they simply cannot betray – all at a cost of living only a little lower than London. Sensitive to the probe, your friends carry their secrets away with them through crashing metal apartment-block gates into stone hallways, up in their unconvincing lifts, across cardboard-matted thresholds, and, their goodnights touched with both courtesy and shame, disappear behind doors padded against the cold into a secret life that remains as harsh as the Russian winter.

> An actor who's taken two or three parts tolerably well no longer bothers to learn his lines, puts on a silk hat and thinks himself a genius.

My report for the *Independent* fits in between a season with Peter Hall's Company at London's Old Vic and another at the Piccadilly. The repertoire last year included *The Seagull*: I played Trigorin, with Felicity Kendal as Arkadina, and Dominic West and Victoria Hamilton as Konstantin and Nina. When I looked out across the lake with Nina –

> It's paradise here...just lovely...a beautiful place...

– what I generally saw was a photograph I'd taken from a train near Yaroslavl in 1983. It may turn out that my only contribution to the history of Trigorin is a laboriously created wig of my own design, based on the look of Maxim Gorky, which had the critics positively rolling in the bars; but I was glad to discover Trigorin's greediness, and ate continuously in Act Three, as if a writer, like an actor, could never be quite sure where the next cucumber was coming from. To this man, it was natural to discuss life with Masha and to accept Nina's inscribed medallion without breaking munch: he was attentive to both women, but luncheon meats were an unavoidable accompaniment, like a stride pianist's left hand. This was all consistent with the fact that as far as women go, Trigorin is someone who, on seeing a blanket, would assume it was no more than his duty to climb under it.

I was gratified by a reviewer who said that when I opened my mouth in this part it seemed that I was about to speak in Russian; and really the only aspect of the engagement I didn't enjoy was the feeling of being the company's resident expert to whom my colleagues would turn, slightly dead-eyed, to ask the distance to Kharkov, how to drink tea properly or pronounce their names. Rising to the bait, I would offer some things unbidden – how you should cross yourself from the Orthodox right to left, the significance of bread and salt and why you might spit on the floor. In one rash moment I mentioned the Russian tradition whereby a company will sit together for a few quiet moments before undertaking a journey: this was enthusiastically taken up for Arkadina's

Act Three departure, but rather hurriedly, in the last minutes of a certain day's rehearsal, so that the reasons were not much gone into. Everyone ended up inventing their own: to check if they'd forgotten something, to contemplate the poetic vastness of Russia, or to have a quick rest. And in fact, and not to be precious, that's probably right. Meanwhile, ever alert to product for our new company, Hall asked me to revive *Anton Chekhov* as a companion piece.

I had barely done the show, apart from a few nights in Dublin and a brief German tour, since the week in 1986 when, in what we all knew was a last throw, Mum (now with a leg as fragile as Chekhov's mother's), Mark, the great suitcase and I piled onto a flight to Barcelona. The previous week I'd taped *Chekhov in Siberia* for the BBC – thinking inconveniently of Israel and giving a performance of some insinuating gravity, like a sort of Siberian Alan Bennett, but also a certain ponderousness, as if I were indeed wearying of the subject a little. The day before we left, the Arts Council had confirmed their grant for the new touring Shakespeare company which would occupy the next six years of my life to the exclusion of most else, so Chekhov in Barcelona already felt like a quaint revival.

The rain poured, all the time. Little and gallant and tired to the marrow, her hands in her lap, my mother saw the show again and specially enjoyed an off-the-cuff lecture I gave afterwards, which perhaps reminded her of my father. In her yellow pages she noted with satisfaction that I had been 'held in high esteem'. Quite the European lady, she took in Picasso and Miró and the glassblowers at the Pueblo Espagnol; but she seemed most at home in Tarragona Cathedral, and for a moment I wondered if she wasn't having a religious conversion in her discreet way. This is what she must have been like when I'd grown up and they made their trips to Florence and Rome – neither of them religious but delighted by the Renaissance, all of it part of her love for him and of her relief that I was, in some way, on my way.

Effie had seen her job in the world, like my father the demands of liberal justice, as no more than obvious: like the heroine of Eduardo di Filippo's *Filumena*, her true wish had been 'to stay quiet all my life'. A long happiness had now been followed by a limited contentment, though perhaps not three years' worth. I think that much of it consisted in making her notes, for really she was writing to my father, as Knipper continued to do to Chekhov. If not for these messages, how would he know what the Wailing Wall was like, or that she had been fearless in the souk, or that Antonio Gaudi had been run over by a tram, and that his Temple looked like a melting birthday cake? How else could he guess how alive she had felt in front of Caravaggio's *Saint Jerome* (old age to the exact life), or the El Greco in the museum at Montserrat, up in the mountains; or how it felt to hear the Sunday school children in the village square there, fingers of rock hanging above them, echoing the Salve that rang out from the great choir inside the packed church? And if he'd heard her, back home from Jerusalem, telling her friends (it put her somewhat ahead of much of her acquaintance) how a Russian boy and an Italian girl could chat each other up because an ancient Biblical language had been reinvented for the purpose, he might have been so delighted that he wouldn't have interposed to explain the painful history of the Russian Jew.

At all these times, the glimmering light hidden under a bushel for fifty years had peered out with a bright, thin radiance. I think my mother started to become ill the moment my father died, and while abhorring the melodrama of suicide, she now prepared herself to depart without fuss. Two springs after this, she looked carefully around and saw that, what with my travelling life and Mark's need to take wing, it was difficult for everyone to carry on; and she quietly withdrew from us all after a short illness, having seen me safe home from my new company's first season on the road.

As I wondered if I could re-learn my own lines, Mark's first child, Louis, was born, to be followed eighteen months later by his sister, Eve: more than anyone, he looks like my father. I excitedly called Lucien Stryk in Chicago and, most unlike a man who normally spends as long on a new poem as Ike-no-Taiga might on a scroll-painting, he immediately sent me a poem:

> Today my friend and I rejoice…
> Squirrels, rabbits, wildlife in
> the woods begin their gutsy antics,
> birds size up branches leafing into
> spring. And over there, a child is born.

I was shocked to realise that I was now ten years older than Chekhov when he died. Looking at the National Theatre tapes from 1984, I reckoned that I should have been playing him a great deal younger even then, and resolved on an altogether lighter and less gloomy tone. At the Vic I had as ideal a setting as I had had then on the other side of the wall from *Wild Honey*: now I would be in Konstantin's study, suddenly emptied of its ghostly occupants. Also, the Vic stage is very deep, so Chekhov would be able to start by materialising out of blackness in an eerie manner, as if he too were a visitant.

The script needed revision. This being a new political age, I took out Soviet premonitions such as the sinisterly incompetent spy at the Pension Russe. It also seemed obvious now that the opening was too complicated – the black monk, the insomnia business, the review of the life all jostling: so I pruned it back and concentrated on the sheer physical effort of wandering round the house trying to force fatigue to take over. I would still stay on in the interval, but now I'd do a proper curtain call, rather than remaining in character and thanking the audience for their company ('When I'm alone, for some reason, I feel afraid…'), as I rather archly had before.

By now enough people had pointed out that it was perverse to do a whole evening in the company of Chekhov without referring to the theatre at all, or touching on it so very obliquely. So I wrote four pieces of five minutes each about his attitude to the major plays. Late on in the second half, with the audience warmed up, Chekhov would pretend to run dry and step out of the frame to admit that yes, he supposed he should at last speak about them. I gave the audience the choice – *Seagull, Vanya, Three Sisters, Cherry Orchard* – but only one, and only for five minutes. At the end of this an alarm clock on the set would ring (the show was now so internally referenced that I could enjoy what very few people would have known, that Chekhov used to contribute to a periodical of that name). It was a genuine vote – I never simply did the one I preferred – though few people believed that, which was a pity, because the separate accounts were very hard to remember, having certain points in common which arose at different stages in each. All four ended with the same summary – Chekhov admitting that he had one last play in mind, about two men who wait all evening for a third who never comes. As I was about to name it, the alarm clock rang. For this I was chastised by some critics, experts as they are, who thought it a poor thing to take advantage of the fact that *Waiting for Godot* was in our repertoire at the Vic – but Chekhov in fact said this to Alexander Vishnevsky during his visit to Lyubimovka in 1902.

At least, I think he did. No, I'm sure of it – it's in Simmons and I read it on the Trans-Siberian. In fact I don't believe I've made anything up, though I have sometimes convinced myself that things happened in a different order. Chekhov's shelter in the Siberian cottage came not after the carriage crash but at some other time on the road, but it sounds more like a Chekhov story my way. It's also possible that the Romanov's Restaurant he ate in after the *Seagull* fiasco in Petersburg was an even rougher place – in Dostoyevsky's part of town, in fact – run by Vasily Romanov; but, perhaps primly, I've chosen the one nearer the theatre, opposite the Kazan Cathedral and next to where Petersburg's biggest bookshop would one day stand. In all these things, my research, though thorough, was ever a little opportunist: I've alighted on what most corroborated my suspicions. Accurate biography is only a way of helping you guess better; and in the theatre, whatever leads an audience to say, 'Yes, yes, I think that's likely', carries the weight of fact.

So just as Chekhov feared that his impressions of Siberia might have 'more of myself than Siberia in them', I am sure there is as much of me as of him in *Anton Chekhov* – I can hardly complain that the writer or the director or the company have forced me to compromise. Meanwhile Lucien Stryk, ever the gentleman, has never let me see him chuckling at the results of his modest proposal, so hastily spurned: he has watched Chekhov moving in on me with exemplary grace, though he must have been entertained at how often I have wanted, like my subject, to climb under the table rather than answer questions about my 'obsession'. The whole business has certainly engendered some eccentricity: for years I've rhapsodised to friends that I've been looking at the same view that Chekhov saw, sitting where he did on his garden steps or in his study, or that I've come across some wonderfully daft remark, all to a reception best described as tolerant. Sometimes he's resembled some private vice, as I sneaked back to my hotel to do a little more research rather than going out for a companionable drink. In a waking dream, I've tapped on his window and expected him to swing round at his desk to survey me through his pince-nez, his head lifting as Stanislavsky describes, his mouth beginning to open.

A few weeks after going to Moscow in 1998 I found myself on the Russian-Norwegian border at the small town of Kirkenes, up above the Arctic Circle. The town is best known as a base for reindeer safaris, but I was in a tiny municipal art museum, staring at a painting I'd never seen before but which I've talked about often enough: Genrikh Semiradsky's strikingly erotic *Phrynia Naked*. Once it hung in the Academy of Fine Arts in Petersburg, and that's where Chekhov stood in front of it – in fact in 1889, just after the opening of *Ivanov*, but, in my adaptation, on his first visit to the capital, when he mistook girls for bottles and fell asleep over Dostoyevsky:

> There were two attractions in Petersburg at that time – a painting by
> Semiradsky of a girl, naked, and me, fully clothed…

Although I was alone, I found myself turning in foolish delight – to whom? the curator? that familiar shadowy figure? I continued my walk muttering pleasantly to myself, feeling full of resource and quite at home in this improbable place.

Would Chekhov be disarmed by this story or the opposite? To claim a kinship with a great artist is a risky business; however, to feel companionship, certainly with a man like this, is normal. Maxim Gorky, not yet ready to declare that a socialist theatre had greater need of Dickens and Shakespeare, sat down one day to think about his recently-departed friend. He had a temperature and the guns of the Russo-Japanese War were rumbling – if tuberculosis hadn't killed Chekhov, Gorky reckons, this terrible violence would have done it. For some reason he remembers Chekhov's delight at finding a particularly good subject for a story – a Darwinian schoolteacher who fights ignorance and superstition by day, but at night boils up a black cat to extract a bone said to be lucky for love. Gorky seems to be writing for no other reason than that he misses his friend's conversation, his moroseness, his gusts of humour, even his angry knowledge that it is not pleasant to live only in order to die early. This, Gorky says, was a man who lived entirely 'on his own soul': he was himself, inwardly free, and never troubled with what others expected of Anton Chekhov. To remember him, he goes on, brings new energy into your life and reminds you that man is the axis of the world.

And in fact it is always, at the very least, a pleasure to think of Chekhov, in Tel Aviv, Hereford or Nakhodka, when your matches go off in your pocket or when you lack incomprehensible daring ardour. In a life so short it is always a shock to remember the fact, Chekhov lost more friends than most people do by sixty, but he has gained hundreds of thousands who love that fugitive figure, its guardedly attentive attitude, the merciless word in the right place, the moral force lightly carried: one thinks of him in the most unexpected corners of life. Unavailable to account for himself, he has become the invention of his admirers, who may prefer him wary or exuberant, skittishly lyrical, coldly severe, charming or implacable, walking like a girl or tough as old boots. Some get excited by the new Chekhov, now those old-maidish Soviets have got their hands off him to reveal warts on the familiar face: all this does to others is prompt a smile. For what could be more natural for a man with delicate physical difficulties in a barbarous age than to complain daily to his sister about the water closets; and for a consumptive whose euphoria turned erotic at inconvenient times, what more natural than to exploit his new-found fame in Moscow's green rooms or to turn down an alley in a Siberian town? None of this affects our enthusiastic co-opting of his spirit.

It certainly is the case that in Chekhov's company it becomes easier to live something like a good life, in which his responses – tactful, candid or tolerant – become your own. His voice doesn't need to be loud or consistent: he believed that life demands constant work, day and night, and to hell with the rest, but he also, asked for its meaning, said it was the same as with a carrot – it's just a carrot, and that's all we know. He passionately believed in his profession, and that man would only improve when he was shown what he was really like:

> Most of all, dear friend, you must not lie, it's impossible to lie in art. You can lie in love, in politics, even in medicine; you can deceive other people and even the good Lord himself, but it is impossible to lie in art.

But he is equally inspiring in a whisper:

> Please greet the lovely hot sun from me, and the quiet sea. Enjoy yourselves, be happy, don't think about illness and write often to your friends.

So, let him go. If nothing else, I've done one thing that he'd have liked, a tribute to his sense of the silly and his self-esteem, and a better version of the hornpipe I once planned to make him dance. When I admitted at the Old Vic that the audience would want to hear something about the plays, and which one would it be, there was always a great outcry. They would yell the names of their favourites – I remember a few of them standing up – until chaos made it hard to choose the winner. This used to run happily on for a minute or so; I thought as I waited, well, this is it – an excited audience yelling the names of Chekhov plays at someone playing Chekhov, much as at a rock concert when favourite songs are called for. At this point of genial collusion, I felt that a man I had taken many liberties with could probably rest in peace.

ANTON CHEKHOV

by Michael Pennington

The text that follows is the current playing version

ACT ONE

*Night. Chekhov's study, surrounded by darkness. A clock ticking.
His desk, covered with papers, etc., with an oil lamp. Downstage of
the desk, a chair. Upstage of it, Levitan's painting 'Haystacks In the
Moonlight' on a music stand, and a small table with a basin and
pitcher of water, a towel and a saucer. A garden chair with the
Braz portrait of Chekhov on it in the centre and a bentwood chair,
partly covered with dustsheets. Upstage left, a table with chairs,
also covered. Downstage left, a coatstand and an open trunk, packing
cases, one of them green, strong enough to sit on. A doctor's bag.
Piles of books around the trunk, and around the base of the desk.
We glimpse CHEKHOV.*

CHEKHOV: If I were asked what is the essential
characteristic of my life these days, I'd have to say
insomnia.

He comes forward into the room.

Every night I go to bed at midnight exactly and fall
asleep immediately, and then I wake at two o'clock,
feeling as if I hadn't slept at all. I get out of bed and
light the lamp. I step out into my garden. Then I walk
from corner to corner of the room for an hour or so,
looking at all the pictures on the wall. Then, tired of
that, I sit at my desk, without movement, without
thought and without desire. Sometimes I make myself
count to a thousand to occupy my mind. I imagine a
friend's face. I listen for sounds. The cupboard creaks;
the lamp gives a sudden whistle. All these sounds
disturb me somehow.

He sits at his desk.

All tonight I've been thinking about a strange story
I heard – I can't remember where. A thousand years
ago there was a monk, all dressed in black, walking in
the Sahara Desert. At the same moment, several miles
away, some fishermen saw another black monk moving
slowly across the surface of a lake. This second monk

was a mirage. This mirage generated another mirage, then a third, and so on, until the image had been endlessly transferred from one layer of the earth's atmosphere to another. You can forget about the law of optics: this monk can be seen on Mars and on the stars of the Southern Cross. But the point of the story is this. Exactly a thousand years from the day the monk was walking in the desert, he will return to earth and be seen by men. It seems that we are now at the end of the thousand years, and so, according to the old story, we can expect to see that black monk any moment now.

Where did I hear this story? Did I read it? Did someone tell it to me? Or did I dream it?

Never mind.

Reluctantly he registers the audience.

My name is a popular name. Among Russian writers I am number thirty-seven. There's not a single stain on my name. Josef Braz has just finished my portrait, did you see it?

He briefly shows the portrait.

Do you think that looks like me? It's not me, it's some Frenchman. I sat for this portrait for three weeks, eating cherries twenty at a time – which is the best way to eat cherries, by the way – and still it makes me look as if I'd been sniffing grated horseradish. Braz wants to present it to Moscow University. Very suitable. The broken-down buildings of Moscow University, its gloomy corridors and dirty walls, have been an important conditioning factor in the history of Russian pessimism.

He is taking off his coat and moving between the desk and the coatstand, eyeing his books.

I studied there myself, at Medical School. I can't remember what prompted me to choose Medical School at the time, but I've had no reason to regret the choice. In fact, to this day I regard medicine as my legal wife and literature as my mistress: it's very convenient, when I get tired of the one I can slip off and spend the night with the other. Not very respectable, but at least it's not boring.

He begins to pack books into a trunk.

When I look back on my life, it seems to me a beautiful, accomplished composition: all that remains is not to spoil the finale. I've worked hard, I have the stamina of a camel, and I do have talent: I've published six hundred short stories and a poem. Also, as you may know, I have sinned in the dramatic line, but not much, because I don't like the theatre and I can't stand the actors. What nonsense they talk. When they're young they scrape their feet and neigh like donkeys, and when they're old their voices become so hoarse with drinking you can't hear what they're saying. All the same, I have written a few plays: Tolstoy says they're even worse than Shakespeare's. I'm quite afraid of Tolstoy: after all, he wrote, 'Anna Karenina saw her own eyes gleaming in the darkness.' He's a colossus; though I can't help feeling there's more love of humanity in electricity and steam than in chastity and the refusal to eat meat.

To live well and humanly one must work, work with love and faith: and really what I'd like best is to be a little bald old man sitting in a comfortable study at a big desk, writing and writing. But I'm also of the opinion that true happiness is impossible without idleness. My ideal is to be completely idle and love a fat girl. I'd like life to flash by brilliantly, because I know life is short. I'd like to sit on a boatdeck and pop bottles of champagne, and in the evenings, women. I'd like to go to Chicago and India and Constantinople, and so on and so forth...

He has a bottle of champagne and a glass and sits comfortably centre. The sound of the clock has faded and the light brightens a little.

The trouble is, I get homesick and develop a yearning for cabbage soup and buckwheat porridge. My publisher says that whenever we go abroad together all I ever want to see are the cemeteries and the circuses. He says I once lay down in St Mark's Square in Venice and cried out aloud, 'Ah, how good it would be to be lying on the grass in Moscow! Ah, Moscow, Moscow!' But I don't believe I did. It's just that I was tired out with walking: you know what Italy's like. I used to come back to my hotel in the evening feeling as if my feet had been stuffed with cotton wool. Actually I remember Venice very well; partly because if you're a poor degraded Russian and you stand and listen to the organ in the cathedral there you immediately want to become a Catholic; and partly because two Dutch girls used to sit opposite me at dinner, and I would look at them and imagine a little white house with a tower and wonderful butter and cheese and Dutch herring, and a venerable pastor and a quiet schoolteacher, and I decided I wanted to marry a Dutch girl and have our picture painted outside our clean little house. In fact Holland's one of the few places I've not been: I've been everywhere else. I was in Hong Kong, and I was greatly impressed, by the way: movement on the sea such as I've never seen, and everywhere the tender concern of the English for their employees. We Russians criticise the English for exploiting the Chinese, and you do, of course, but in return you give them water, roads, museums, Christianity; whereas we Russians, we exploit, but what do we give in return? On that journey I went swimming in the Indian Ocean too, and then I went to Ceylon – what paradise! I travelled on the railways and had my fill of palm groves and bronze-skinned women. So I shall be able to say to my children: 'Listen, you, your father once had a black-eyed Hindu girl, and would you like to know where? In a coconut grove, on a moonlit night!'

All in all, I think France is my favourite. Especially Paris; to take your own wife to Paris would be like taking your own samovar to Tula. Culture in France oozes from every shop window and wicker basket: every dog smells of civilisation. I used to stay at the

Pension Russe in Nice and live the life of a king. The only thing against the Pension Russe was the other Russians, devil take them all: what fools, one ugly face after another, nothing but malice and gossip. A Russian's such a strange creature: as in a sieve, nothing remains in him. When he's young, he fills himself up greedily with anything he comes across, but after thirty years all that's left is a kind of grey rubbish. I sometimes think that the Russian evolved from a magpie and the German from a fox and the English from – excuse me – a frozen fish; but the French are amazingly courteous and considerate, don't you think? My chambermaid used to smile at me constantly, smile like a stage duchess; though underneath I could tell she was tired, terribly tired. And the life in the streets is so wonderful – I would just go out of my hotel in the evening and drift with the crowd, anywhere: it's as if there really were a sort of universal soul. No, it's really good to travel abroad; and of course we could go mad amidst all your European culture and art. All the same, our Russian painters are more solid than the French – in fact, there's not a single European landscape artist to compare with my friend Levitan.

He indicates Levitan's painting.

Levitan's a king. One evening I was feeling melancholy for the fields of central Russia, and he grabbed up some board and his paints and in half an hour he'd done this for me – *Haystacks In the Moonlight* – wonderful.

Levitan once went on holiday to Italy, and as soon as he got off the boat he began to miss his Russian landscapes so badly he turned on his heel and came home again. What nostalgia we all feel for our homeland. When I'm abroad I think constantly of the southern steppes of my childhood. I used to spend my summer holidays with my grandfather in Voronezh Province, on the estate where he worked, and he would put me in charge of the big steam threshing machine, and it would whistle and whine, with a cunning, playful expression, and it seemed to me that it was human, and the men working it were the machines...

I have a memory too of travelling with my grandfather
to Rostov on Don when I was still a schoolboy. It was a
blazingly hot day, quite exhausting. Our eyes were
gummed together and our mouths were dry with the
heat and the wind blowing up the dust. We didn't feel
like talking or looking or thinking. We stopped at a
place called Bakhchi Salakh to feed the horse at the
house of a rich Armenian my grandfather knew. I can
remember sitting on a green chest in the corner of the
room, exhausted and covered with dust.

*He is moving towards the packing cases stage left, where the
light begins to intensify.*

The wooden walls were unpainted, and the furniture
and yellow floorboards reeked of wood baked by the
sun. Everywhere I looked there were flies, flies.
Grandfather and the Armenian were discussing sheep,
and I knew it would be another hour before the
samovar went on, then another hour for tea, and then
grandfather would have to sleep off his tea for two or
three hours after that; so a quarter of my day would be
spent waiting, and then there'd be more heat and more
dust and more jolting on the roads. I began to hate the
steppe, the sun and the flies.

Just then I heard hurried footsteps, and a girl of about
sixteen came into the room, wearing a simple cotton
dress and a white shawl. As she rinsed the crockery and
poured the tea she had her back to me, and all I could
see was that she was slender and barefooted, and that
her small heels were covered with long trousers.

The Armenian was offering me tea. As I sat down (*He
does so.*) I glanced up at the girl, who was handing me
my glass, and all at once it was as if a fresh breeze had
run across my soul, sweeping away the day's
impressions in all their dustiness and dreariness. I saw
the bewitching features of the loveliest face I've ever
seen, asleep or waking. She was a beautiful girl, and I
could see it at a glance, like lightning.

Sometimes, you know, clouds huddle in disorder on the horizon, and the sun behind them paints the sky with every imaginable shade: crimson, orange, gold, violet, pink. One cloud becomes like a monk, another like a fish, another a Turk in his turban; the sunset glistens on a church cross or the windows of a manor house; it's reflected in the rivers and it quivers on the trees. Far away, a flock of wild ducks flies homewards. Everyone who looks at the sunset – the boy out herding his cows, the surveyor on the mill dam, the fine gentleman out for a walk – all gaze at it and find it beautiful; but wherein its beauty lies, no-one knows, no-one can say.

Well, in exactly the same way I'm ready to swear that that Armenian girl was a real beauty, but I can't prove it to you. I gazed at her. I wanted to say something pleasant to her, something honest and beautiful, something as beautiful as herself. This appreciation of mine was rather strange, because it was not desire, nor joy, nor pleasure that she excited in me, but a kind of painful, pleasant sadness, vague and hazy as a dream. For some reason I felt sorry for myself, sorry for grandfather and the Armenian, even sorry for the girl herself; I felt that the four of us had somehow lost something important and necessary for life, and we'd never find it again. Perhaps I simply regretted that she wasn't mine and never would be, that I was a stranger to her; or perhaps I had the idea that such rare loveliness was an unnecessary accident, and like everything else on earth, not long to last. Who knows.

At any rate, my hours of waiting had passed unnoticed. Our driver walked down to the river and began to bathe the horse and harness it, and the wet horse snorted with pleasure and kicked its hooves against the shafts. Grandfather woke up, the Armenian girl opened the creaking gate, and we all got into the carriage and drove out of the yard in silence, as if we were angry with each other.

And when Rostov on Don appeared in the distance two or three hours later, our driver, who had been silent throughout the journey, suddenly looked round and said: 'She's a fine girl, that Armenian's daughter.' And he whipped the horse.

Silence. The light gradually returns to normal.

So you see I fathomed the mysteries of love rather early in life: but really there was no childhood in my childhood. My grandfather was known as the Viper: he was a serf who bought his freedom and beat my father and then my father beat my brothers and me, with a rope soaked in tar – we felt like little convicts. My home town was so poor that only the Mayor and one of the Greek merchants was permitted the luxury of a chamberpot. My father ran a small grocery store: he used to short-change his customers and give thanks to God – he was a religious man. I remember once a rat dying in a big vat of oil in the store: Father called in a priest to reconsecrate the oil and went on selling it. He put me to work as soon as he could, selling candles across the counter from dawn to dusk – how cold it was in there! I remember the lavatories were half a mile away on waste ground, and sometimes I'd find myself face to face in there with some old tramp who was sheltering for the night – what a fright we both got!

As a schoolboy my trousers were so tight that the other children used to shout: 'Look out, here comes the macaroni.' Idea for a short story: a young man, the son of a serf, a grocer, choirboy and student, brought up to respect rank and kiss the hands of priests and worship other people's ideas, giving thanks for every piece of bread, often whipped, going to school without galoshes, fighting, torturing animals, dining with rich relations, playing the hypocrite before God and man; how this young man squeezes the slave out of himself drop by drop, till he wakes one morning to find that the blood flowing through his veins is not that of a slave but a real human being...

He has a bad coughing fit, and crosses to his desk, attempting to hide it.

I'm terribly sorry. Everyone has something which he hides. Life is quite an unpleasant business, isn't it – but it's not so very hard to make it wonderful. You don't have to win a lottery or marry a beautiful woman: all these blessings are transitory and liable to become a habit. To be continuously happy, even in times of misfortune, here is what you need: One, to be satisfied with the way things are, and Two, to rejoice in the knowledge that they could have been much worse.

Now. If your matches go off in your pocket, rejoice, and give thanks to heaven that your pocket's not a gunpowder magazine. If your relatives come to call, exclaim triumphantly: 'How very lucky it's not the police!' Be glad that you're not a tramway horse, or a tapeworm, or a pig, or a donkey, or a bear led by gypsies, or a bedbug. When they take you to the police station, rejoice; and if your wife has proved unfaithful to you, be glad that she has merely betrayed you and not her country.

There now. You follow my advice, good people, and your lives will be full of happiness – which, after all, is not a supernatural condition. Shouldn't happiness be the normal state of man?

He is moving upstage right to wash himself.

However badly your dogs or your samovar behave, winter will always be followed by spring, just as youth is followed by age, and unhappiness is always followed by happiness – and vice versa. But I do believe that to secure a truly happy life, you must attain a certain degree of what I can only call culture – by which I mean something more than having read *The Pickwick Papers* or memorised a monologue from *Faust*. For instance, a cultured man requires more of a woman than physical relief and horse sweat. If he has talent he respects it, and his heart aches for something that can't be seen with the naked eye. He believes in constant work, day and night, incessant reading, and will always lie down with a book, even if it's only Turgenev.

Heaven knows what I was like as a young man – a very harsh person, liable to flare up at any moment – well, you can understand why: it's taken me years to learn how to restrain myself. Even after I moved to Moscow, my life was hardly conducive to culture. My four brothers and my sister and my parents and I lived in rooms the size of a chest of drawers and I was having to support them all; I was treating infant syphilis at Medical School all day, and then up all night producing newspaper articles and short stories like smelts – one story sold, one smelt to take home to the family for dinner; running round the city like some crooked journalist looking for copy – bad pavements, cockroaches in the bakery, the terrible lavatories at the Maly Theatre. But then, if I was completely stuck for a story, I'd go and visit old Liodor Palmin. What a wonderful fellow he was. You won't have heard of him, I know, but he was one of the real veterans of literature, the kind of influence a young writer can't do without.

He moves across to the upstage left table where the light intensifies, as if Palmin was there.

He used to live in an airless basement, never eating or seeing the sunlight; and often I'd try to get him away to the country, if not for his talent's sake then at least for hygiene's, but he'd never come. Instead he'd go wandering around Moscow with his trousers unbuttoned and his coat all covered with stains and his tie round the back of his neck, and always five or six stray dogs following him around, and I used to wonder how such a poetical spirit could survive in such a run-down body.

But the gods had entered Palmin's flesh and blood, and he was in a state of perpetual ecstasy, with his head stuffed full of themes and ideas, so I used to sneak off to him like a thief in the night and he'd open his heart to me. The last time I talked with him was just before I went to Petersburg, when my work was first being taken seriously, and as usual he brought out a plate of cucumbers and a quart of vodka, and then at five o'clock exactly his fat wife came in, as she always did at five o'clock exactly, always with exactly the same words:

– Liodor Ivanovich, isn't it time you had your beer?

– What did you get married for, Liodor Ivanovich (I'd say to him)? Love lets you down, it brings you less than you expect, and a woman will deceive you five times over before she's worn out a pair of shoes.

– Anton Pavlovich, I think Shakespeare has already spoken quite adequately on this subject.

– Well, I shall never get married. When somebody says the same thing to me day after day, I become quite wild. No. As I shall lie in the grave alone, so I shall live alone.

– Anton Pavlovich, a wife is a wife. A wife is a wife.

– Well I shouldn't write any better for being married and fussing around a wife – unless you could find me one like the moon, that doesn't appear in my sky every day. And I'm famous now, Liodor Ivanovich, and reading the critics about myself. My brother Nikolai says I should die soon and become really famous. To think that such a genius would emerge from a privy. I'm off to Petersburg in the morning to meet the publisher Suvorin, he's going to produce my new volume of short stories; but I don't know what to call it. What shall I call it, Liodor Ivanovich?

– Call it *Buy This Book Or You'll Get A Punch In The Mouth.*

Well, so off I went to Petersburg the next day, and I must say I was treated like the Shah of Persia.

He moves away, downstage centre, and the light moves with him.

There were two attractions in Petersburg at that time – a painting by Semiradsky of a girl, naked, and me, fully clothed. People pointed me out in restaurants and

treated me to sandwiches; I picked up a liking for
cigars and got so drunk I mistook girls for bottles and
bottles for girls. I went to meet the publisher Suvorin: I
remember I had a good wash and put on my new shoes
with the pointed toes and took a cab to his office. His
secretary greeted me as if I were her fiancé, so I bowed
low to her and scraped my new shoes and said How Do
You Do and so on. Then Suvorin rushed in and even
offered me his hand. 'Work hard, young man!' he cried,
'I'm pleased with you, but be sure to go to church and
don't drink too much vodka. Let me smell your breath!
Don't waste your money! Pull your socks up!' Then he
gave me a glass of tea as black as pitch and we took a
boat trip on the Neva, which impressed me greatly.
Suvorin's a talking machine: we shall probably both die
from inflammation of the vocal cords. After that we
went to Dominique's restaurant and he bought me a
meat pie and a vodka and a cup of coffee. Then I went
home and fell asleep trying to read *The Brothers
Karamazov*. Oh dear, oh dear.

He sits downstage of his desk.

So long-winded and indelicate. Too pretentious. Writers
like Dostoyevsky think we should be solving great
questions, like God and pessimism. But we have
specialists who deal with specialised subjects like that.
For the most part people have dinner, that's all they do,
they have dinner, and yet during this time their
happiness is established or their lives are falling apart. I
mean, why should I write about a man who climbs into
a submarine and goes to the North Pole in order to
achieve a reconciliation with the world, while at the
same moment his beloved hurls herself with a shriek
from the belfry? No. You should write about ordinary
things. Pyotr Semionovich married Maria Ivanovna.
That's all.

He looks at his watch. He is back in the present.

Well, of course, I learned the virtues of brevity very
early. For the Moscow magazines, the rules were five

kopecks a line, maximum a hundred lines; if you went over, back would come your answer: 'Dear sir, you don't bloom, we fear. Your latest story is long and colourless, like the paper ribbon a Chinaman pulls out of his mouth. We shan't print. You are fading. Very sad.' To hell with them. When I think of those editors now, it's as if I'd swallowed a woodlouse.

Angered, he is again moving between the desk and the trunk, packing books.

But I did learn to write about anything, straight off, and I can't remember a single story I spent more than a day on. Writers nowadays complain they've no subjects. It's absolute nonsense, everything's a subject; you can dig them up by the spadeful. For instance, you might see a monk going from place to place begging a bell for his monastery, and you can feel an excellent subject coming; there's something tragic about that black monk against the pale background of the dawn... Or this wall, it seems to hold absolutely no interest at all, does it? But if you look really closely at it, you'll find something unusual there, something no one else has noticed, and then an excellent story can come out of it. And I do think a good story should be brief and to the point, so that reading it's like swallowing a glass of vodka. Alphonse Daudet once asked a bird: 'Why are your songs so short?' And the bird replied: 'Because I have so many songs, and I'd like to sing them all.' Well, as you write, your subject has to seep through your memory like a filter, leaving behind only what is important and typical. For instance, you might want to describe a moonlit night. Well, forget about shimmering light and the sound of a piano in the scented air – you should write: a single star lit up a piece of broken glass in the milldam. Or think of a man in a field of rye on a sunny day. Now Dostoyevsky would write: A tall, narrow-chested man who had a short red beard sat down on the green grass, already trampled by passers-by, sat down noiselessly, timidly, fearfully glancing about him... I'd write: The man sat on the grass. You have to be objective. Little details. The sun rises. The birds sing. It's a hot and sultry afternoon. Not a cloud in the sky…

As he begins to invent this story, he moves downstage left, while the light brightens to match his description.

The grass is parched by the sun and has a melancholy air to it, as if the rain will never turn it green again. The forest is quiet and still, looking out from its treetops, as if it were waiting for something.

Along the edge of the scrubland comes a tall, narrow-chested man, about forty, trudging along in a red shirt, patched trousers and big boots. On his right the green of the scrub; to his left, as far as the eye can see, a golden ocean of rye. He's red in the face from the heat, and on his blond head he wears a white jockey's cap. He has a hunting bag on his shoulder and a crumpled woodcock hangs out of it. He's holding a double-barrelled shotgun in his hand and with his eyes screwed up he watches his scraggy old dog, who's running ahead and smelling at the bushes. Everything is quiet… not a sound…every live creature is hidden away from this heat.

– Yegor Vlasych!

The hunter starts, looks round and frowns. Beside him, as though she's sprung out of the earth, is a pale-faced peasant woman, about thirty, with a sickle in her hand. She looks into his face and smiles timidly.

– Oh, it's you, Pelageya…mmm…what are you doing here?

– The women from our village work over here, Yegor Vlasych, and I work with them.

– Hmmm…

And they walk along together in silence, about twenty paces. Pelageya looks fondly at the man's rippling shoulders.

– It's such a long time since I've seen you, Yegor Vlasych. Not since you came into our house in Holy Week for a drink of water. We've not seen you at all since then…yes, you came in for a minute in Holy Week, and goodness knows what state you were in… you were drunk…and you swore at me and beat me and left…and I waited and waited, looking out for you. Oh, Yegor Vlasych, if only you'd come just once!

– What for?

– Well, not for anything of course, but still, it is your house: you could have seen how things were going, you're the master. Oh look, Yegor Vlasych, you've shot a little woodcock. Come, sit down and have a rest.

Pelageya is laughing like a girl. She looks at him and her face breathes happiness.

– Sit down? Yes, why not? You, sit down too.

CHEKHOV sits on a case downstage left.

Pelageya sits in the hot sun. Two minutes go by in silence.

– Couldn't you come just once?

– What for? (And Yegor sighs, and takes off his cap, and mops his brow with his sleeve.) There's no point. If I visit you just for an hour or two it gets you all muddled up, and I couldn't bear to live in your village all the time. You know me, I'm a bit spoiled: I need a good bed and good tea and good conversation. Now I have all that, but in your village there's only poverty and dirt, I couldn't stand it for a day. You know, if they made a law that I had to live with you come what may, I'd burn your house down or shoot myself. There's nothing to be done – I'm just spoiled.

– And where are you living now?

– With the master, Dmitry Ivanovich. I'm his huntsman. I provide all the game for his table.

– That's not a respectable life, Yegor Vlasych…

– You're silly; you don't understand anything. You've never understood what kind of a man I am, and you never will. You think I'm crazy, a lost soul, but among people who know, why, I'm the best shot in the district. The gentry all know that. I've been written about in a magazine, even. There's no-one who can match me. You know, since I was a boy, I've done nothing without a gun, it's what I know…and if they took away my gun, I'd take up a fishing line, and if they took away my fishing line, I'd go hunting with my bare hands; and when I'd the money I'd go to the fairs for the horsedealing. Well, you know yourself, once a peasant takes up with the hunting and the horsedealing, then it's goodbye to the plough. Once that free spirit's entered a man, you'll not get it out: it's like when one of the gentry takes up with the players, he'll not go back to his desk. You're a woman, you don't understand, but you ought to.

– I do understand, Yegor Vlasych…

– No you don't, not if you're going to cry about it.

– I'm not crying, Yegor Vlasych, it's just that it's wrong. It's been twelve years since I married you, and we've had no love, no love…

– Love. (And Yegor scratches his head.) How can there be love? To you, I'm just a wild man, and to me you're just a peasant girl. Do you think we're a match? I'm free, I'm pampered, I'm my own man, and you, you're a worker, you live in the dirt, you've no time to straighten your back even. What kind of a couple are we?

– Yes, but we are married, Yegor Vlasych…

– Yes, because Count Sergei Pavlovich got so jealous that I shot better than him that he got me drunk for a month, and when I'm drunk you can make me change my religion, let alone get married. So he paired me off to you: the huntsman and the cowgirl! What did you do it for? You could see I was drunk. You're not a serf, you don't have to do what he says. Ah, but it's a good catch for a cowgirl, a huntsman, isn't it? Well, now you suffer and you cry and you bang your head on the wall, and the Count just laughs at you.

Silence. Wild ducks fly over the scrub. Yegor watches them until they drop down below the forest, three tiny white dots…

– How do you live then?

– I work, Yegor Vlasych, and in the winter I take a little baby from the orphanage and feed him from the bottle. A rouble and a half I get for that.

– Mmm.

Silence again. From a strip of land that's been harvested comes a quiet song, but it stops as soon as it starts. It's too hot for singing…

– I hear you're building a new house, Yegor Vlasych. For Akulina. You must be fond of her.

– Ah well, such is life. Be patient, little one. Look here, I've been sitting here talking too long… I've to be in Boltovo by nightfall.

And Yegor stretches and hitches his gun over his shoulder.

– When will you be coming to our village again?

– No point. I never come when I'm sober, and I'm no use to you when I'm drunk. I get so mad when I'm drunk. Goodbye then.

– Goodbye, Yegor Vlasych.

And Yegor puts on his cap, tilting it backwards, calls to his dog and walks on. Pelageya stands still, looking at him as he goes…she can see the movement of his shoulders and the back of his head, his lazy, casual walk, and her eyes fill up with sadness and tenderness…her gaze runs over her husband's tall figure, touching him, cherishing him…Yegor seem to feel her look and turns. He is silent, but from the look on his face and his slightly lifted shoulders Pelageya can tell he wants to say something. Timidly she goes up to him and looks into his face, pleading.

– Here, that's for you.

It's a worn rouble note. She accepts it automatically.

– Goodbye, Yegor Vlasych.

He walks along the road; it's long and straight as a leather belt. Pelageya stands motionless and pale as a statue, catching his every step in her eye. Then the red of his shirt mixes in with his dark trousers, she can no longer see his steps, she can no longer tell which is his dog and which are his boots. She can only see his little white cap, and then…suddenly Yegor turns sharply into the scrub and his cap disappears into the green.

– Goodbye, Yegor Vlasych, Pelageya whispers, and stands on tiptoe, trying to get a last view of that little white cap.

The light snaps back to normal and the clock starts ticking again. Otherwise silence. CHEKHOV moves across to his desk and his teaglass. A long silence.

Just going to have some tea.

He moves away to the back of the set.

Interval.

ACT TWO

The lights snap on, warmest in the downstage left area. CHEKHOV is discovered there, above the suitcases, with a glass of tea. He is bright and vigorous.

CHEKHOV: My Siberian hostess just wiped this teaspoon on her behind and gave it to me. Tea is a real blessing on the road, it warms you up and banishes sleep. My God, how rich Russia is in good people. I can see her in the next room making bread; the morning sun is streaming over her brow and her breast and her hands, so that it looks as if she's kneading sunlight into the dough. Were it not for the cold, Siberia would be the richest and happiest of lands. People don't belch in front of you or examine their corns or search for insects in their hair – it's absolutely wonderful. The one bad thing is the sausage, which tastes like a dog's tail covered with tar. However, at every station on the road there are good water closets, and on the Volga riverboat there was one with four steps leading up to it: anyone with less experience than me would have taken it for a royal throne.

He puts down his tea. He seems older.

I'd caught a new disease. Mania Sakhalinosa. I had the feeling my trousers weren't hanging right: I wasn't writing as I should, in fact when I thought about my work it was as if I were eating cabbage soup from which a cockroach had been taken – if you'll forgive the comparison. So I decided to make a journey across Siberia, to the island of Sakhalin, where there's a penal colony, and write a report on the conditions there. Our government uses Sakhalin to resettle our Siberian exiles when their sentences have run – rather as you did with Australia. Exile. What a terrible thing for a Russian. We've let millions of people rot in prisons all across the continent, and then we've driven them through the Siberian cold for thousands of miles and infected them with syphilis and debauched them, and then blamed it all on the red-nosed prison warders. But it's not the red-nosed prison warders who are to blame – it's us. All of us.

Well, of course my friends all thought I'd gone mad: they said no-one's interested in Sakhalin and assumed I must be on the run from some love affair. But the way I saw it, if literature is my mistress and medicine my wife, then I'd been behaving towards my wife like a pig; so I bought myself some boots and a sheepskin coat and a revolver and a knife to cut sausage with and keep the tigers at bay, and thus armed from head to foot, off I set. I knew it would be solitary and full of hardships, but then to the lonely man the desert is everywhere.

He sits on a suitcase downstage left. He is younger again.

I go along in a sort of wicker basket drawn by a pair of horses: I sit in this vehicle and look down on God's earth like a baby, without a thought in my head. Heaven only knows where the Siberian plain ends: brown earth, the bare branches of the birch trees covered with hoar frost like powdered sugar, lakes all covered with ice, a cold wind pricking my cheeks. Wild ducks take wing from my carriage wheels and fly lazily off into the birch trees: never in my life have I seen such a multitude of ducks. My carriage jolts over the hillocks, turning my innards inside out, but I'm used to it now and no longer notice how morning turns to noon and noon to night. My socks blow their noses. The inside of my felt boots feel like a water closet. All that keeps me going is some incomprehensible daring ardour.

Mind you, I might have had to return home a headless horseman. I was driving along in the early hours of this morning watching the grass being burned by the side of the road when we collided with a mailcoach coming in the opposite direction and I was thrown out of the carriage with my bags on top of me. The drivers climbed down and started cursing each other. How horrible it was, and what grossness of spirit it took to think up such language, dragging through the mud all that's most precious to man. There I stood before dawn in the open fields, looking at the broken shafts of the carriage and the flames eating up the grass and my smashed bags and the horses in a black mass on the ground, and I felt as if I was in another world and that soon I'd be trampled to bits. You can't imagine how desolate it was.

So we repaired the carriage and I took refuge in this peasant's hut, by which time it was already light and there were golden tones in the sky and the heathcocks were calling. I fell asleep for a time and dreamed of my own bed in my own room: I dreamed I was sitting at my own table and telling my friends how I was nearly killed by a carriage on the Siberian highway. Then I woke and realised where I was. I had a good look round: it's quite charming. The peasant and his wife have decorated their walls with sweet wrappers and vodka labels, and someone's painted a tree on the door growing out of a vase, and some red flowers, and birds that look more like fish. The demand for art is here, but the good Lord has sent no artists. How can a peasant think about art? For nine months of the year he can't even take off his mittens and straighten his fingers, and when the summer comes his back aches with labour.

My first visitor was grandpa, very interested in me.

– Are you from Russia, your Honour?

– Yes, that's right, from Russia.

– Never been there. Round here, if a fellow's been to Tomsk he puts on airs.

– I've been to Tomsk. It's like a pig in a skullcap, isn't it, in bad taste. Why is it so cold in Siberia?

– It's God's will. I was just looking at your gun, your Honour. I was wondering how much it cost. Do you think there's going to be a war, do you?

– No, no, my gun is for self-defence only.

– Think of that… The newspapers are saying there's to be a railway built round here, your Honour. But how can that be? It'll work by steam, I understand that. But if it has to go through the village isn't it going to knock over the houses and crush the people?

I explain about the rails.

– Think of that…

Just then the door opened and an idiot boy wandered in, carrying firewood. His arms were as thin as little sticks. He peered at me and mooed like a calf.

– Mooo…

– Get out of here. Go on, be off with you. Now, your Honour, what I want to make plain to you is this. Here in Siberia people have darkened minds. They can't make anything, they can't even fish. It's a crying shame, because a Siberian's a good man. He's soft-hearted and honest and he doesn't drink – he's a treasure, not a man, but his life is wasting, like a mosquito, shall we say, or a fly. What's he living for, your Honour?

– Well, I suppose he works and eats and clothes himself. What more does a man want?

– Your Honour. A human being is not a horse.

The old man sat staring at the table. The wick of the candle was crusted with soot. The rain was beating on the windows now and I was thinking again of home. In Russia it's May now, and the forests are green, and the lilac and acacia are in bloom. But it seems to me that there too the wick of the candle is crusted with soot and someone is mooing. Moooo…

He stands, centre. The light is cold.

The ferry crawls. The water doesn't boom or roar, but seems to be knocking on the lids of coffins at the bottom: it's a dismal effect. From the banks come the strains of miserable accordions and the figures that we pass, standing stockstill on the barges in their ragged sheepskin coats, seem petrified by some endless sorrow. A bittern calls, as if on purpose to say: 'Don't be afraid, I am here!' I can just make out the lights of a harbour. Forest fires belching sparks and flames, and beyond them the mountains. A lighthouse on a promontory throws its beams into the darkness and lights up three reefs rising from the white spray of the breakers at the entrance to the port. These reefs are called the Three Brothers; but they look like three great black monks. I seem to have reached the end of the world: Sakhalin.

– What's your father's name?

– I don't know.

– You live with your father but you don't know his name?

– He's not my real father. He just lives with my mother.

– Is your mother a widow, or is she still married to someone?

– She's a widow. She came here for my father. She murdered him.

– Do you remember your real father?

– Never knew him; I was born on the way here.

Yegor has been sent to Sakhalin for killing his wife with a hammer. She was a beautiful woman and he was very much in love with her, but one day they had a quarrel and he knelt down in front of the icon and vowed to kill her. Every day after that he heard a voice in his ear saying: 'Kill her. Kill her.' Afterwards he gave himself up immediately and now he's here on Sakhalin. He sits philosophising all day – or giving lessons, as he calls it

– and whenever he sees a group of children he always shouts: 'Where there are fleas there are children too.' Once when we were out walking he suddenly burst out: 'Revenge is a most honourable thing!' He lives in the most meticulous way on Sakhalin, in a tidy little room, and above his bed he keeps a portrait of his wife.

Sometimes a convict will stand at a window and stare in silence at the roof of a neighbouring house. What is he thinking about? Or he'll talk about some trifle, looking sideways at you, with a look in his eyes that says: 'You, you'll be going home soon.' Since I arrived on Sakhalin I've worked for three months from five in the morning until late at night, and still I feel like a man at the zoo who's seen the insects but missed the elephant. I've visited every hut and made a card index of ten thousand convicts for my survey. I've talked to men chained to wheelbarrows. I've enough for four doctoral dissertations and a feeling in my innards as if I'd been eating rancid butter. I've developed headaches and there's something wrong with my eyes.

He steps aside, stage left. As he narrates the following, the light reduces on him and intensifies in a small area centre stage.

The doctor listens to the prisoner's heart. Then he goes and sits behind his desk.

– You're innocent, of course, aren't you; you're all innocent. It's just that people are so suspicious, aren't they? Did you have pleasant dreams last night?

– I can't remember, your Honour.

The prisoner stands half-naked. He is trembling.

– Well, here's some news for you. You're sentenced to ninety strokes of the lash. Come with us.

And the doctor slaps the prisoner on the forehead.

We walk to the warder's office. In the doorway we meet a medical assistant; he seems to be begging for alms.

– Your Honour, your Honour, may I watch the man being flogged?

Inside the office is a sloping bench with openings for the prisoner's hands and feet. The executioner nods to the prisoner: the prisoner lies down without a word. The executioner slowly pulls the prisoner's trousers down to his knees and ties him to the bench. The inspector is glancing casually out of the window. The doctor is strolling up and down the room. The executioner approaches the prisoner.

– Would you like a glass of water?

– Yes, yes please, for God's sake, your Honour.

While he drinks, the executioner slowly untangles a whip with three leather thongs.

– Now then. Bear up.

He strikes the first blow casually, without swingin g the whip, as if he were practising.

– One! cries the warder, like a church deacon.

For a moment the prisoner is silent and his face doesn't change. Then suddenly a shudder runs along his body and he lets out not a scream but a squeal.

– Two!

The executioner stands to one side and guides the whip across the body. After every five strokes he walks slowly round to the other side, giving the prisoner half a minute's rest. The prisoner's hair is stuck to his forehead and his neck is swollen. After the first five strokes his body has turned from red to purple and the skin breaks with every blow. He manages to gasp out:

– Your Honour. Your Honour. Why are you beating me?

After twenty strokes he's muttering like a delirious man or a drunk.

– God help me. I'm done for. God help me. Your
Honour. Your Honour.

Then he pokes his head out in a peculiar way and
makes a sound like vomiting. He doesn't speak again:
there's only a rasping sound coming from his throat.
We seem to have been there an eternity. But the
warder's only shouting, 'Forty-three! Forty-four!' I step
out into the street. It's quiet there apart from the sounds
coming from inside. A convict comes shuffling past: he
steals a glance into the office. A look of terror comes
into his face: he shuffles away. I go back inside.

– Eighty-nine! Ninety!

The prisoner's hands and legs are quickly untied and
they help him up. His back is purple with bruises and
dripping with blood. His teeth are chattering. His face
is yellow and damp, his eyes are wandering. When they
give him something to drink he convulsively bites the
glass. They sponge his face down and take him to the
surgery. On the way out we pass the medical assistant
who's asked to watch. He is enchanted.

– I love to watch the floggings. Worthless scoundrels. I
love it.

The light slowly changes back to normal.

God's world is good. Only one thing in it is bad –
ourselves.

Before my journey to Sakhalin, Tolstoy's *Kreutzer
Sonata* seemed to me a great event; afterwards it
seemed ridiculous. Either I'd grown up or I'd gone out
of my mind, I couldn't say which. I wrote a report on
Sakhalin and went to Moscow with it, to the university,
to submit it for a doctorate, and the Dean turned on his
heel and walked out of the room. When it was
published, the critic Burenin complained about
'mediocre writers who lose the ability to look straight
at life and so wander off to Siberia and Sakhalin'.
Perhaps I should shoot myself. All the time I was in

Moscow some strange feeling of ill will seemed to
surround me: people wined me and dined me, but I'd
the feeling they wanted to eat me alive. I went to a big
dinner to commemorate the abolition of serfdom: all
the literary men were there to welcome me, kissing me
a lot and wanting to know about Siberian women.
Gorky and I did have an interesting cough together. We
all drank champagne and made loud speeches about
freedom, and all the time serfs in tailcoats waited at
table and our drivers stood in the freezing cold waiting
for us to finish. It felt like lying to the Holy Spirit.

Well, so I flew out of Moscow like a bomb, obeying the
first law of physics, and in fact since I came back from
Sakhalin, I've never lived in the city again. First I
bought a house a little south of Moscow – six hundred
acres of birchwood and pasture and a nasty little river –
and then I moved further south, to the Crimea, where I
have orchards and running water and every American
convenience. Freedom, freedom! What bliss to hear the
larks and the starlings and to get the newspapers and
reviews from another world. What bliss to step out into
my garden at five o'clock in the morning, knowing I
don't have to go anywhere and no-one's coming to see
me. If I hadn't been a writer, I'd have been a gardener,
I'm sure. The soil hereabouts is so good that if you
were to plant a shaft in it, in a year's time a cart would
grow out of it. And I've so many cherries in the
summer I don't know what to do with them. And
because I used to be beaten for eating cherries when I
was a boy, I'm still fearful when I stand under my
cherry tree. I've little apples too, the size of three
kopeck pieces, and gooseberries and potatoes and
divine cabbage. How can you get along without
Russian cabbage soup? I've a pond a few steps from the
house, so I can fish straight out of the window, and
sometimes the hares stand up on their hind legs and
look through the window at me. How I love to fish! It's
a wonderful occupation, a quiet sort of insanity. Just to
catch a perch or a ruff, how delightful it is! And you
don't have to think!

I'm the only doctor in the district, so I have to treat my peasants, of course, for free. The men from the village bow respectfully to me, as Germans do to their pastor, and the old women cross themselves when they see me coming, as if I were a saintly half-wit. They brought a woman to me today, a country wife who'd been out carting rye and had fallen out of her cart with a dreadful crash. She had concussion, her neck muscles all terribly jarred and so on, vomiting, in great pain. I felt such a fool, dismally discouraged and ashamed of myself and my science, trying to keep my composure. Her relatives all bustled round her, and she was moaning and crying and imploring God for death, but all the time her eyes were fixed on the old peasant who was carrying her, and she was muttering, 'Leave the lentils now, Cyril, thresh them later, but be sure to thresh the oats now.' Well, I told her that talk about oats could be postponed because really there was something of a more serious nature to think about now. 'But he's got such good oats,' she whispered. A bustling, greedy country wife. Sometimes it's terrible to live among them like this, but there's nothing in a peasant's life you can't understand: terrible labour that makes the body ache all night, cruel winters, crop failure, overcrowding, no help or anywhere to look for help. And when a peasant dies of consumption, he always says, 'There's nothing I can do, I'll be gone with the spring rains.'

I have visitors all the time, most of them welcome. Levitan especially. 'Isaak Ilyich!' I write to him, 'Come and stay with me! If you don't, I hope your trousers come undone, in public, right in the middle of the street!' He's a Jew who's worth five Russians, with a passionate thirst for life, though his romances are a terrible worry. Once he tried to commit suicide over a girl, and then he went and shot a seagull near a lake where he was living and laid it at the lady's feet. Next he fell for my sister Masha, and she didn't know what to do. I advised her: 'Don't you marry Levitan! Levitan needs a woman out of Balzac.' I hope he doesn't shoot himself again. He shot a little woodcock once when we were out walking. It fell into a puddle at our feet with its wing wounded. So I picked it up. It had a long beak and big black eyes and beautiful plumage. It looked at us in wonder. What to do? Levitan closed his eyes and begged me to smash its head against his rifle butt, but I couldn't do that. He kept shrugging with nerves and twitching his head and begging me, and the woodcock kept looking at us in wonder. I had to do it in the end. And so two idiots went home and sat down to dinner, and there was one beautiful enamoured creature less in the world.

I have other visitors, less welcome. The ones who ask me: 'Anton Pavlovich, what is life?' You might as well ask: 'What is a carrot?' Or clever people who want to start serious conversations, about my plays and so on. These are my guardians. (*A pair of binoculars.*) I use them when I see the visitors approaching. If it's daytime I look at the sea, if it's night time I look up at the sky. Then my visitors think I must be pondering something profound and significant, and for fear of breaking my mood, they stop talking.

Sometimes they send me presents, antique embroidery. (*He shows us.*) Do they think I'm an archaeologist or something? What am I do with such things? What a shame. You should never give a silver pen or an antique inkwell to a writer. It's out of the question. Besides, I'm a doctor – you should give me a catheter. You could give me a new pair of socks. My wife doesn't look after me. She's an actress. I go about in torn socks. I write to her, 'Look here, darling, the big toe on my right foot's sticking out.' 'Wear it on the left foot,' she says. I can't live like this, but at least it's better than discussing literature with Moscow intellectuals. I have to go to Moscow for business of course, to supervise my books, or to see my wife, but I usually come back ill, especially when I've seen…one of my plays… I suppose I must talk about these plays of mine. Do you want me to?

He comes forward out of the set, and the auditorium lights up a little.

All right, but only for five minutes. There are plays I've written that I can't bear to think about, but in the main, there are four that matter, and they've all been done by a private theatre in Moscow with little-known actors, the Art Theatre: two comedies, *The Seagull* and *The Cherry Orchard*, one which is really just some scenes from country life, called *Uncle Vanya*, and a drama called *Three Sisters*. I can talk about one of them today, I don't mind which, you can choose, but only for five minutes. I'm going to set my alarm clock while you decide. (*He does so.*) Now, which one will it be? *The Seagull? Uncle Vanya? Three Sisters? The Cherry Orchard?*

The audience chooses a play. He discusses their choice for five minutes. The following is an outline only; in performance the accounts vary, with additional anecdotes, etc.

A. *The Seagull*

I made a bad start with the theatre: as a young man I saw Sarah Bernhardt in *La Dame Aux Camélias*. What a soulless actress she was; no spark, just an acting lesson carefully learned by heart. But it wasn't wasted, because I remembered her when I wrote about an actress in *The Seagull*, which is a play with a view of a lake, much talk of literature, not much action and several hundredweight of love. The Alexandrinsky Theatre in Petersburg put it on first, as part of a benefit for a comic actress. This was a mistake. The sets were old-fashioned, and so were the actors. They just declaimed; they didn't understand that the whole meaning and drama of a person's life lies inside, not in outward manifestations. They didn't know their lines, they didn't come to rehearsals, they weren't interested, so why should the public be? I missed most of the rehearsals, and went to the opening. There was booing, and a sense of shame in the theatre, and people turned their backs. I could no more forget that night than I could forget a punch in the face.

Two years later I was approached by this Art Theatre for permission to do the play in Moscow. I was reluctant, you can imagine, but they said it had the very pulse of Russian life in it, and wanted to give it a second chance. This time I went to the rehearsals but missed the opening. As a matter of fact I fell in love with the actress playing the actress. Some of the production was absurd, especially the realistic sound effects: frogs croaking, and dragonflies, which is as stupid as to stick a real nose on a painting of a face. I said to them, the next play I write, the hero will come on at the start and say, What wonderful silence! No birds, no cuckoos, owls, clocks, no sleigh bells, no crickets!

On the first night I heard that the actors were very nervous and smelt of valerian drops, and Konstantin Stanislavsky played the writer Trigorin like an impotent man recovering from typhoid. And, by the way, he should have worn check trousers, as a bad writer would. Then my actress was taken ill, and they had to cancel some performances. What terrible luck, I thought, if I marry an actress I shall father an orang-utan or a porcupine. But I did marry her in the end: in fact she was to become the last page of my life. And *The Seagull* was a success at last. I even had a letter from Fyodor Chaliapin, and when I saw the play later I couldn't believe it was I who had written it.

B. *Uncle Vanya*

I wrote this play out of an old play of mine, *The Wood Demon*, which I decided was too sentimental. For instance, in *The Wood Demon* I made the hero shoot himself, but in *Uncle Vanya* he tries to shoot himself and misses. I went to Petersburg one day for the first performance of another play of mine, *The Seagull*, and put *Uncle Vanya* in my bag; but *The Seagull* failed so badly that I brought *Vanya* home again. But it was performed in the provinces for the next two years after that and it made me a thousand roubles.

For the Moscow production I decided at first on the Maly Theatre – it's the oldest theatre in Russia and I'd always wanted to have a play put on there. But it happened just then that this new Art Theatre had had a success with *The Seagull*: in fact, they gave it life. So I offered *Vanya* to them. For the first time, I attended all the rehearsals. The actors kept asking me about the inner significance of their lines, and all I could say was, 'I've written it all down, it's all there…' Olga Knipper played Yeliena. Actually it was not her best part, I must say. Konstantin Stanislavsky was Astrov – he quite misunderstood the part, always weeping. The point is, the whole meaning and drama of a person lies inside, not in outward manifestations. The big outward events in a life are just unrepeatable accidents.

Well, I was here in the south when the play opened in Moscow, and it was the first time my own fame had kept me awake: every time I dozed off the telephone rang and I ran in my bare feet in the dark to hear more congratulations, went back to bed and then the telephone would ring again. There was something false about all the enthusiasm though, and sure enough there were bad reviews, in fact with all my plays it took a season or two for them to become really accepted. I only saw the play, in fact it was the first time I'd seen the Art Theatre give a performance at all, when they brought it down here to Sevastopol not long ago. The town band played polkas in the park next door to the theatre, all the way through – how sentimental it all was. But all that was wrong with the production was the realistic sound effects: frogs croaking, dragonflies, which is as absurd as to put a real nose on the portrait of a face. The whole company stayed here for ten days: it was wonderful, parties and friendship, and when they left they gave me the bench and swing from the production for my garden.

The main thing about all this playwriting is that it brought me my wife Olga Knipper, the last page of my life, great actress of the Russian land, and at last I had found a company I could write for. I tell you, they will provide the best page in a book yet to be written about the Russian theatre. As long as they control their sound effects. By the way, I heard that Tolstoy was at the first night in Moscow. He sat in a box and the audience applauded him. He didn't like the play though: 'Where is the drama? What does it consist of? These people are idlers, no good. Where do your characters take you? From the sofa to the junk room and back.' I expect he's right...

C. *Three Sisters*

Well, there I was living in the Crimea with my hair falling out, eating nothing but soup, and Olga Knipper, the last page of my life, was in Moscow, working in the theatre and going to balls in a plunging neckline. She kept asking me to join her in Moscow, but I pretended to be writing a play; and in the end I did write a play, with a fine part for her.

Years ago I used to stay sometimes in a garrison town called Voskresensk, where the officers had the dullest military routine, which they broke up by endlessly sitting around philosophising. At another time I'd stayed on a country estate at Luka with three sisters called Lintvaryev, so in my mind I put these two groups together to see what would come of it.

I gave *Three Sisters* to this Art Theatre, which had done two of my plays before and were getting well-known by then. When they read it, the actors complained it wasn't a play at all, just an outline, and it made them gloomy – but what I had written was really a comedy, almost a farce. When the play opened I was in Italy, and they cabled me there that it was a success, but I found out it wasn't really true. The audience had been very quiet, and the critics misunderstood it. My publisher Suvorin hated it. It was the same with all my plays – it took a season or two for them to become really accepted.

I saw the play the next year, by which time I was married to Olga, and the actors called it 'Two Sisters' as

I'd stolen away the third. As usual there were far too many realistic sound effects: the actors made the noise of cooing doves as the curtain went up at the start. You must do without such details: let the characters take over. But in general the production was perfect: in fact it improved on the play as I'd written it. The next year it was performed in Petersburg in front of the Tsar; the Art Theatre was famous at last and I made eight thousand roubles.

The main thing about all this playwriting is it brought me my wife, Olga Knipper, great actress of the Russian land, and at last I had found a company I was happy to write for… I tell you, they will provide the best page in a book yet to be written about the Russian theatre. As long as they control their sound effects.

D. *The Cherry Orchard*

By the time I wrote this play, I'd already had three others performed by the Moscow Art Theatre, and now I had the idea to write a four-act farce, with parts specially planned for the actors I knew. There was to be a man who buys an estate where his father and grandfather were serfs and he wasn't even allowed into the kitchen. Cherry trees like a sea of white, an unusual sense of distance in the outdoor scenes. I remembered from my youth the kind of very old, very large house that's usually pulled down nowadays for summer cottages, and a family in it going bankrupt as fast as possible, but with style. At the same time I wanted to say something about the poverty of the workers, and how the family were living off them, if I could get that past the censors.

How hard it was for me to write this play though: the characters kept going stale on me, and one day a whole section I'd just written got blown away by the wind – and do you know, I couldn't remember a word of it. The theatre needed the play rather badly: they had come to depend on me for one every year, but I couldn't work any faster.

When I finally sent it to them they immediately told
the newspapers it was a work of genius – which of
course robbed it of half its chances. My doctor wouldn't
let me go to rehearsals: he kept me at home in the
Crimea, eating eight eggs a day. So each morning I was
sending telegrams, telegrams: I was terribly anxious
and afraid of what they'd do to the play. For instance,
the youngest girl, Anya, is unimportant, but she must
speak in a ringing voice, and they had cast an old-
fashioned girl with a squeaky voice. From what I heard,
it seemed everyone was crying. But these snivelling,
whining characters have nothing to do with me. When I
write in my plays 'through tears' that's only to indicate
the characters' mood, not actual tears. The point is, the
whole drama and meaning of a person lies inside, not
in outward manifestations.

My wife Olga Knipper, the last page of my life, a great
actress of the Russian land, was playing the owner of
the estate. I told her the part's easy: you have to be
kind and absent-minded, always smiling. Stanislavsky
directed the play, and I told him: Lopahin, who buys
the cherry orchard, is not a crude peasant, or a typical
merchant, he's a gentle person – decent, dignified,
nothing petty – after all Varya is a serious, religious
girl, and she loves him.

As usual Stanislavsky wanted to put in realistic sound
effects: crickets, doves and so on, which is as silly as to
put a real nose onto the portrait of a face. While they
rehearsed, I stayed in the south, waiting for permission
to come to Moscow – apart from anything else I felt
like seeing my wife. Really, it was difficult. The point
is, this *Cherry Orchard* is a comedy, in places a farce,
with a cheerful last act – the whole thing light-hearted
and frivolous in fact, but Stanislavsky was determined
to make it a lament for some splendid dying class –
well, he was a rich man himself. He was nervous about
the play's chances, and arranged the first performance
for my birthday. They made a big public celebration
for me, a jubilee, but I can't endure that sort of thing.

But they insisted that I come. It was dreadful. Toasts, gifts, long speeches; and not a chair to sit on.

The Cherry Orchard was the same as all my other plays: it failed with the critics at first. This time they said I'd put too many jokes into a social tragedy. So it's clear that Stanislavsky had ruined it, and the less said about him the better. And whether it amounted to anything I can't really tell. Perhaps if I had been healthy I could have dealt with the theme better.

In the case of each play CHEKHOV finds his way back to this point.

But really all this is nothing special, because, all things considered, I'm a mediocre playwright. When I write a play, I'm uneasy, as if someone were peering over my shoulder. I have one more idea though, though time is going on and I may not be able to write it. In it two characters will discuss the arrival of a third, who never comes. Then they get a message to say that he's died. I've even got a title for this play. I'm going to call it…

He is interrupted by the sound of the alarm clock. He switches it off and returns to the room. A suggestion of moonlight downstage left. The clock starts ticking again.

What a superb night it is. I can see the sharp points of my garden fence and my little wizened tree under the window – the road, and the dark strip of the wood. A smell of hay, and some other scent, very nice. The moon bright and peaceful, not a cloud in the sky; everything quiet, not a leaf stirring. It's as if all these things were watching me, waiting for me to start dying.

All country people know these long, quiet nights, when even the clocks are tired of ticking. It's so fiendishly dull, the very flies drop dead. I know what I can show you.

He digs out a portfolio of maps.

This is a special pleasure I allow myself about once a month, not more; I entertain myself with these for an hour or two in the evening, and then I become warm and peaceful and the crickets chirp. (*He shows the first map.*) This is a map I've made of our district as it was fifty years ago. The green is forest, about half the whole area. Where I've drawn red over the green we used to have deer and goats, and swans and ducks and geese used to live in this lake, 'a power of birds' as the old people used to say, all kinds of birds flying about like clouds. Hamlets and villages and settlements, little farms, huts and watermills scattered all around. This blue represents cattle and horses: every home had an average of three horses. Now. (*A second map.*) This is how it was twenty-five years ago. Only a third of the area under forest by this time. No goats now, but still some deer, and the green and blue areas are paler. And so on and so forth. And this (*A third map.*) is our district today. Only a little green, and all in patches, and the deer and swans and geese have all disappeared, and no trace of the settlements and farms. In fact this is an unmistakable picture of gradual decay, and in ten or fifteen years' time it will be complete. Well, you may say, that's the influence of civilisation, the old way of life giving way to the new and so on, and I'd agree with you if only on the site of these ravaged forests there were roads and railways, workshops, factories and schools, so that people were healthier, better off, better educated. Not a bit of it. We have the same swamps and mosquitoes, the same poverty, typhus, diphtheria and fires. This is a decay caused by inertia and ignorance and complete irresponsibility, as when a sick, hungry, shivering man instinctively clutches at anything to satisfy his hunger and keep him warm, and in so doing destroys everything, without a thought for tomorrow.

He looks hard at us.

But I can see from your faces this doesn't interest you at all. Perhaps you don't have such problems. But I must tell you that this Russia of ours is such an absurd, clumsy country that one day events will take us unawares, like sleeping fairies. You know how we always philosophise and say things will be better in a hundred years, and better still in two hundred years, but nobody bothers about improving things tomorrow. For example, I've been catching cholera by the tail all summer: I'm responsible for twenty-five villages, four factories and a monastery, all with one dish, no thermometer and half a pound of carbolic. I treat my peasants all day, and then I get up behind my mangy old horses and go bouncing over unknown roads in the dark, trying to raise money for clinics as if I were begging for bread. I've proved myself a first-rate mendicant, and now we have two well-equipped hospitals, and five fairly well-equipped – well, quite bad, actually. But I'm exhausted, just stupefied with tiredness – tired of thinking about nothing but diarrhoea, running out in the middle of the night with somebody knocking and the dogs barking, trailing round the countryside in some unspeakable vehicle. I ride through the forest on a dark night, and if I see a light in the distance I forget how tired I am and I forget the prickly branches lashing my face, but mostly there's no light in the distance.

He has difficulty getting to his feet.

Oh dear, I feel as rickety as an old wardrobe.

Still, we do make some progress: in the old days the peasants used to lynch the doctors. Socialist agitators would persuade them that we were spreading cholera on behalf of the government. Russia is an enormous plain across which wander mischievous men, convincing our people that their crass prejudices are the truth, as if some beautiful future could justify deceiving them now. I think politically minded people ought to have to take an oath never to betray the present for the sake of the future, even if they're offered a ton of bliss for every pennyworth of lies.

I seem to have fired off a leading article from a radical newspaper at you. But really, I'm not a liberal, nor a conservative, nor a transitionalist, nor a gradualist, nor an impartialist, nor an indifferentist, nor a monk. I'd like to be a free artist and nothing else, and I regret that God hasn't given me the strength to be one.

He sits centre.

I still write a little every day: only a little, but I do write. And then in the evenings Levitan might come knocking at my window – 'Are you there, crocodile?' – and I let him in and we talk. He has terrible fits of melancholy these days, but if I tell him a funny story he rolls on the floor with pleasure and kicks his feet in the air. But his work is deteriorating: he no longer paints with a feeling of youth, but with a sort of bravura. I think the women have worn him out. It's impossible to paint a landscape without a feeling of pathos, of ecstasy, and ecstasy is impossible when you've gorged yourself. If I were a landscape artist I'd live quite an ascetic life: I'd have intercourse once a year, and I'd eat once a day.

Also, it's terrible to be a doctor, because I know Levitan won't come tapping at my window much longer. His heart doesn't beat, it puffs and blows. May the heavenly kingdom be his. May his memory last for ever. Death is a cruel thing, isn't it, a disgusting punishment. People take you to the cemetery, make speeches, and then they go home and have tea. Disgusting. Once when seances were all the rage in Moscow I managed to call up Turgenev's ghost and he told me my life was drawing to a close. Well, I thought, death is a dreadful thing of course, but it's not as bad as the thought that you might live for ever. In any case, I'm not going to die: joyous visions fire me, I'm breathless with excitement. I have a terrific longing for life. What if, by some miracle, this present turned out to be a dream, a hideous nightmare, and we were to awake renewed and cleansed, strong, upright and proud? Why do we never try to stand again when once we've fallen? When we lose one thing why don't we search for another? I want our lives to be holy, sublime and solemn as the vault of heaven. Let us live! The thief on the cross had hope even though he had less than an hour left to him, and the sun only rises once a day, so take hold of what's left of your life and save it. My holy of holies is the human body, health, intelligence, talent, love and the most absolute freedom imaginable, freedom from violence and lying, whatever form they may take. That's the programme I would follow if I were a great artist.

The clock has stopped ticking. CHEKHOV comes forward.

I walked down my path to the river, disturbing the sandpipers. The last rays of sunlight were still on the pines, but on the water it was dark. I crossed by my bridge and found myself in a wide field of young rye. There was nothing – no house, no sign of life. It seemed as if the path where I was standing would lead straight to the unknown place where the sun had just gone down and the evening glow was flaming in the sky.

What space. What freedom, what stillness, I thought, as if the world were watching me, waiting for me to grasp its meaning. At that moment a wave ran across the rye and a soft evening breeze touched my face. Then came another, stronger gust – the rye rustled and behind me I could hear the hollow murmur of the pines. I halted. On the horizon there rose, from earth to sky, a tall black column like a whirlwind, or a sandstorm perhaps. Its outline was unclear, but it was not stationary, but moving with terrific speed towards me, and the closer it approached, the smaller and more distinct it became. I just had time to plunge into the rye at the side of the path.

It was a monk, all dressed in black, his arms crossed on his chest, his hair grey, his brows black, his bare feet not touching the ground. He came rushing past. What a white, fearfully white, thin face. He nodded at me, in a friendly way. Then, swelling again, he flew across the river, crashed without a sound into the clay cliffs and the pines, passed straight through them and vanished.

Some years passed.

He moves to his desk.

I moved to the Crimea, reaching Sevastopol one
evening, and I stopped at a hotel there to rest before
coming on to Yalta the next day. I was tired. I stepped
out on to my balcony. It was warm and I could smell
the sea. The wonderful bay reflected the moonlight: it
had a colour difficult to define, a soft blend of blue and
green. In places the water had the dark blue of vitriol
and in other places it was as if the moonlight had
turned to liquid and filled the bay in place of water.
What a symphony of colour. What a feeling of peace
and calm and repose.

From the ground floor beneath my balcony I could
hear laughter and women's voices. A party, obviously. I
went back into my room. I knew from experience that
the best cure for melancholia is work. You have to sit at
your desk and force yourself at all costs to concentrate
on a single idea. From my bag I took a notebook that
contained some work I'd planned to do if the Crimea
became boring. I sat at my desk and started writing,
gradually feeling a calm and resigned mood creeping
over me. The work led me to reflect on the hustle and
bustle of the world. What a price life exacts from man
in return for its commonplace rewards. To come this far
I had had to work day and night for twenty years,
endure a solitary life, and do a number of stupid and
unreasonable things that are best forgotten. I saw
clearly that I was a mediocrity, and I was glad, seeing
that everybody should be satisfied with what he is.

A light wind blew in from the sea, sending my papers
to the floor. I went out onto the balcony again. Now the
bay was like a living thing, looking at me with blue,
turquoise and fiery red eyes. It seemed to beckon me.
Beneath my balcony a violin started to play and two
female voices started to sing. I caught my breath. There
was a sadness in my heart but also a sweet, long-
forgotten delight which made me tremble.

I went to bed and started reading – a French novel.
Soon the clock struck three. I put out my candle and
lay down to sleep. I lay for a long time wakeful, my
eyes closed, the room terribly hot. Then at half past
four I re-lit my candle, and there, sitting in the chair
beside my bed, was a man of medium height with his
grey head bare, all in black, barefooted like a beggar.
On his deathly white face his black brows stood out
sharply. The black monk.

He nodded amiably at me.

– Greetings.

– What are you doing here, I said. You're a mirage,
why are you sitting in my chair?

– A mirage? A mirage is the product of an overheated
imagination. I am an apparition.

– So you don't exist?

– Think as you choose.

– What an old, wise face you have. It's as if you really
had lived for a thousand years. Why do you look at me
with such delight? Do you like me?

– Very much. My friend, your ideas, your work and
your life have been dedicated to everything rational
and beautiful, to the eternal, in fact. You are among the
chosen people of God.

– How pleasant it is to talk to you.

– I'm glad to hear it.

– But you are an hallucination, aren't you? Am I
mentally deranged?

– What if you are? You're ill now because you've
overworked and tired yourself out. You've sacrificed
your health to your ideas and soon you will sacrifice
your life to them. What could be better than that? That
is your goal.

I tried to answer, but blood was pouring from my mouth. I didn't know what to do. I covered my chest with my hands and they became covered in blood. I tried to call out.

– Olya! Olya!

I fell to the ground and raised myself on my arms. I called on Olya. I called on my garden, its flowers all covered with dew, the parkland, the pines with their twisted roots, the field of rye, the steppe, my life's work, my youth, my daring and my joy, on my life which had been so lovely. I could see a great pool of blood on the ground near my face. I was too weak to speak, but a boundless happiness flooded me. When my wife woke up and came out from behind the screen, the monk was gone and I was lying with a blissful smile on my face.

The last thing I remember was…they brought me champagne. I was very glad of it. It's a very long time since I last drank champagne.

Please greet the lovely hot sun from me, and the quiet sea. Enjoy yourselves, be happy, don't think about illness, and write often to your friends. Every hour is precious. Keep well and cheerful, and don't suffer from indigestion and bad temper.

He drinks slowly and puts the glass on the desk. The lights slowly fade.

INDEX

INDEX